MERV GRIFFIN

On stage fright:

"I was terrified. The shaking of my legs was clearly visible through my pants. The celebrity audience thought this was hysterical because while I was singing these romantic ballads, my legs were keeping their own separate beat."

On how to liven up a TV show:

"I can handle almost anything in my life except boredom. And this job on a morning show was boring me to tears. Several times a show, the announcer stood there with a long sheet of paper and read the temperatures and forecasts from around the country. One day—and I still don't know what made me do this—I leaned over and lit the bottom of his weather report on fire. The poor guy panicked. Even though his copy was only burning slightly around the edges, he yanked off his toupee and threw it across the room. By the time the fire was out, the damage was done."

On his business dealings with Donald Trump:

"Donald Trump is the Vince Lombardi of developers. For Donald, winning isn't everything; it is the only thing. What he doesn't understand is that you can only beat someone who chooses to play your game. I never did."

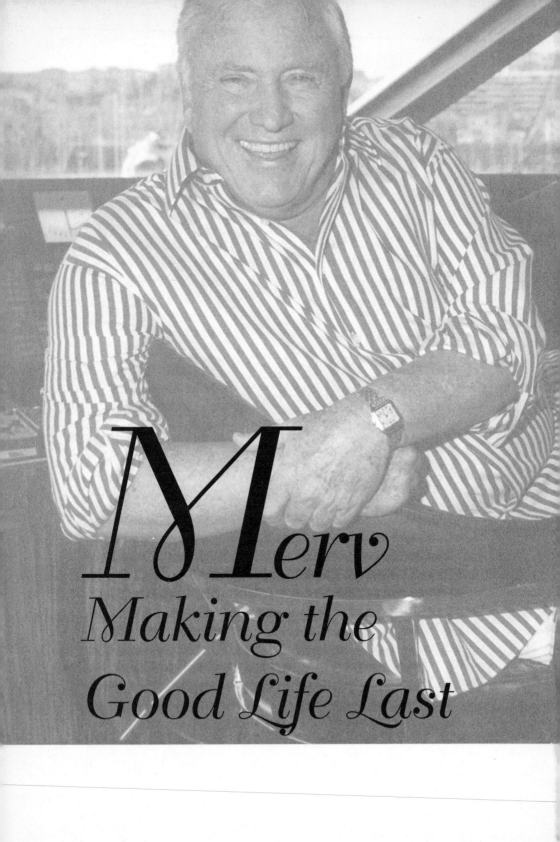

Merv
Making the Good Life Last

Merv Griffin

with David Bender

Pocket Books

New York London Toronto Sydney

Pocket Books

A Division of Simon & Schuster, Inc.

1230 Avenue of the Americas

New York, NY 10020

First Pocket Books trade paperback edition October 2007

POCKET and colophon are registered trademarks of Simon & Schuster, Inc.

For information regarding special discounts for bulk purchases,
please contact Simon & Schuster Special Sales at
1-800-456-6798 or business@simonandschuster.com

Designed by Karolina Harris

Manufactured in the United States of America

10   9   8   7   6   5   4   3   2   1

ISBN-13: 978-0-7434-5696-8
ISBN-13:   0-7434-5696-3

Acknowledgments

Writing a book is much like putting out to sea for a lengthy voyage—you leave your loved ones behind and come to rely on the steadfast support of your traveling companions as you navigate new and uncharted waters.

The authors wish to express their great appreciation to Michael Korda for providing the compass for this journey, as well as to Chuck Adams for his keen editorial eye that never wavered from the horizon. Our sincere thanks also go to the team at Simon & Schuster—Ted Landry, Cheryl Weinstein, Veronica Jordan, and Karolina Harris—whose yeoman efforts were essential to guiding this book safely into port. Likewise, we are very appreciative of B. G. Dilworth and Bill Klemm at Authors & Artists Group, whose diligence on deck ensured that we never ran aground.

Last, but certainly not least, we are deeply grateful to our agent, Al Lowman, who christened this project with his passion and then blessed it with patience, impatience, intelligence, creativity, and love.

MERV GRIFFIN: I want to acknowledge these friends and associates who have been on this wonderful journey with me and have truly made my life a good one with their lasting contributions: Jim Bradley, Dick Carson, Ernie Chambers, Larry Cohen, Warren Cowan, H.R.H. Princess Elizabeth of Yugoslavia, the Eyre family, Tom Gallagher, Michael Hathaway, Nancy Jones, Al Krivin, John Lauderdale, Mort and Judy Lindsey, Bob and Audrey Loggia, Bob and Lynne Murphy, Bill and Rose Narva, Jean Plant, Nancy Reagan, Gloria Redlich, Murray Schwartz, Bob Shanks, Jack Sheldon, George Vosburgh, and Ron Ward.

And I want to give a special acknowledgment to David Bender, who wrote my ramblings in such a colorful way that, as a result, I'm looking back on my own life and smiling. It wasn't as tedious as I thought it would be—there were so many joyous moments of laughing and remembering with David, that a chore became a fiesta. Thank you, David.

DAVID BENDER: For never letting me sink below the waves, I wish to thank the following people for their love and friendship: Dave Baird, Emily Black, David & Jan Crosby, Jerry Haft, Michael Hong, Jim & Marian Hong, Michael Jensen, John Keefer, Chad Raffety, Joyce Rebhun, Robert Sedor & Carol Chappell, Blair Sabol, Adam Sofen, Caroline Thompson, and Rick & Andrea Weidman.

In addition, I'd like to acknowledge Ben & Cindy Kollen of Country Store Antiques in Saugatuck, Michigan, who, in a lovely bit of serendipity, sold me Merv's first book, and Shaun Robinson, Margaret Morton, and the staff of Merv Griffin's Scottsdale Hilton Resort and Villas for all their kindness to a wandering writer.

Finally, I need to say a word about the captain of this ship, Mervyn Edward Griffin, Jr. I didn't know Merv (except as a fan) when I signed up for this voyage, but I've come to understand why the whole world loves him. He is smart, generous, compassionate, and uproariously funny. And he loves dogs.

I think the last word on the "dear boy himself" rightfully belongs to his longtime sidekick, the late Arthur Treacher, who knew him better than most. "Merv," he wrote, "is a natural-born friend."

For Tony & Tricia

And for Farah and Donovan in the hope that this book will help you to know your grandfather a little bit better when you grow up . . .

Contents

One:
Dreams

When I was five years old, my family lost our house to the bank and we were forced to move. It was the height of the Depression and my father's job in a sporting goods store wasn't enough to keep up the mortgage payments. We lived (and I was born) in San Mateo, a bedroom community twenty miles south of San Francisco. Even today I can remember the exact layout of that house: my sister's bedroom on the top floor, my parents and I on the second floor, the big kitchen that always seemed to be filled with people. Somewhere I still have the picture of me and my sister, Barbara (who was two years older), sitting together on the front stairs looking sad, while we watched our possessions go out the door.

As it turns out, we did leave a few things in the house. One item that apparently remained behind was our original toilet seat. I heard recently that it was sold at an auction to benefit a charity in San Mateo. You know those signs—"George Washington Slept Here"? I can only imagine how they described it in the catalogue: "Merv Griffin – – – – Here."

I still remember crying when we finally left our house. And believe me, those early childhood experiences stick with you in a powerful way. I'm certain that because I was a Depression baby, there have been times as an adult when I've placed far too much value on material things. That's an instinct I've had to wrestle with my entire life. And although it's taken me seven decades to do it, I honestly believe that I've finally got it beat.

We moved in with my maternal grandmother and her two other daughters, Claudia and Helen, both of whom were older than my mother. How can I describe my mother and her sisters? Each of them had brown hair and deep brown eyes. None of them wore makeup— they didn't need it. When people see a picture of my mother as a young woman, they frequently remark on her strong resemblance to the actress Anne Baxter (remember *All About Eve*?). My Aunt Helen was a gifted ballet dancer with a lithe dancer's body who once performed with the legendary Isadora Duncan. She moved through a room and across a stage with incredible grace. Aunt Claudia had the most luminous skin; she looked strikingly like one of the angels you'd see depicted on a holy card.

Even before we moved in, Aunt Claudia had begun teaching me how to play the piano. I'd started at the age of four when I was still so tiny that I could only play standing up, my small fingers banging away on the keys. I was her little "Buddy" (the nickname my mother had given me to minimize confusion between my father, Mervyn Sr., and me), and she was my best friend. When I wasn't practicing the piano, Claudia would sometimes take me fishing at Coyote Point, not far from our house. We'd sit out on the end of the wharf all day catching jacksmelt, the small silver and blue fish that populated the San Francisco Bay. Those were idyllic days; the sky was bluer and the sun warmer. Looking back, I know how lucky I am to have grown up in such a close family.

Probably as a result of my family's financial worries, I became a very entrepreneurial child. The first things I ever did, I didn't consider to be jobs at all—they were just fun to do. At four, I had a magazine route, selling *The Saturday Evening Post* and *Liberty* door-to-door. I carried them in a little white canvas bag on my side. I mowed our neighbors' lawns. Years later, when I was in my twenties and already an established performer, that particular job experience would come in handy. I had become great friends with Frank Loesser, the brilliant composer who wrote *Guys and Dolls*. On Saturdays he would invite me to his house to rehearse his songs with him. But he also had a not-so-hidden agenda. Every week, without fail, he'd look out at his yard and say, "That lousy gardener didn't show up again. Would you help me cut the lawn, Merv?" And every week, without fail, I'd cut his damn lawn. Still, it was worth it just to spend time with him.

At seven, I decided to start my own two-penny newspaper, *The Whispering Winds*. It covered all of the breaking news in our corner of San Mateo. I ran it off on something called a hectograph, which used a gooey purple substance similar to Jell-O. By the time I got the paper out every day, my skin had taken on a definite purplish hue. (Picture a kid in a Barney costume and you'll get the idea.)

I was like one of those young newsboys in the movie *Mr. Smith Goes to Washington*, running everywhere, spreading truth to all the neighbors, whether they liked it or not. Once I included some gossip about the people who lived next door to us. They bought up all thirty copies of the paper before canceling their subscription. My journalistic career lasted until the day I printed an off-color joke told to me by an older kid. I was too young to understand the joke, but the neighbors got it and they were not amused. Our phone rang off the hook with cancellation orders and that marked the end of *The Whispering Winds*.

Larry King often calls me the "Merv of All Trades." He doesn't know the half of it. Growing up, I had other jobs including setting up pins in a bowling alley (I was once "double-balled"—before I could get out of the way, a bowler released his second ball and I became the spare); selling war bonds on street corners (my rhyming patter was very effective—I was the world's first rapper); and selling Christmas wreaths to the wealthy residents of Hillsborough, an affluent community north of San Mateo. I worked right out of the phone book: "Excuse me, Mrs. Van Smythe, I was passing by today and I noticed that your beautiful home on Maple Street doesn't have any holiday decorations up yet. I'm sure you're very busy, but it just so happens that I have some very lovely wreaths that I'd be happy to bring by and show you." If they already had one, I just apologized and moved on to the next name in the book. There's an old Irish term for this—we call it "chutzpah."

After several years of piano lessons, Aunt Claudia knew that I had gone way beyond what she could teach me herself. Instead of being proprietary about her favorite student, Claudia loved me enough to push me out of the nest. She and my mother arranged for me to study with a trained classical teacher, Madame Siemmens, who taught at Mercy High School, a private girls school in nearby Burlingame. I eventually outgrew her as well, and not a minute too soon—she used to rap my fingers with her ruler. After Madame Siemmens, I took lessons at a music conservatory and studied under a gifted man named Lesley Growe, who taught me to play some of the great classical piano pieces.

Although I couldn't know it then, the experience of regularly going in to San Francisco as a piano student would soon play an important part in my relationship with Aunt Claudia.

All through grammar school, I'd race home in the afternoon and shout, "Aunt Claudia, I'm home!" But starting around the time I was thirteen, I'd call out her name and, quite often, she wouldn't answer. Then I'd knock on her bedroom door: "Aunt Claudia?" Nothing. So

I'd quietly turn the knob and push the door open a crack. There she was, kneeling on the floor in front of a large picture of the Sacred Heart, her body swaying slightly as she murmured her prayers. This generally lasted for about an hour. And no matter how many times I looked in on her she never seemed to hear me. I'd usually just shut the door quietly and wait for her to come out. When she emerged, she was invariably glowing, as if she'd just had the most profound religious experience right there in our little house in San Mateo.

Eventually I asked my mother about my aunt's strange ritual. She told Barbara and me not to mention it to anyone, including Claudia. She reminded us that as a girl, Aunt Claudia's only ambition was to enter a convent, but my grandmother wouldn't let her go.

After a few months of keeping watch on her, I came home one afternoon and found a note on the kitchen table: "Please don't worry. I must be about my father's business." I recognized the quote—it was Luke 2:49—but the import of it didn't really register until my mother got home. We waited for two days without a word and everyone was frantic with worry. My father was getting ready to call the police (Chief Burke was a family friend), when the wall phone rang in the kitchen. I ran to answer it—it was Aunt Claudia. She'd walked the eighteen miles from our house all the way in to San Francisco, stopping only to sleep in the Daly City cemetery.

For the past day she had been wandering the streets, preaching the gospel to anyone who would listen. I begged her to stay on the phone and talk to my mother, but she hung up. I flashed the receiver (something you can't do anymore) and the operator came on the line. "Yes, sir. May I help you?" I lowered my voice and said, "This is Chief of Police Burke. Give me the location of the last call on this line." "Yes, sir. Just a moment." A few seconds later she came back on the line—the call had been placed from a phone booth in central San Francisco.

The next morning I got up at six o'clock and took the bus into San Francisco. Fortunately, my time spent studying piano had also given me a working knowledge of the city's geography. I quickly found the phone booth, then I just started walking in wider and wider circles until I found the closest Catholic church. I sat through two Masses and, suddenly, there was Claudia, coming down the aisle carrying a large cross with a figure of Jesus on it. She stopped at the communion rail and knelt down, placing the cross beside her. I went up, knelt next to her and said softly, "It's me, Aunt Claudia. Buddy." She just bowed her head and began sobbing. I cried with her. Finally, I helped her to her feet and we went to a nearby breakfast room to talk. She described her experiences on the street—how the sailors would pass her by and jeer because she was preaching for peace, at a time when the entire country was preparing for our entry into World War II. I listened uncritically to everything she had to say, then I told a white lie that I knew I would be forgiven for: "Aunt Claudia, we all need you too. Your brother Joe [who lived nearby in the city] is very ill and he really wants to talk to you. Will you call him tonight?"

I left her without really knowing for sure what she'd do. The whole family drove up to Uncle Joe's that night and waited anxiously until Claudia finally called. My parents picked her up and drove her to a hospital for observation. She was given a clean bill of health and released a few days later, but her religious fervor never wavered throughout the remainder of her life.

Just as Aunt Claudia gave me early direction by teaching me to play the piano, my father's brother Elmer was also a strong influence in my young life. Uncle Elmer was the first person to help me see the world beyond San Mateo, a world that previously existed only in the movies I'd seen.

In order to fully appreciate my Uncle Elmer, you first have to understand the important role that the game of tennis has always played in the Griffin family.

There were five Griffin brothers—Frank, Clarence (known as Peck), Elmer, Milton, and my father, Mervyn. Collectively they were referred to as "those Griffin boys with their lace curtain Irish names." (Until I started this book, I never knew the actual meaning of the name my father and I share: "Merv" means both "from the sea" and "a famous friend.")

All the Griffin men were about 5'9", except Uncle Peck, who at 5'7" was the bantam of the group. And they all had athletes' faces—those classically ruddy Irish features. My father and Elmer looked very much alike; each had a strong, athletic body and thinning hair. Uncle Milton had jowls, four double chins, and a potbelly, so he was never much of a sportsman. Neither was Uncle Frank, but nobody could play the piano like he could. Oddly enough, although my father and Uncle Elmer were both champion tennis players, it was the smallest brother, Uncle Peck, who was the national doubles champion, a fact he never let his brothers forget.

Peck's title notwithstanding, it was generally conceded that my father was the best tennis player in the family. For a time he even coached Don Budge, one of the all-time greats of the game. But of all the brothers, my father was the only one who chose to get married and have children. Since tennis was still only an amateur sport in my father's day, his decision to support a family forced him to leave the tennis circuit when he was only twenty-one. Ironically, in today's game even mediocre players are earning seven-figure salaries. I've often wondered how far my father might have gone had he been born fifty years later.

I was always grateful to my dad for one thing. As much as he loved tennis, he never pushed his kids to play it professionally. (Neither my father nor my mother were the kind of parents who tried to live vicariously through their children.) It's true that he did try to teach Barbara and me the rudimentary features of the game. Yet like most athletes, he had a terrible time coaching his own kids. He would take us out on the court, but what he ended up doing was just running us back and forth until we got dizzy and fell down. That was his idea of fun.

Elmer also had a lot of fun with the game. So much so that his exploits earned him three separate mentions in "Ripley's Believe It or Not." Once he won three Oregon state titles all in the same afternoon. Then he won a match while wearing roller skates (his opponent wore sneakers). My favorite Ripley's entry was the time he defeated one of the great players of all time, U.S. men's champion William "Little Bill" Johnston. Uncle Elmer beat Johnston without using a racquet, by catching and returning every serve and volley with only his bare hands. He won the set 6–1.

In 1926, Elmer founded the Beverly Hills Country Club as a place where film executives and stars could meet, socialize, and conduct business. It quickly became a favorite spot for Hollywood stars to see and be seen. Some of the early members included Cesar Romero, Humphrey Bogart, and Errol Flynn.

It was almost beyond comprehension to me that my own uncle knew movie stars like Errol Flynn *personally!* Flynn was my favorite screen hero, leaping from ship to ship, brandishing his sword gallantly in the cause of justice. Invariably in the last reel he would vanquish the villain, then sweep the leading lady up in his arms and kiss her passionately. Fade to black.

When I was sixteen years old, I made my first solo trip to visit Uncle Elmer in Los Angeles. It happened that Errol Flynn was actually staying with him, as he often did between wives and girlfriends. I was literally trembling with excitement when I walked into my uncle's house. What I didn't expect was that my film idol, fresh from the shower, would be sitting *starkers* in Elmer's living room. Now, how shall I put this? I think it's fair to say that Errol Flynn brandished a sword both on and *off* the screen.

At thirty-two, Flynn was twice my age chronologically, but a thousand years older than I was in terms of life experience (his scandalous trial on statutory rape charges wouldn't take place until the following year). Like a sponge with ears, I absorbed everything that I heard during my brief stay. I particularly remember Flynn talking scathingly about his then boss, the powerful (and often punitive) studio chief, Jack Warner. Although Flynn always credited Warner with having the vision to cast him in his first starring role as the swashbuckling hero of *Captain Blood*, it was no secret that the two men had a tumultuous relationship, due primarily to Flynn's alcohol-fueled escapades off the screen. Flynn's absolute fearlessness in dealing with Warner was fascinating to me. I couldn't possibly imagine that in little more than ten years I would also be under contract to Warner Brothers, and that what I'd learned from Flynn would one day prove quite useful in my own dealings with the tyrannical "J.L."

Since early childhood my fantasy had been to do what Mickey Rooney and Judy Garland did in the movies, which was to clear out a barn and have it became the stage set of a Broadway musical. I never could figure out how they did it; they would get this old barn, and then out would come this million-dollar set. Happened every time. But my secret dream was really to play opposite Judy. In the darkened theater, while she was singing "Dear Mr. Gable" up on the screen, I always imagined that the face in the picture frame was mine, not Clark's.

In truth, I didn't yet have any ambition to be on center stage myself. I just wanted to make things happen. You have to remember that at the time I didn't think of myself as a singer at all. I knew that I had a talent for playing piano, but in the beginning that was as far as it went.

At this point in my life, having only studied classical music, I admit that I was something of a musical snob. I had little awareness of pop music until I was twelve and my family went to visit my sister, who was spending part of the summer at Camp Imelda up on the Russian River, north of San Francisco. They had a camp show every night where the campers sang or put on skits. One of the kids sang a brand-new Rodgers and Hart song called "Where or When." We didn't use the phrase back then, but I was blown away. I'd never heard a song that sounded so beautiful to me. As soon as we got home I taught myself to play it.

Shortly after that I had my first—and ill-fated—singing experience with the choir at St. Matthew's Church, which I attended every Sunday with my mother, Aunt Claudia, and Aunt Helen. When I first joined the choir, I was often asked to do the solos, because I had a high soprano voice. One day, without warning (and in front of the entire congregation), puberty struck. I was a soprano no more. Instead I was stunned to hear a croaking sound coming from my throat that sounded like someone was strangling that frog-voiced kid from the Little Rascals. From then on I was only a piano player. I certainly never planned on singing in public again.

In the summer of '42 (wasn't that a movie?), I graduated from San Mateo High School. I was seventeen. At 5'9" and 240 pounds, I would fail ten consecutive physical examinations before the military finally decided to give up on me. During the last physical they even detected a slight heart murmur for which I had to be hospitalized. When they released me, the induction officer (whose name, fittingly, was Grimm) said, "That's it, son. You're done. We ain't gonna pay you no veteran's benefits for some heart condition. You ain't goin'."

I may have been 4F, but I was determined to make some kind of contribution to the war effort. So I took a job at the big naval shipyard out on Hunters Point in San Francisco. They put me to work in the supply depot, helping to organize provisions that were being loaded on giant transport ships bound for the Pacific Theater. At the same time (and only to please my parents) I took a few classes at San Mateo Junior College.

Although I was still very confused about my future, I did know one thing for certain—I was not cut out for academic life. After twelve years of school, that may have been the only lesson that I'd learned well enough to merit an A+. Unfortunately for me, they didn't give out grades for a lack of interest in school. Don't get the wrong idea. I love to read and I'm willing to match the depth and breadth of my knowledge against anyone with a college degree. Heck, I invented that game—it's called *Jeopardy!* But I'm also someone who's always resented being told what to do, particularly when someone says "it's for your own good."

I honestly believe that's one of my greatest strengths. Making my own choices has allowed me to be more creative than I ever could have been if I was simply following someone else's lesson plan or job description. More than that, it's meant that I've always had to take responsibility for my own decisions. If it works, I can take pride in knowing that the achievement is truly my own. Should I fail—and believe me I have—then I certainly can't blame anyone else for it. Creativity and responsibility. Shouldn't we be encouraging those things in school? Okay, I'll get off of my soapbox.

July 6, 1943. My eighteenth birthday. It was a Tuesday afternoon and I'd just taken the commuter train home from my new position in the checking department at the Crocker Bank in San Francisco. Just in case you're wondering about my credentials for the job, let me clear that up for you: my father taught tennis to the Crocker family.

Instead of going directly home from the station, for some reason I decided to take a long walk along the railroad tracks. Loosening my tie, I draped my jacket over my arm and headed south toward—where *was* I going? Boy, was that ever the $64 question. (Believe it or not, that was still the top prize on one of the most popular radio quiz shows of the forties, *Take It or Leave It.* Ten years later it moved to television. The show's producer added three zeroes to that figure and *The $64,000 Question* was born.)

My thoughts were jumbled that day, but running through my head—almost like the soundtrack of a movie—were the words to "Where or When," the Rodgers and Hart tune that was the first pop song I'd ever learned to play. The lyrics seemed to carry a special significance that day:

> When you're awake, the things you think
> Come from the dream you dream
> Thought has wings, and lots of things
> Are seldom what they seem
> Sometimes you think you've lived before
> All that you live today
> Things you do come back to you
> As though they knew the way
> Oh the tricks your mind can play

Perhaps my mind *was* playing tricks on me that afternoon, because I was suddenly overwhelmed by a sensation unlike anything I've ever experienced in my entire life—before or since. With a clarity and power that caused me to stop right there on the tracks, a thought—actually it was more of an awareness—came into my head: "You will never again be a private person."

I began to cry. The pent-up emotions of eighteen years were released in that single transformative moment. *When you're awake, the things you think, Come from the dream you dream* . . .

All my life I've been a dreamer. But from then on I knew that my dreams weren't just childish fantasies. Something clicked inside me that day. My dreams—both waking and sleeping—were no longer mere abstractions; I now understood that I had to act on them. Sometimes that's meant trusting my hunches and taking large risks, despite the odds. Other times I've literally followed the dream itself. And I'm not talking here about grandiose dreams like "someday I'm going to buy the Grand Canyon" (or, as Donald might call it, "Trump Canyon"), but actual precognitive dreams. Dreams that cause me to wake up in the middle of the night and write down every detail I can remember.

Even today, when I'm on the phone and doodling abstractedly, I find myself writing down the words, "Where or When." But I do it in a very odd way. All the letters are connected like this: WHEREORWHEN. I have no idea what that means, but it gets weirder. A year after my epiphany on the railroad tracks, I was given a chance to sing on a nationally syndicated radio program called *San Francisco Sketchbook* that was broadcast from our local station, KFRC. The very first question that Lyle Bardo, the orchestra leader, asked me was, "Do you know 'Where or When'?"

That was on a Friday. On Monday, the name of the program was *The Merv Griffin Show*. I was exactly twenty years old.

While I was at KFRC I made it into the record books in a rather interesting way. With my friend Janet Folsom, I formed my own little record label, Panda Records. We chose four songs and I recorded them at a studio in San Francisco. It just so happened that the recording engineer there had recently returned from the war in Europe, where he had been doing experimental recording with something called magnetic tape. In 1946, *Songs by Merv Griffin* became the first American album ever to be recorded on tape. (If you're looking for a copy, you can find it in the Ampex Museum.)

After three years on the air, the first *Merv Griffin Show* developed something of a following. I had no way of knowing that one of my regular listeners also happened to be one of the most popular orchestra leaders in the country, Freddy Martin. That all changed one morning in 1948 when a young woman (she couldn't have been any older than I was) named Jean Barry called the station and asked to meet me for lunch. She identified herself as Freddy Martin's secretary.

Over lunch she told me that Freddy's singer, Stuart Wade, was leaving the band after its current stand at the St. Francis Hotel in San Francisco. Then she dropped her bombshell: "Freddy wants you for the job, Merv."

At first I didn't believe her. I realized that she was serious only when she invited me to come see the band's show at the St. Francis and meet Freddy in person.

Even before I walked into the elegant Mural Room of the St. Francis Hotel, I had pretty much made up my mind to say yes. At twenty-three, I was eager to expand my horizons beyond San Francisco—and this seemed like the perfect opportunity to do exactly that.

If I had any doubts about whether I was making the right choice, they were forever dispelled that night. Before I even told him that I had decided to accept his offer, Freddy asked me to come up to the microphone and do a guest song. I went up on stage and, whispering in my ear, he asked me if I could sing—you guessed it—"Where or When." You *betcha*, Mr. Martin.

The next day I walked into the KFRC manager's office and said, "Sir, we don't have a contract and I've been here three years. I think that I've done my job well, and you've been very generous, but I quit."

The manager, whose name was Bill Pabst (no relation to the Blue Ribbon), was amazed. He said, "You quit?"

"Yes, sir. I have an offer to go with the Freddy Martin band as their singer for a hundred fifty dollars a week."

Despite the realization that he was about to lose his star, Pabst couldn't help but be amused. "Let me see if I understand this, Merv. You make a hundred dollars per show here and you do eleven shows a week. So you're talking about a weekly salary cut of almost a *thousand dollars*. You don't understand very much about economics, do you, son?"

What he didn't understand was that money by itself was never that important to me. Don't get me wrong, I was glad to have it. But I never dreamt about it. I still don't.

What I *did* dream about was being able to perform on the glamorous stages all across America that I'd only read about or seen in the Movietone newsreels. The Starlight Roof in New York. The Cocoanut Grove in Los Angeles. Even the Mural Room in the St. Francis seemed like a distant and exotic world to me.

My parents were very proud of me. Still, I don't think they believed it all right away; it took a while for my success to sink in. First they had to cope with the fact that I had become a local celebrity who was now making more money in a week than my father made in a month. And they had to accept that their youngest child would be leaving home to travel all over the country as the featured singer of a famous orchestra.

To their credit (and my great fortune) none of that ever changed how they treated me. To them, I was just Buddy.

I took my mother to opening night with Freddy Martin at Ciro's nightclub in Los Angeles. I was terrified. The shaking of my legs was clearly visible through my pants. The celebrity audience thought this was hysterical because while I was singing these romantic ballads, my legs were keeping their own separate beat. Of course, whenever people know you're a newcomer, they're extremely forgiving and very generous with their applause. Afterward, all my mother could say was, "They really *like* you, don't they?"

The exhilaration of performing in front of an orchestra is something that, even today, I have trouble describing in words. This much I can tell you—after doing it for more than fifty years, I still feel it. The moment those violins come in I get a physical sensation of . . . I suppose the only word for it is *joy*. That wonderful feeling passes right through my body, the way Judy Garland's voice passed through me whenever I saw her perform.

It was also during this time—for better or worse—that I began my lifelong association with coconuts.

In those days, the Cocoanut Grove in the Ambassador Hotel was the hottest nightspot in Hollywood. And when we were in town, the Freddy Martin Orchestra *was* the Cocoanut Grove. I sat in front of the band every night—occasionally I'd shake the maracas—watching with amazement as every movie actor I'd ever seen on the screen came through those doors. Say a name and they'd appear, as though conjured up by some musical magic—Elizabeth Taylor, Bing Crosby, Lana Turner, Doris Day—it was a nightly parade of stars.

Of all the celebrities who came into the Cocoanut Grove, perhaps the most interesting, and certainly the most unusual, was Howard Hughes. When we played there he was in the audience every night, and I really do mean *every* night, of what were sometimes three-month-long engagements. He always had a fabulous girl with him, although it was rarely the same girl twice. And although his date was dressed to the nines, Hughes always wore beat-up old sneakers and a tattered sport coat. A creature of habit, he would first order a dish of vanilla ice cream and then he would invariably request the same song, a rhumba that I sang in Greek called "Miserlou." (Down the road it would become clear that these habits were the first inklings of Hughes's obsessive-compulsive personality, but back then he only seemed like a harmless eccentric.)

For someone so famous and powerful, Howard Hughes was almost painfully shy. Maybe it was because I was so young, but for some reason he felt comfortable with me. I can't say that we ever became friends, yet night after night he'd see me out front and he'd stop to request his song. I liked him.

Years later, Noah Dietrich, who was Hughes's assistant for twenty years, wrote an extensive biography of his former boss. When he appeared on my talk show, I hadn't yet read the book.

With great seriousness, as if he was telling me something of extreme importance, Dietrich said, "Merv, do you realize that you were Howard Hughes's favorite singer?"

After Dietrich made this shattering pronouncement, he clearly expected me to be impressed. I wasn't.

Puzzled, he asked, "You're not thrilled?"

"Well, not really," I replied, knowing that would inevitably lead to the next question: "Why not?"

"Noah, the man was *deaf*. Maybe he liked me because he couldn't hear me."

In 1950, I recorded a novelty tune called "I've Got a Lovely Bunch of Coconuts." I sang the whole silly song in a cockney accent and, don't ask me why, but it shot to number one on the Hit Parade. All of a sudden I had real *fans*, not just people who enjoyed my singing. The song was so popular that when we got to Los Angeles, rather than doing our usual stand at the Cocoanut Grove, we were booked into the Palladium, a ballroom with a capacity of 10,000. I will never know what Elvis or the Beatles went through, but those Palladium shows gave me a taste of it. Thousands of screaming girls chanting "We Want 'Coconuts'!" is an image that you never forget. Backstage, I even met the president of my newly created Hollywood High School fan club, a skinny girl with a big voice and a marvelous laugh whose name was . . . let me see if I can remember it . . . wait a minute . . . oh yes, her name was Carol. Carol *Burnett*. Go figure.

Without even knowing that I was doing it, I had transformed the Freddy Martin Orchestra from a dance band into a show band. The success of "Coconuts" prompted Freddy to commission pieces that were written especially for me, like "Back on the Bus," the story of a band on the road. Unlike "Coconuts" (which, when I hear it now, makes me cringe), "Back on the Bus" was an *intentionally* funny song with very witty lyrics. The audience waited for it every night.

It was certainly an appropriate song for me, because for most of the four years I was with Freddy Martin, I basically lived on a bus. My seat was always directly behind the driver, which allowed me to carefully observe the ingrown hairs on the back of his neck. (In case you're curious, they were in the shape of a checkerboard square.) There was one stretch where we did seventy-four one-nighters in seventy-four days as we traveled east across the United States. I may not have seen the country before, but I was certainly seeing it now. And I loved it.

Well, most of the time. There was a tradition among traveling musicians that I wasn't made aware of until the band was safely out on the road and I was a long way from home. Bluntly speaking, the boy singer was used as bait. Here's how it worked. I'd be sitting downstage near the audience, with the band behind me, when all of a sudden I'd hear a trumpet player say, "Hey, Merv, get me *that* one. The one in the white blouse."

We were doing a one-night stand in the coal mining town of Mahanoy City, Pennsylvania, a couple of days outside New York. I was onstage singing as dozens of young couples twirled across the dance floor below. Suddenly, there was an urgent whisper in my ear, "Red dress." It was the voice of the saxophone player, one of the lead wolves in our traveling pack.

Dutiful lamb that I was, I spotted Miss Red Dress and started smiling at her, as if she were the only girl in the room. The problem was that she was dancing with her boyfriend at the time. Whenever he'd swing her around so that he was facing the stage, I looked away. As soon as his back turned toward me again, I continued putting the look on his date. This went on for a good ten minutes and she was clearly getting my message. And so was her boyfriend's best buddy, a big hulking fellow who looked like he could dig coal with his bare hands. I watched the whole thing play out right in front of me, like a horror movie in slow motion. Big Lenny comes lumbering right out on the dance floor and starts talking to his friend and pointing up at me. The band is playing and I'm singing, trying to pretend that I'm not seeing any of this. Then the boyfriend starts yelling at his girl, and she's shaking her head back and forth, as if to say, "Don't blame *me*. I didn't do anything. He was the one looking at me." At this point they had both stopped dancing. Other people were starting to look up at me and point.

I don't think that I've ever sung so fast in my life. After what seemed like an eternity, the music finally stopped. Unfortunately this also meant that I could now *hear* what was being said to me. Some of it was pretty ugly—and quite specific: "Come down here, pretty boy. Let's see how cute you look with that microphone shoved up your . . ."

Obviously I survived, but the only reason I didn't need medical attention was that the entire band (including the now sheepish saxophone player) surrounded me as we walked out of the ballroom. The coal miners may have been tougher, but they were unarmed. All the musicians held their instruments over their heads like weapons, fully prepared to whack anybody who came near us.

Finally, we arrived in New York where we played the Strand Theater on Broadway (now the Warner Theater) and I realized one of my dreams by singing at the Starlight Roof of the Waldorf-Astoria. Even as I continued to work with Freddy, I also began to have a bit of success on my own. My girlfriend at the time was a beautiful young redhead named Judy Balaban (her father, Barney, was president of Paramount Pictures). Life seemed endlessly interesting and exciting to me then, as it does when you're young. (Actually, life still seems that interesting to me now. You know the old expression, "you're only as old as you feel"? That's not quite true. Sometimes I feel older than dirt. What *is* true is that you're only as old as you think. Ask anyone and they'll tell you that I'm the oldest kid they know.)

One of my first solo gigs in New York was as a guest singer on what was then the top-rated radio program in the country, *The Big Show* on NBC. *The Big Show* was hosted by a woman whose picture can be found in the thesaurus next to the phrase "larger than life"— the outrageous, caustic, bawdy ("but never *boring, dahling*") Miss Tallulah Bankhead.

Before I go on, you need to be familiar with the backstory here. At the same time that I was booked to appear on her radio program, Tallulah Bankhead was also involved in one of the biggest celebrity-scandal trials of the era. Her maid had been charged with stealing from her and, very reluctantly, Tallulah was forced to testify in the case, thus opening the door to testimony about the lurid details of her personal life.

Compared to, say, the O.J. trial, this was a celebrity case with quite a lot of funny moments. In fact, Tallulah was warned repeatedly not to laugh during the testimony of the other witnesses because her throaty guffaw would break up the entire courtroom, including the judge. But she couldn't control herself. "Oh your honor, *dahling*," she'd say to the judge, "really, I am sorry." She was eventually banished from the courtroom except for when she had to give her own testimony. (By the way, do you know how I knew that O.J. was bad news long before the rest of the world found out? Simple. Sophia Loren once told a story on my show about how Simpson hadn't paid up when he lost to her in poker. In other words, "the rules don't apply to me.")

Okay, back to *The Big Show*. At the afternoon rehearsal, everybody gathered around a large table to go over that evening's script. Let me tell you who else was there that day: Ethel Merman, Phil Silvers, and Loretta Young. And fresh from her matinee performance in New York Superior Court, our host, Miss Bankhead.

Now, everyone in that room knew that in court Tallulah had been accused of being a flagrant pot smoker. Anyone else would have been on her best behavior, knowing that the slightest impropriety would surely make its way into print. But not Tallulah. Draped in a full-length mink coat, she sauntered leisurely into the room (late, as usual, which guaranteed her an audience) and stopped in front of the NBC orchestra. She looked at Meredith Willson and the hundred musicians seated behind him, paused for effect, then in that gruff Southern voice that earned her the nickname "the Alabama Foghorn," she asked, "Has anybody got a reefer?"

After the waves of laughter finally subsided, Ethel Merman resumed telling a story to Phil Silvers that had been interrupted by Tallulah's grand entrance.

"So, Phil, I was just saying that I bumped into that singing teacher we used to have." She mentioned his name and Phil Silvers said, "Oh *him*. I thought he was dead. He's a son of a bitch."

Loretta Young, who was very religious and quite proper, said, "That will be one dollar for the swear box." Phil Silvers dug into his pocket, pulled out a dollar, and put it in a cardboard shoebox that was sitting in the middle of the table.

"Well, honey," continued Ethel, "you remember that little rat who was our first manager? I thought he was dead too, but I saw that lousy bastard in Sardi's just last week."

Like a missionary among heathens, Loretta was undaunted. "Ethel," she said, primly, "that will be another dollar for the swear box."

And so it went, back and forth like a tennis match for about ten minutes, until the shoebox was stuffed with cash. Tallulah had been uncharacteristically quiet throughout these exchanges until, finally, she could stand it no longer.

"Loretta, *dahling*," she drawled, "how much will it cost me to tell you to go *fuck* yourself?"

Loretta slumped down in her chair as if she'd been struck. And that was the end of the rehearsal.

Along with my solo gigs in New York, I still had a steady job with Freddy Martin. In fact, we even landed our own weekly television show on NBC. In early television, every show had a single sponsor. Ours was Hazel Bishop lipstick, which was a very famous brand in the fifties—"Won't smear off. Won't rub off. Won't kiss off."

"*The Hazel Bishop Show* featuring the Freddy Martin Orchestra" originated live every Wednesday night at ten o'clock from the Center Theater in New York. (Now remember this detail; you'll be tested on it later. The Center Theater had a giant movie screen above the stage so that the studio audience could see everything in close-up, just like the audience at home.)

There actually *was* a Hazel Bishop. She was the laboratory technician who had discovered a revolutionary no-smear formula for lipstick. Unfortunately for her, there were also a few problems with her product that hadn't quite been worked out yet. One particularly annoying side effect was that after putting on the lipstick, a girl's lips swelled up as if she had been kissed by a bee. The band got free samples without realizing any of this and we gave them out to all our wives, girlfriends, mothers, and sisters. It wasn't pretty. Of course we couldn't say anything negative about the lipstick without offending our sponsor.

Every week those of us who were soloists were required to do a commercial with the spokeswoman for Hazel Bishop (not Hazel herself). Inevitably, my turn came to do the commercial.

The bit was that I would be singing and the spokeswoman would lean over in the middle of my song and kiss me. I'd act surprised and pull out my handkerchief to wipe off the lipstick. Then I'd look at the handkerchief before I turned it to the audience. "Amazing," I'd say holding it up, "no lipstick smears!"

Because very bright lights were required for those early television broadcasts, we needed to wear a lot of makeup. I rehearsed the commercial without it. That night, of course, I had full makeup on for the cameras.

So the big moment came and the girl kissed me. (Don't forget, this whole thing was *live*.) On cue, I wiped it off, but when I looked down at my handkerchief, there was a huge, gooey makeup stain on it. I knew immediately that on black and white television screens that smudge would read like lipstick. But I had to do something. I flipped the handkerchief over quickly so that only the white part was showing and, with a terrified deer-in-the-headlights look, said, "See, no lipstick smears!" Then I shoved it back in my pocket as fast as I could. I don't know how it played at home, but the live audience saw the whole thing on the big screen. They screamed with laughter for two solid minutes.

When I went backstage, the real Hazel Bishop was there waiting for me. She was red-faced and shaking with anger. Hazel didn't give a damn about her company. All she said was, "You embarrassed me in front of my friends!" My "first blush" of success became a very famous clip, one of the original bloopers from early television.

A side note: the crew of *The Hazel Bishop Show* would go on to enjoy extraordinary success in the years to come. The director was Perry Lafferty, who would later become the West Coast head of CBS. The front stage manager was Arthur Penn, who went on to direct *The Miracle Worker* and *Bonnie and Clyde*, among many great films. And the backstage manager was Bill Colleran, who ended up as the director of *Your Hit Parade* and, later, *The Dean Martin Show*. Bill married Lee Remick, and I became godfather to their daughter, Kate. It was an all-star crew and we became very close friends, never imagining what the future held in store for each of us.

In July of 1952, my own future arrived in the form of a draft notice: "Greetings. Please report to 39 Whitehall Street for your pre-induction physical." Although I had flunked those ten physicals during World War II, the new slimmed-down Merv (I'd lost eighty pounds since then) was certain to pass muster.

Like a man condemned, I got all my affairs in order. First, I informed Freddy that Uncle Sam had invited me off the bus. Then I sent all my belongings back to my parents. My friends in New York gave me a big farewell party. Finally, the day came and I took the subway downtown to the main induction center on Whitehall Street (made famous by Arlo Guthrie in the song "Alice's Restaurant"). Sure enough, I was now a perfect physical specimen. As I gathered my clothes and walked back to the desk for final processing, I remember thinking, *I wonder how long it will take me to learn Korean?*

I was still lost in thought when the desk sergeant looked up at me and barked, "What the hell are you doing here?"

"Reporting for duty, sir!"

"Reporting for duty my ass, you're too old. They changed the law six months ago. Twenty-six is the new cutoff." I had just turned twenty-seven.

Stunned, I managed to say, "What do I do now, sir?"

"Go home. Next."

What *was* next? I didn't go back to Freddy Martin, but as a personal favor, I did agree to appear with him in Las Vegas for a two-week booking at the Last Frontier Hotel and Casino when his newly hired singer (my replacement) had a last-minute family crisis.

It was during this engagement that my life once more changed drastically. Again it would happen with dizzying speed, much in the way it had when I was given my own radio show after only three days or when Jean Barry asked me to lunch and, a week later, I was singing with Freddy Martin.

This time the angel of my good fortune was one of the biggest movie stars of the fifties—the former Doris Von Kappelhoff, better known to the world as Doris Day.

I was in my dressing room between shows (we were doing two shows a night), when I heard a light knock on the door.

"Yes?"

No one answered so I went over and opened the door myself. Standing there was a little boy who must have been about ten years old.

"Mr. Griffin?"

"What can I do for you, young man?" I smiled down at him, already feeling for a pen in my pocket to give him an autograph. (People never have their own pens.)

"My name is Terry and my dad wants to sign you for the movies and my mom wants to make a movie with you." I'd heard a lot of good stories, but this was a new one on me.

Playing along, I said, "Hey, that's great, kid. So who's your mom?"
"Doris Day."

I stared at him blankly for a moment. He might as well have said
Queen Elizabeth. When I found my voice, all I could think to say
was, "I love your mother."

He ran out and brought both of his parents back to meet me.
Needless to say, his mother really *was* Doris Day, and his stepfather
was her husband and manager, Marty Melcher. Doris was under contract at Warner Brothers and she told me that I'd be perfect for the
kind of musicals that she was making there. Doris and Marty promised to arrange a screen test for me right away.

Elated, I flew to Los Angeles immediately following my final show
with Freddy. After taking my screen test a few days later, I signed my
name on a long-term contract with Warner Brothers for the stagger-
ing sum of $250 a week. (*"You don't understand very much about eco-
nomics, do you, son?"*)

The ink wasn't even dry when the studio started trying to "fix" me.
They began with the name I'd just affixed to my contract.

"We don't think your name works. How about *Mark* Griffin?"

I said, "Well, I've had my own radio show and a number one
record with that name, so I think it works fine."

"Okay, then how about changing the spelling? We can add a second 'e.' You'll be *Merve* Griffin."

I resisted the temptation to say, "Hey, you guys have got some
merve." Instead, I politely thanked them and said that I couldn't
change the spelling because it would greatly upset my father, whose
namesake I was. (It didn't much matter what I wanted. I spent the
next ten years telling reporters "I don't *care* what it says. There's no
second 'e,' damnit!" Dan Quayle would later have the same problem
with "potatoe.")

My salary of $250 climbed to a whopping $300 a week after I
starred in *So This Is Love*, with Kathryn Grayson. The public didn't
realize it, but as a contract player you could be the star of a major
motion picture and when it was over you were still poor.

Today they pay actors these astronomical sums, sometimes as
much as $20 million a picture. Even so, I believe it's smarter to do
what Jack Nicholson did on films like *Batman* and *As Good as It Gets*:
take a low salary in return for a percentage of the profits on the back

end. If the film is a hit, you'll make far more than you would have as a salaried actor, no matter how much you're paid up front.

My bookkeeper, Gloria Redlich, who's been with me over forty years, always tells people about a remark I made to her when we first met: "You'll never get rich on a W-2." I still think that's true.

It turned out that *So This Is Love* was the only serious film role that I would ever have. The press screening was held at the Pantages Theater in Hollywood. Louella Parsons and Hedda Hopper were both there, confirming the importance of the event.

It was in that theater that I saw myself, for the first time, on the big screen. I had never watched the rushes (the partial film clips shown at the end of each day's shooting), so I had no idea what I looked like on film. As the picture unspooled, I found myself sliding further and further down in my chair. By the time it ended, I was under the seat, on the floor. Before the credits even finished rolling, I snuck out into the lobby, hoping to make a quick exit. But Hedda and Louella were there, blocking my path. "Oh, you darling boy," they cooed at me in unison, "you're going to be the biggest star in the world." They kissed me and hugged me and I thought, What's going on here? Could they be telling the truth? Nah.

That night, I just lay there in bed, unable to fall asleep. Finally, I decided that Hedda and Louella were right. I *was* the biggest star in the world. I drifted off and dreamt that I was thanking the Academy for the great honor it had bestowed upon me.

Unfortunately for my Oscar, I woke up.

To be fair, it wasn't only *my* performance that sank *So This Is Love*. The day before our picture opened, Twentieth Century–Fox released *The Robe*, the first motion picture ever shot in CinemaScope ("*The modern miracle you see without glasses!*"). For months afterward, all anyone could talk about was "widescreen."

From then on, I was given small parts and voice-over work in a dozen other movies, none of which meant a thing. Of course you remember that dramatic radio bulletin in *The Beast from 20,000 Fathoms*: "*Well, folks, here's another one of those silly reports about sea serpents again.*" That was me.

Finally I called my manager and said, "How do I get out of here?" It got so bad that one day the casting director called my house and I answered the phone as if I barely spoke English.

"Can I speak to Mr. Griffin, please?"

"He no home! He no home! You call back!"

Shortly after that, I bought out the remainder of my contract. I wasn't sure what I was going to do next, but I knew that I wouldn't be giving that Academy Award speech anytime soon.

Short-lived as my film career proved to be, it did earn me a small footnote in cinema history. Judged by today's standards, my achievement seems almost comical. Believe it or not, when I kissed Kathryn Grayson in *So This Is Love*, it was the first time an open-mouthed kiss had ever been shown in theaters. At the time, it was a big deal. Really.

In December of 1953, I found myself back in Las Vegas, the town where, only two years before, Doris Day "discovered" me. (Show business may be the only profession where you can work for years to become an overnight sensation.)

Right after my release from the Warners contract, my agent got a call from the Sands Hotel in Las Vegas. To celebrate their first anniversary they'd brought in none other than the great Tallulah Bankhead herself and asked her to create a variety act especially for the occasion. I was hired as her opening act.

On the second day of our two-week engagement, I developed laryngitis and had to take the night off. I was back the next day, but to my surprise, Tallulah wasn't speaking to me. I thought she was going to fire me. I finally cornered her and asked her what was wrong.

"You little prick." She was smiling, so I knew my job was safe.

"You know I hate it when people get sick around me. I start to take on their symptoms, dahling. If I'm around someone who stutters, I stutter. When somebody tells me that they've been in a car accident, I feel injured myself. Just don't cough on me, dahling."

I made a mental note: find another job where you won't get fired if you lose your voice.

On our last night at the Sands, Tallulah and I had more than a few too many. Feeling no pain, and in violation of house rules that strictly forbade performers from gambling, we hit the tables. By dawn, I had almost $30,000 in my pocket, including my paycheck. (There was a grim moment later than afternoon when, having spent the night in my car, I woke up and couldn't remember where my money was. I finally found it pushed down in my shoes.)

I decided to parlay my Vegas winnings into a new start in New

York. So when I got back to L.A., I called the girl that I was seeing at the time, a singer-dancer named Rita Farrell.

"I'm out of here, Rita. I'm going to New York to start my career."

She didn't try to talk me out of it. "I'm going with you," was all she said.

I got a deal on a new Ford convertible and the two of us hit the road. Once again I was headed to New York in search of fame and fortune. But this time it would be different (or so I thought). There was no Freddy Martin to answer to, no studio executives to argue with. I was now the captain of my own ship.

Maybe so, but anybody who saw me during that cross-country trip must have thought my ship was a garbage scow. Rita and I were both wearing old clothes and looking slovenly. We barely even stopped for food along the way, so by the time we got to Pennsylvania, I hadn't shaved in almost a week.

My new Ford convertible blew up at the Harrisburg exit on the Pennsylvania Turnpike. The engine block cracked and steam came pouring out; we had to have it towed into the local dealership.

Looking (and probably smelling) like two escaped prisoners, Rita and I were stuck at that Ford dealership in Harrisburg waiting for word about our car.

Finally, the manager broke the bad news: "You need a new motor."

I was dumbfounded. "It's a brand-new car. I just bought it. You've got to fix it."

"I'm sorry," although he clearly wasn't, "but you're over the mileage limit on your warranty."

"You've got to be kidding." We were talking big money for that kind of job.

"There's nothing we can do about it. Those are the rules. I'm sorry."

Now, there's something you should know. The year before, when I was still at Warner Brothers, I'd performed at a private show for all the top brass of the Ford Motor Company at the Pan Pacific Auditorium in Los Angeles. Many of the big Warner stars were on the bill and, afterward, all of us were introduced to the three Ford brothers, Henry, William, and Benson.

So I said to the manager, "Could I use your phone to call Mr. Ford?" He looked at Rita and me as if we were lunatics.

I ignored his attitude and calmly repeated, "Please let me use your phone. I want to call Benson Ford."

Clearly annoyed, the manager said, "Would you *really?*" But he decided to call what was certainly my bluff.

So he turned to his secretary and said, "Get Mr. Benson Ford on the phone and tell him—what's your name?—tell him *Merv Griffin* wants to speak with him."

Luckily, he had a primitive kind of speakerphone in his office, so after she placed the call, I did all the talking.

"Mr. Ford's office. May I help you?"

"Mr. Ford please, it's Merv Griffin calling."

"Oh yes, Mr. Griffin," said Ford's secretary. "Hold on, please, I'll get him." At that point the color began to drain from the manager's face.

"Merv! How are you?" The booming voice of Benson Ford blasted over the speakerphone.

I replied, "Terrible, Mr. Ford, just terrible."

Now the manager is suddenly looking at me with a mixture of awe and fear, like I'd just called God (which to him, I had). I explained our predicament to Benson Ford. When I'd finished my tale of woe, he simply said, "Put that manager on the phone."

The manager, who was listening to all this over the speaker, said, somewhat hesitantly, "I'm right here, Mr. Ford."

"Now you listen to me. Give that boy a new motor. Give him anything he wants. Just charge it to me. Got that?"

"Yes sir, Mr. Ford. Right away, sir." Oh boy.

They gave us a new motor and we were back on the road two days later. If I'd asked him to, the manager would have driven us to New York himself.

I had a leg up when I arrived in New York because I was already represented by MCA, then the largest talent agency in the country. Marty Kummer, who also handled Ed Sullivan and Jack Paar, was my agent there, and he was devoted to me. He had that rare quality in an agent—he treated you with the same enthusiasm and attention whether you were making ten dollars or ten thousand dollars.

For a while Marty got me a lot of singing jobs, usually one-offs (a single night's work). Since I was a quick study, I developed a reputation as being a reliable utility singer ("We're on in twenty minutes? Get that Griffin kid.").

Finally, after about six months of this, I called Marty Kummer and said, "I don't want to sing anymore."

"What do you mean, Merv? You're a singer. That's what you do."

"But I don't want to do it anymore, Marty."

There was silence on the line. For a second I thought he'd hung up. Then, quietly, almost like he was talking to a child, he asked, "What is it you *want* to do, Merv?"

"I want to MC."

"Merv," he said patiently, "you know that singers aren't accepted as MCs. They can't talk. Have you seen *The Eddie Fisher Show*?"

I *had* seen it. It was a train wreck. "That's different, Marty. He can't talk. I can."

By this time, Marty was resigned to losing the argument, so he shifted gears. "Okay, fine. Right now, there aren't any MC jobs out there. I'll put your name in if something opens up, but it could take quite a while. And there's no guarantee you'll even be seriously considered. So what are you going to do in the meantime? You've got to eat."

"I don't want to depend upon my singing voice anymore, Marty. I don't think that's the career for me. I'll wait."

I hung up the phone and thought, What the hell have I just done?

There's an old Irish saying that God watches over drunks, fools, and little children. I'm not exactly sure where I fit in, but apparently He was watching over me anyway. Within a few months of that telephone call to my agent, a hosting job opened up on *Look Up and Live*, a Sunday morning religious show on CBS. I jumped at it, if only for the opportunity to prove that I could cut it as an MC.

Look Up and Live was a show that ran its entire script through the TelePrompTer, so I had to learn to read my lines while making it look like I was ad-libbing. One day I was midway though an earnest conversation with a Protestant minister when the whole show, quite literally, unraveled. The early TelePrompTers were little more than long rolls of paper. Suddenly the entire thing scrunched up and the paper tore, then completely ripped apart.

I looked at the minister and, without pausing, I said, "Isn't that right, Reverend?"

He glanced at me nervously. "What?"

"What I just said. Isn't that right?"

"Oh yes," he said, still not sure of what he was agreeing to, "that's exactly right." (He wasn't listening either.)

I'd just dumped it all on him. At least he could fall back on Scripture, even without the TelePrompTer.

Very early in my career, I had discovered something important about myself. When that red light came on, I didn't have a single nerve in my body. It was like stepping out of reality and becoming someone else.

While I was doing *Look Up and Live*, I became quite friendly with Mahalia Jackson and Sidney Poitier, both of whom were regular performers on the program. Mahalia sang gospel songs and Sidney acted out various Bible stories.

Sidney was about my age and, like me, he was frustrated at the direction his career was—or wasn't—taking. But unlike me, he loved acting. He'd even started his own drama school up in Harlem. One morning we were having breakfast and he asked me what I'd do if I couldn't get work as a host after this show. I thought about it, and then realizing how much I'd come to admire my agent, Marty Kummer, I said, "I think I might try my luck at being an agent." Sidney said that if things didn't pan out for him soon, he'd quit acting and run his drama school. After we left the show we lost touch with each other, and I didn't see him again for more than twenty years. One day we ran into each other in Sardi's, where we were both having dinner. By this time, I had a national television show running five nights a week and he had my Oscar.

We greeted each other warmly. "Sidney," I asked earnestly, "do you still have your acting school?" Without missing a beat, he said, "No, Merv, that didn't work out for me. Are you still an agent?"

After I finished my run with *Look Up and Live*, CBS gave me an even bigger opportunity. It was a slot on their version of the *Today* show—*The CBS Morning Show*. Even though they wanted me as a singer, I took the job because it was the same show where Jack Paar got his start.

After Paar, CBS had given the host's job to John Henry Faulk, the great American humorist (who was subsequently blacklisted on charges that were eventually proven false). Faulk was the host when I was hired.

American Airlines was our sponsor and they served us breakfast on the air between seven and eight in the morning. Every day they gave us these huge portions of pancakes and bacon. I suppose they wanted people to think that these were airline-size portions. Right.

Because we had to repeat the show for the West Coast at nine (no tape in those days), we had to eat the same damn breakfast all over again . . . *and* look like we were enjoying it. Well, I was already annoyed at having to go to work at 4:00 A.M. (an hour I far prefer at the end of my day rather than the beginning), but having to eat those stupid meals twice a day on camera was beginning to put me over the edge.

I can handle almost anything in life except boredom. And this job was boring me to tears.

Now several times during the show, the announcer stood up and gave a weather report on camera, much in the same way Al Roker does it now on the *Today* show. However, in those primitive days of television, there were no maps and charts and satellite photographs. He just stood there with a long sheet of paper and read the temperatures and forecasts from around the country.

So, one day—and I still don't know what made me do this—I leaned over and lit the bottom of his weather report on fire. He screamed, "I'm on fire!" although it was only his copy that was burning slightly around the edges. The poor guy panicked. He wore a toupee and, fearing that it would soon ignite, he yanked it off his head and threw it across the room. By this time the fire was out, but the damage was done. He turned to me and said, on camera, "That was evil." Stifling the urge to laugh, I said, "Oh, I guess it was. I'm very sorry."

I'm not sure how you would describe my behavior in those days. I don't think I was brash . . . well, perhaps setting the weatherman's copy on fire *was* brash. But it was entertaining.

Shortly after that, Faulk was let go. We learned that his replacement would be a young disc jockey from New Orleans who'd only done local television; his name was Dick Van Dyke. This would be his big national break. CBS flew him to New York, he had a great rehearsal, and everything was set for his debut the following day.

The next morning we were all at the studio at four, everybody except Dick. Five o'clock comes, then six, and still no sign of our new host. Finally it was five minutes to seven, and the producer comes rushing out and says to me, "We've looked everywhere. We can't find him and we're going on live at seven. You're going on in his place." Maybe it was because I was too young to know any better, or maybe it was because this scene was already very familiar to me from all those Judy Garland–Mickey Rooney movies where somehow the show always managed to go on, but I wasn't nervous at all. I just said, "Okay, I'm ready. Let's go."

At two minutes to seven the producer handed me a bunch of public service announcements ("Don't forget this is National Bunion Awareness Week") and said, "Read these." I looked at them and said, "These are diseases. It's seven in the morning. Trust me, nobody wants to think about getting sick when they're not awake yet. I'll just wing it." I handed him back the papers and before he could argue with me, the red light came on and we were off to the races. For the next three hours, I MC'd the show without a script and when it was over, I thought to myself, This is fun. I can *do* this.

Oh, maybe you're wondering whatever happened to Dick Van Dyke. It turned out that he was so nervous he slept through his wake-up call and all the frantic calls from the production staff that followed. He never did show up that day. By the next day he was fine, and he had a great run as host of the show. Obviously, CBS never lost confidence in him. A good thing too—ten years later he was their biggest star. Dick and I have laughed over this story many times. He takes credit for launching my career as a talk show host and I point out that he's just lucky I didn't set him on fire.

Two:
Always Bet
on Yourself

When I decided to leave *the CBS Morning Show* the following year, it wasn't because I didn't want to do television anymore. On the contrary, I was now convinced that my future was hiding somewhere inside that large box with the small screen. I couldn't see it clearly yet, but I knew that it was only a matter of time before my life came into focus.

I still didn't want to take singing jobs, but I rationalized that any job which gave me more experience in television was—for the time being—worth taking.

Then I met Robert Q. Lewis.

Lewis was a radio personality who'd occasionally substituted for Arthur Godfrey on *Talent Scouts* (the first *American Idol*, for those of you who are generationally impaired). Based on these few appearances, CBS decided to take a chance on him with his own half-hour variety show. With his black horn-rimmed glasses and perpetual smirk, Lewis was an odd fit for television. He seemed more like a dyspeptic accountant than the urbane host he thought himself to be. He wasn't humorous, and I don't think he was very inventive. But as so often happens, he had a gargantuan ego that was not commensurate with his talent. And as I was soon to discover, he was also insane.

I'd been brought in by CBS producer Irving Mansfield (Jacqueline Susann's husband) to help save the show, which was floundering in the ratings. Lewis didn't want me there, but he couldn't fire me. Our first confrontation came very early on. As the featured singer, I had to do two songs every day. And he insisted that they be new songs, often from the latest Broadway shows. But there was no way anyone could learn that much material on a daily basis. That meant the lyrics had to be put on the TelePrompTer, which Lewis insisted remain on the floor below the camera, not behind it. Because of this, I had to look down while I was singing, never an impressive way to perform.

So one day (which also happened to be Yom Kippur, the highest holy day in the Jewish faith) I came in and started to rehearse one of my two new songs—"On the Street Where You Live" from *My Fair Lady*. I'd only sung a few bars before Lewis (whose real name, I should note, was Bobby Goldberg) shouted, "Stop the rehearsal!"

He was in the back of the studio, the disembodied voice of God. Over the speaker comes the sarcastic question, "Mr. Griffin, on St. Patrick's Day, we all sang St. Patrick's songs. What are you going to do on this high Jewish holiday? *That* song?" I responded calmly (which I knew infuriated him), "Well I'm rehearsing it. That's what the show selected." But he wouldn't let go. Again the voice came back from out of the darkness, "Aren't we going to do something for the Jews?" With just a hint of a smile, I replied, "Would you like 'Onward Christian Soldiers'?"

The entire cast and crew fell apart laughing.

Lewis failed to see the humor. He came rushing out of the darkness waving the script in the air. "Griffin," he screamed, his eyes bulging behind his glasses, "whose name is on the cover of this script, yours or mine?" He threw it down at my feet and stalked off, kicking chairs and banging on tables as he departed.

Did I mention that he was crazy?

Thirty years later, I was seated in St. Germain, an elegant restaurant on Melrose in Los Angeles that I used to go to for lunch when my show was taping in Hollywood. I'd just started eating when Robert Q. Lewis walked in. (I need to tell you that at this point my first book, *Merv*, had just come out and was already on the *New York Times* best-seller list. And unfortunately for Bob, I have an extremely good memory. My account of our time together was probably very unpleasant for him to read, precisely because it was completely accurate.)

So Lewis sees me and walks over to my table, the familiar scowl still on his face all these years later. "I read your book," he snapped. And I said, "It's good, isn't it? Oh, and by the way, Bob, whose name is that on the cover?" He just glared and walked away. I never saw him again.

Surprisingly enough, I will always be grateful to Robert Q. Lewis. You see, I married his secretary.

Born with big dreams in the small town of Ironwood, Michigan, Julann Wright arrived in New York in 1954 determined to break into show business. Her first love was the theater, but like me she'd been forced to compromise in order to gain experience—and eat. Lewis hired her as a secretary-assistant on his Saturday radio program, which had continued to run even after he got the television show.

One day when Lewis was on the air, Julann came quietly into the studio with his coffee. On a whim, Lewis just started talking to her, live on the radio.

"Oh, Julann, thank you so much for the basketball that you gave me for Christmas."

Of course, she hadn't given him anything for Christmas, but Julann was so quick, nothing fazed her. Like a redheaded version of Judy Holliday, she replied, "Oh, you're welcome. I knew you had a hoop."

The audience ate it up. After that Julann played the part of his daffy secretary every Saturday. (Nothing was further from the truth. Like Judy Holliday, Julann used her talent for playing dumb to conceal an extremely sharp mind.)

Even though she only appeared on the radio show, our paths inevitably crossed and we quickly fell in love. She was (and still is) one of the warmest, funniest people I've ever known. Two years later, after our marriage was announced in the papers, Lewis told people that I had purposely married Julann just to get back at him. In his mind, even our marriage was about *him*, that's how egocentric he was.

Eager to escape Lewis's lunacy (and to take Julann with me), I actively pursued other opportunities. You want to know how desperate I was? When "Buffalo" Bob Smith had a heart attack and couldn't work for a while, I came *thisclose* to filling in for him on *Howdy Doody*. In the end, even *I* couldn't rationalize that playing second banana to a dummy was a good career move. (I confess, however, that I've long had one regret about my decision. I pride myself on spotting and developing new talent. Had I taken the *Doody* job, I would have always been remembered as the man who introduced Gumby to the world.)

Fortunately, the producer who offered me *Howdy Doody*, Martin Stone (who would become a lifetime friend and mentor to me), came back with another prospect that was far more attractive. ABC, then the fledgling third television network, was launching a Miami-based variety show called *Going Places* and they wanted me as the host. In a few short years, Marty Kummer's admonition that "singers are not thought of as MCs" was no longer valid. Increasingly, singers were replacing comedians as television hosts. That year (1957) more than twenty shows were being MC'd by singers ranging from Perry Como and Dinah Shore on NBC to Frank Sinatra, Pat Boone, and Julius La Rosa on ABC.

Although it meant commuting to Florida from New York every weekend, I didn't hesitate in accepting the job. This would be my first solo effort as a host, and I was ready—eager—for the chance.

Although it was fun, *Going Places* wasn't exactly my road to stardom. More like an off-ramp, actually. One of my first interviews was with the mayor of Miami, who, for some reason, thought my name was "Herb." Another guest referred to me as "Mirth," while the orchestra leader kept calling me "Mark" (shades of Warner Brothers). But the final blow to my pride came the day after the broadcast when the *Miami Herald*, in its review, credited me as "Mery" Griffin. At least *she* got a good review.

When I spoke with my parents on the phone that night, neither of them mentioned any of the miscues. To them, I was now a television star. In the manner of a typical Irish-Catholic father of his generation, my dad was gruff but proud. "Ya did good, Buddy. Keep it up and keep your nose clean. Here's your mother." My mother told me that I looked too thin (ah, the good old days), but very handsome.

Ultimately, *Going Places* went nowhere and ABC canceled it after eight months. I'm sure very few people remember it today, even the people who put it on the air. Yet for me, it will always be a special experience for reasons having nothing to do with my career.

Right before the second show was going out live from the Gulfstream racetrack in South Florida, I received a long-distance call from my sister, Barbara, in California. My father had just suffered a massive heart attack.

"I'm sorry, Buddy," she was crying. "He didn't make it."

I just stared at the phone in my hand. This wasn't happening. It *couldn't* be happening. He was only fifty-five.

"Buddy? Are you there?" I heard my sister's voice as though it were being filtered through an echo chamber.

"Yes. Yes, I'm here. I'll take the first plane back. I love you."

Fifteen minutes later I was on live television bantering with my guests as if I didn't have a care in the world. It was like an out-of-body experience. "Mirth" Griffin was doing my show for me. Buddy was watching from the sidelines, crying. I didn't tell anyone until the show was over. I knew that if anyone had offered me so much as a word of sympathy, I would have lost it right on the air.

Of all the thousands of television hours I've logged in my career since then, that first installment of *Going Places*—one week before he died—was the only time that my father ever saw me hosting my own show. For that reason, I've always believed that silly little program in Florida was something I was meant to do.

That year was very hard for me. Not only because of the loss of my father, but after I returned to New York, it also seemed as if I might be losing my career as well. Day after day I sat in my apartment on West 57th Street (which I'd sublet from Marlon Brando), waiting for the phone to ring. Occasionally I picked it up to see if there was still a dial tone. Given my dire financial straits, this was often a fifty-fifty proposition.

I've always been an enthusiastic, energetic person. Waiting around doesn't work for me. For the first time in my life, I began to doubt myself. What if I'd made a huge mistake by giving up singing? Although I'd only received $50 for it (Freddy got the rest), I had a number one hit song with "Cocoanuts." Now I owed my mother money.

In the middle of the longest summer of my life, I turned thirty-two. Some swivel-hipped kid named Presley was the nation's new singing sensation; even if I'd wanted to, I could scarcely call myself a boy singer anymore.

Up to that point in my life, I'd always bet on myself. What I mean by that is I followed my instincts and made my own choices. It's a very difficult thing to gamble on oneself. It can be scary. But in the end, it's the only bet worth making. Because when it pays off, the rewards are all your own.

And until that summer, even when the bet was a long shot, my self-confidence was usually justified. Now, I wasn't so sure.

If life were a movie, this would be the scene where the phone finally rang. But in reality, it never did.

Finally, I got so tired of waiting around in New York that I took a vacation from being unemployed. Using what little savings I had (If the phone wasn't going to ring, why give it any money?) I found a cheap flight to the Caribbean.

While I was down there, my agent, Marty Kummer, who'd never given up on me, sent me a telegram that read:

GOODSON-TODMAN AUDITIONING HOSTS FOR NEW SHOW
STOP THEY LIKE YOU STOP NEED YOU HERE FRIDAY STOP
MARTY

Mark Goodson and Bill Todman were the most successful game show producers in television. They'd developed a string of popular programs during the 1950s, including *To Tell the Truth*, *I've Got a Secret*, *What's My Line*, and *Beat the Clock*. Possibly the only good thing about having a lot of time on my hands was that I got to watch television in the morning. I'd seen all of them. A lot. This was something I could do. And I'd be following in Jack Paar's footsteps yet again. In the early fifties, he'd hosted *I've Got News for You* and *Bank on the Stars*.

I made my way back to New York and showed up at the Goodson-Todman offices at the scheduled time, seven o'clock on a Friday night. Marty Kummer was supposed to meet me. When I got off the elevator on their floor, no one was there. No receptionist, no staff, nobody. I could hear the sound of laughter coming from somewhere deep inside the offices, but the connecting door was locked, so I was stuck outside in the reception area. Finally a secretary came out and asked me to wait. After about a half an hour of cooling my heels (as I've told you, I'm not good at waiting), I got up, said "to hell with it," and punched the elevator button. Literally. When the elevator door opened, Marty Kummer stepped out, just as I was getting in.

"Where are you going?"

"Home. They've been in there laughing and shouting for almost an hour now, Marty. They don't want me. It sounds like they've got someone anyway. And I don't even know what the show is. What's the point of hanging around?"

Ever the patient man, Marty put his arm around me as the elevator closed without me in it. "Come on, Merv. They wouldn't get you up here if you didn't have a shot. Trust me. They'll love you."

At that moment the secretary reappeared and said, "They're ready for you now."

I looked at Marty. "Just read the cards, Merv. You'll be great."

Well, I *was* already there. I might as well see it through. It would probably be good for a laugh. And in those days, I needed all the laughs I could get.

As I walked through the door, somebody said, "Now, here's the star of our show . . . Merv Griffin!" I found myself standing in a conference room full of Goodson-Todman employees, posing as a studio audience. All of them were applauding as I entered the room.

I turned to Marty, who was right behind me. "I guess we're playing for keeps, huh?" Which was fine by me. Adrenaline pumping, I stepped right up to the podium and began interviewing the faux contestants. I read the cue cards and discovered that the show was called *Play Your Hunch*. For the next thirty minutes we played the game, which involved a series of stunts that tested the abilities of the players. The host needed to sing, dance, lead an orchestra, perform in skits—and be funny the whole time. By the time I was through, the applause was clearly genuine.

Then the diminutive producer, Mark Goodson (who I later learned was a fellow San Franciscan), said, "Merv, are you sure you've never done a game show before? You're a natural!" Marty was smiling broadly, although he had the decency not to say "I told you so."

I did the pilot for *Play Your Hunch* and, during the six months it took CBS to buy it, I returned to my grueling regimen of staying home and watching television. Occasionally, I even appeared on it. For those months I became the "go-to guy" when they needed a substitute or replacement host on some of the daytime shows. I replaced Carl Reiner as moderator of *Keep Talking* on ABC, and I was a frequent substitute for Bud Collyer on *To Tell the Truth*. (On one of those appearances, my panel included a young comedian who already had his own game show: the host of *Who Do You Trust?*— Johnny Carson.)

But even though I was now getting occasional jobs during the day, I was *always* home by 11:30 P.M. to watch *The Tonight Show*. Almost from the moment Jack Paar made his debut as host on July 29, 1957, I was an unapologetic "Paar-tisan," as his fans were quickly dubbed. With the distance of time, it's hard to explain just how riveting he was or how obsessed with him America became, almost overnight. It was like watching a high-wire walker work without a net. Or, as one columnist put it, "would this be the night that Jack finally has a nervous breakdown on the air?"

Jack's emotions were never far from the surface, every night. This made for compelling, if exhausting, television. His feuds were legendary. Powerful newspaper columnists like Walter Winchell and Dorothy Kilgallen were no match for the emerging power of television, and Jack knew it. Once, he literally threw Mickey Rooney off his set.

Yet for all his volatility, Jack was also an extremely bright and engaging interviewer. He was fascinated by the world and he shared that fascination with his viewers. When Castro came to power in Cuba, Jack went to Havana to interview him, for which he was roundly criticized in the press. He sought out Albert Schweitzer in Africa and then he took his show to Berlin, so we could watch that terrible Wall go up on live television.

Jack was at the height of his influence in 1960. His interviews with Vice President Richard M. Nixon and Senator John F. Kennedy were considered as pivotal to the outcome of that closely fought presidential election as Oprah's chats with Bush and Gore would be forty years later. In fact, the president-elect's father, old Joe Kennedy, sent Jack a note afterward that read: "If we had had five more Jack Paars in the United States . . . we wouldn't have had to wait almost twenty-four hours before we knew we were elected." (*"We?!"*)

That same year Jack's emotions finally took him over the edge, and we went right along with him. It seemed innocent enough at first. In his opening monologue, Jack told a joke that included the phrase "water closet," an innocuous nineteenth-century euphemism for toilet. What happened next would become headline news for the next month. The NBC censors decided that the term "water closet" was offensive to the American public and, since the show was done live on tape, they edited out the *entire* joke. In its place they inserted a three-minute news broadcast.

Jack was understandably livid, but with Paar that was only the beginning. NBC accused him of being "thin-skinned." Jack shot back, "It's *my* skin."

Obviously enraged (and fighting back tears), Jack played his ace: "I am leaving *The Tonight Show*," he told his stunned audience. "There must be a better way of making a living than this."

NBC may have won the battle of the water closet, but it lost the war of public opinion. After weeks of public outcry, both the chairman and the president of the network issued abject apologies to their victorious star. His first words after returning to the air were vintage Paar: "As I was saying before I was interrupted . . ."

Being the host of *Play Your Hunch* every day was like doing improvisation in acting class. I got to ad-lib everything, which to me was the best job in the world.

We had lots of big-name stars on the show, including Bob Hope, Boris Karloff, Jonathan Winters, and the Three Stooges. In a lucky coincidence that I couldn't appreciate at the time, one of those celebrity guests was a very tall, "veddy" British character actor named Arthur Treacher.

Harpo Marx was another one of the celebrities who came on *Play Your Hunch*. In 1961, I returned the favor by appearing with him on an NBC program called *The Wonderful World of Toys*. The premise of the show was that Harpo and Carol Burnett led a tour through Central Park and along the way discovered various interesting toys. Two things stand out in my memory of that experience. The first was standing in the middle of the park with the cameras rolling and, just as I was about to do my song, a pigeon crapped on my head. Harpo, who famously never spoke on camera, shouted "Wonderful! That's good luck!" Unfortunately for Harpo fans (but luckily for my dignity), that footage never aired.

The other thing I remember about that Harpo special was that it was the first time I ever met a young Hungarian actress named Eva Gabor, who was also a guest on the show. We didn't become friends then, but I remember thinking, "God, she's *beautiful.*"

Long before Woody Allen became an Academy Award–winning filmmaker, he was a television writer and stand-up comedian. In the fifties, along with Neil Simon and Carl Reiner, he was part of Sid Caesar's comic brain trust on *Your Show of Shows*. By 1961 he had taken a tentative step toward a performing career of his own by developing a stand-up routine in some of the small clubs around Greenwich Village. Around this time I was on my sofa at home watching Jack introduce this "talented young writer" as his first guest.

Out walks this twenty-something kid with black-framed glasses, wearing a sport jacket and tie. If I'd seen him on the street, I would have given him my keys and told him to be careful parking the car.

Although his timing and delivery were superb, Woody seemed as if he'd been plugged into an electric socket and someone had flipped the switch. His hands never stopped moving, his head bobbed up and down, and his facial expressions ranged from nervous tic to epileptic seizure. But he was brilliant.

The difference between sex and death is, death you can do alone and nobody will laugh at you.

At home, I was having convulsions from laughing so hard. He said things you'd never heard before on television. Remember, we were barely out of the fifties, a decade where a husband and wife couldn't be shown in bed together unless one of them kept a foot on the floor. (Which, of course, begs the question, where *did* Little Ricky come from?)

At the end of Woody's routine, the camera cut back to Jack, who was plainly furious. He said, "Whoever booked that man and knew what he was going to say, I want to see in my office immediately following this show."

It was a frozen moment. At home I thought, "Oh God, someone is going to get fired."

Shortly after that I had my own run-in with Jack Paar—luckily with much better results.

I was doing my daily hosting duty on *Play Your Hunch* when, suddenly, there was a gasp from the studio audience, followed by tremendous applause. I turned around and standing behind me was Jack Paar, who had just come through the curtains.

I looked at him like Stanley must have looked at Livingstone. Instead of "Mr. Paar, I presume?" the best I could come up with was "What do you want?"

Jack replied, clearly confused, "What are *you* doing here?"

"Taping my show, *Play Your Hunch*."

"Play your what?"

"Hunch. It's a game show."

By this time Jack had noticed the studio audience, which was eating this up.

"Oh. Okay, then. Sorry to have disturbed you, Merv." With that, he waved to the crowd and disappeared back through the curtains.

"No problem. Drop in any time," I said to Jack's retreating back. The audience roared its approval.

It turned out that Jack always cut through that studio on the way to his office. On that particular day, he came to work much earlier than usual. Because he was such a creature of habit, nobody had ever thought to tell Jack that somebody else used *his* studio in the morning. So when he walked through those curtains, he had no idea that he'd be walking onto a live stage.

Marty Kummer had been pitching me for months as a possible fill-in for Paar on his regular Monday night off. Shortly after our close encounter, Marty ran into Jack at a restaurant.

"Hey Marty, don't you represent that sharp kid on *Play Your* . . . whatever it's called—that game show MC?"

"That's Merv Griffin. He's the same guy I've been telling your producer about."

"Well, let's give the kid a chance."

Marty couldn't wait to tell me. He called me from a pay phone in the restaurant with the big news.

When it was over, the night of Monday, January 29, 1962, felt like the longest *year* of my life. I made it through on sheer willpower and the generous support of a twenty-nine-year-old staffer named Bob Shanks. As low man on the *Tonight* totem pole, Shanks had been stuck with the thankless assignment of producing the Monday night shows in Jack's absence.

I was so panicked that, during the first commercial break, I tried to leave the show before it was over.

"I can't do this, Bob. Get somebody else. *You* go out there."

To his great credit, the normally soft-spoken Shanks found his producer's voice at just that moment.

"You *can* do it, Merv. And you will! Now get back out there!" With his hand in the small of my back, he pushed me back onstage. (Only much later, when I could laugh about the experience, did it occur to me that this was exactly how Mickey Rooney must have felt when Paar heaved him *off*stage.)

I learned three things that night. One was that Aretha Franklin (who had made her first talk show appearance that night and killed) was a phenomenal singer. The second was that Bob Shanks, although he'd never produced a television show before, was a natural at it. I promised him then and there that if I ever got my own show, he was going to be my producer.

The final lesson I took away from my first *Tonight Show* experience was how to deal with stage fright. Since I'd never had it before, it was something that I'd never considered until that moment.

I realized that you shouldn't fight your fear; you could use the tension it causes around you to create a more exciting atmosphere. "Controlled chaos" was how Jack Paar would describe it to me later, as he was complimenting me on my performance. All of a sudden those countless nights where I'd watched Jack do his high-wire act came back to me. *That's* why he worked without a net. If he wasn't scared, we would have stopped watching.

I must have done all right because I was invited back the following Monday. I asked Bob if he could book that writer "Jack doesn't like" as one of my guests.

"You mean Woody Allen?" asked Shanks. "I'd love to have him back. I was the one who originally found him down at the Bitter End. After that show Jack told me to stop going down to the Village to look for talent. It would be great to give him another chance."

I told Bob to book him. Fortunately, Jack gave his guest hosts complete latitude to bring on whomever they wanted (probably under the theory that if they screwed up, he'd look even better on Tuesday).

As usual, Woody was a riot:

> I was in analysis. You should know that about me. I was in group analysis when I was younger because I couldn't afford private sessions. I was captain of the latent paranoid softball team. We used to play all the neurotics on Sunday morning—the nail biters against the bed wetters.
>
> But if you've never seen neurotics play softball, it's really funny. I used to steal second base, then feel guilty and go back.

If I hadn't booked him on *The Tonight Show* after his debacle with Jack, Woody's stand-up career would have struggled a lot longer. There's no question that his talent would have made him a star eventually, but Jack's hostility was a big obstacle for any young performer to overcome.

Ironically, for the last forty years Jack has taken credit for giving Woody Allen his first break on national television. I kid you not.

That year Jack finally quit *The Tonight Show* for good. After five tumultuous years, he needed a break. As soon as the announcement was made, the jockeying to succeed him began.

I was also getting tired of my day job, having done *Play Your Hunch* almost as long as Jack had done *Tonight*. (There's a delicious twist to what happened after I left *Hunch* that July. For a brief time it was hosted by Gene Rayburn, who was then replaced by none other than . . . Robert Q. Lewis. I had to chuckle when I read that the show was finally canceled while he was the host. Did some junior network executive tell him, "I'm sorry, Bob, but *you're* no Merv Griffin"?)

Paar's replacement was slated to begin that fall. During the summer I hosted the show for a total of six weeks. Although I had no great expectations of getting *The Tonight Show* myself (there were persistent rumors that Johnny Carson had been promised the job already; they later proved to be true), I went along with what was a rather strange nonaudition audition process.

On one of those summer shows, I had a free-for-all lineup that included the Smothers Brothers (another act that Paar wouldn't book), my wife, Julann (whom Jack once seriously considered as a regular à la Dody Goodman), and that British actor I'd met on *Play Your Hunch*, Arthur Treacher. Arthur was a spry sixty-eight-year-old whose dry wit was perfect for the talk show format.

At one point in the show, Tommy Smothers got a little crazy and pretended that *he* was the host. So I went with it. I gave him my chair and let him take over the show. While he "interviewed" Julann, I moved over on the couch and spoke quietly with Arthur. I told him then that if I got *The Tonight Show* job, or any show like it, I wanted him as my "gentleman's gentleman." His words—and I remember them exactly—were "you dear little man."

NBC couldn't fathom the huge ratings I was getting during the summer. I was subsequently told by a network executive that I'd done so well during those six weeks that they wondered openly if they'd made a big mistake in committing to Carson so early.

So they decided to hedge their bets by offering me an hour-long daytime talk show that would air at two in the afternoon, one of the worst time slots imaginable. It would begin in the fall, on the same day that Johnny Carson would take over *The Tonight Show*.

I wasn't thrilled at the prospect of launching a new show simultaneously with Carson's debut, but as Bob Shanks (a devout Cubs fan) astutely observed, "Merv, they want you warming up in the bullpen in case Johnny gets shelled."

One big incentive for me to take NBC's offer was that I could package and produce the show myself. I'd formed Merv Griffin Productions for just that purpose. Not only was this a good idea economically, but it would also provide me with the kind of creative control that would make the show fun to do.

If the deal was to work, there were a number of points that needed to be ironed out. My attorney, Roy Blakeman, had been talking with Herb Schlosser, the network executive (later NBC president) who'd been given the task of signing me.

While negotiations were going back and forth between Roy and Herb, I happened to be in one of the NBC control rooms. A monitor was carrying the closed circuit feed from the network affiliates convention in Houston. I wasn't paying much attention until I heard my name mentioned.

"And starting in October, Merv Griffin will be a wonderful addition to our daytime schedule." *I will?*

The president of NBC had just announced me in their lineup when I hadn't yet signed a contract. That was good news for me. Even better, nobody at NBC—particularly Herb Schlosser—had any way of knowing that I possessed this valuable information.

I called Roy Blakeman and, telling him what I'd heard, informed him that "I'm going with you to meet with Herb Schlosser."

Roy was horrified. "Merv, you can't. Talent *never* participates in negotiations. It's not done."

I said, "Well, there's a first time for everything. What time is the meeting?"

The following day we arrived at Schlosser's office and Roy whispered to me, "Let me do the talking, Merv. I think they're going to make us a very good offer." I didn't say anything, so Roy assumed that I'd be a good boy and sit quietly while the grown-ups took care of business.

Schlosser put his offer on the table. Eight thousand dollars a week for me as the host.

"That's awfully generous, Herb." Roy was smiling. He'd been right. Or so he thought. "Are you *happy* with that, Merv?" he asked in a slightly patronizing tone.

"Of course not." I was implacable. Now they were both looking at me with a mixture of curiosity and annoyance.

Then Herb Schlosser asked, "How much *do* you want, Merv?"

"Eighteen thousand."

"What? Merv, that's impossible," sputtered Schlosser. "Nobody makes that kind of money."

"Well, Herb, I don't care about *nobody*. I know what my record was for you during the summer and I want $18,000 a week. That's it. There's no more negotiation. My lawyer may have told you that $8,000 was a generous offer, but *I* didn't say that. It's $18,000. Let me know what you decide."

I got up, shook hands with Schlosser, and left the office. Roy followed me out into the hallway, shaking his head. "Merv . . ." he began.

I cut him off. "Don't even start, Roy. I know what I'm doing. And next time check with me before you accept an offer on my behalf, okay?"

Needless to say, NBC caved. As I'd guessed, they were over a barrel having already announced me to their affiliate stations.

When Herb Schlosser called to tell me that NBC had agreed to my terms, he said, "Merv, if you ever decide not to perform anymore, I'd hire you in a second for our negotiating team."

I caught one more unexpected break in putting the deal together. Of all places, it came from the United States Supreme Court. They'd finally issued a decision on a case that had been working its way up the judicial ladder for years. The upshot of their ruling was that talent agencies couldn't wear multiple hats without violating the Sherman Antitrust Act. That meant that MCA (which also owned Universal Pictures) was effectively out of the talent agency business. And it also meant that I didn't have to pay them a hefty packaging fee for the sale of *The Merv Griffin Show*. Timing, as they say, is everything.

Just as starring in a major motion picture hadn't been nearly as glamorous as I'd once imagined, my first day at NBC was a rude awakening about what it actually meant to be a network "star."

In the early sixties, the NBC studios at Rockefeller Center seemed like a warehouse badly in need of a coat of paint. Furniture was scattered and mismatched; the "art" on the walls looked like something you'd pass up at a garage sale. My office was a 9 x 12 cubbyhole with a low ceiling and no windows. Perhaps as a concession to my soon-to-be star status, there was a drape covering one of the walls, behind which there *might* have been a window.

And you know what? I didn't care a bit. I was having the time of my life. In August, Bob Shanks and I sat down and planned out the first month of Merv Griffin shows, which would begin on October 1. The first thing I did was hire three talented young writers. Dick Cavett and David Lloyd were friends at Yale who had become a writing team working for Paar (David would go on to be an Emmy-winner for such classic sitcoms as *The Mary Tyler Moore Show*, *Taxi*, *Cheers*, and *Frasier*). The third member of our team was a large, incredibly funny man named Pat McCormick, who you'll probably remember as a comic actor (he was "Big Enos" in the *Smokey and the Bandit* movies).

They were a great bunch. One time I asked them to come up with some gag songs that I could do on the show. I'd pretend they were examples of some of the terrible songs that people would write "*especially for you Merv*," and send me in the mail.

Here's one that Dick wrote (I wrote the music):

> Happy Thanksgiving Day
> I've got a drumstick in my teeth
> Goodbye to summer
> I wouldn't have a drumstick in my teeth
> If I hadn't picked a fight with the drummer

Once the writing staff was set, we started booking talent. My first move was to put Woody Allen under contract to appear on the program every Friday. Then I called in some chits. I'd known Joan Crawford slightly back in San Mateo (my old Panda Records partner, Janet Folsom, was friendly with her), so when I called to ask her to appear on my new show, she quickly agreed. Then I called Adela

Rogers St. Johns, the prominent newspaperwoman and author, who used to play tennis with Uncle Elmer. She was delighted to know that her former ball boy was doing so well, and she also agreed to be one of my first guests.

Those two months went by unbelievably fast. One day I woke up and—bang—my calendar read October 1. Only nine months had elapsed since Bob Shanks shoved me back onstage to finish that first terrifying show, but I wasn't the same guy. From the moment I walked into Studio 6B (the same studio Carson would use at night), I felt like I was home.

That first week of shows was a blur. I remember asking Joan Crawford at one point if she had any romantic feelings toward any of her onscreen leading men. She gave the standard studio reply about how "they were all just friends and nothing more."

Adela, who suffered neither fools nor liars, couldn't let that one go by. "Now, Joan," she said, "you *married* three of them. You must have had *some* feelings."

It was going very well. From NBC's standpoint, possibly *too* well. Few people remember it now, but for the first six months of *The Tonight Show*, Carson had a lot of trouble getting big names to come on the air with him. He was an unknown quantity and they weren't willing to trust their careers with him—at least not yet. On the other hand, major stars like Danny Kaye, Montgomery Clift, and Harry Belafonte all agreed to do my show because I'd already proven myself subbing for Paar. The *New York Times* ran a feature story that said "*The Tonight Show* looks better in the afternoon." And my most important critic—my mother—gave me her highest praise: "Buddy, I like your show better than *Lawrence Welk*."

The problem for the network (and ultimately for me) was that *The Tonight Show* generated four times more in advertising revenue than my little afternoon show.

After only three weeks on the air, *The Merv Griffin Show* was preempted by the Giants-Yankees World Series, which was broadcast on NBC that year. During the break, we took the show over to London to tape some interviews.

Our big coup in England turned out to be landing the first American interview with a young actor named Peter O'Toole, who'd just completed shooting a motion picture called *Lawrence of Arabia*. I'd been following the press reports about this soon-to-be classic film even before O'Toole was cast in the part. (I'll bet you didn't know that Marlon Brando had initially agreed to play Lawrence—it was announced in the newspapers—before changing his mind and backing out. Then Albert Finney was given a screen test, but he turned down the role as well. Try picturing either of them on that camel crossing the desert. Can't do it, can you?)

The Columbia press agent had pitched Peter O'Toole to us aggressively. After all, he was still a virtual unknown and no one had actually seen the film yet. So when we agreed to tape the interview, the studio people were tremendously excited. They arranged for us to meet the actor at his home in Blackheath. On the appointed day, we caravanned out to this quiet residential neighborhood in three huge television trucks and a line of cars. When we pulled up in front of O'Toole's house it resembled a parade. Bob Shanks went up to the front door and rang the bell. The maid answered and politely informed him that, "The mister is not in. May I tell him who rang?" We were madder than hell (but not very smart; he was in the corner pub, a block away). We spent the entire trip back to our hotel cursing out the press agent, who was mortified.

There is only one real job requirement for a press agent and that's an unlimited capacity for humiliation. This guy had no shame. The next day he was back on the phone to us, apologizing profusely and begging us to give O'Toole another chance. "I'll lose my job," he pleaded. I thought of pointing out to him that with clients like this, he'd be better off unemployed. But I finally relented.

That afternoon the handsome brown-haired actor with piercing blue eyes came to our hotel and gave one of the funniest interviews I've ever done. He did a funny recounting of all of the accidents that happened to him during the making of *Lawrence*.

When we were done taping, I said, "Peter when are you coming over to the States?"

"In three months, for the premiere in New York." He turned to the press agent, who looked very relieved now that the interview from hell was finally over.

"Mark this down," said O'Toole, grandly. "I will *only* do Merv's show when I'm in America."

True to his word, when he arrived in New York that December we booked O'Toole for an exclusive interview. As was my custom, I didn't see him before the show (I'm always afraid that any conversation I have with a guest prior to taping will spoil the interview's spontaneity).

The moment arrived for him to walk out and I gave him a huge buildup.

"Remember when we spoke with this brilliant young actor in England just a few months ago," I told the audience. "Now he's joining us again on the eve of the release of *Lawrence of Arabia*, which I believe will be regarded as one of the great films of all time. Ladies and gentlemen, please welcome, Peter O'Toole!"

Out walked a light, almost platinum-haired man who, as far as I could tell, *wasn't* Peter O'Toole.

A thought flashed through my head: This is a gag. The staff and O'Toole put some guy up to this.

I said, "Hello?"

"Hello Merv," he responded, sitting down.

"You're not Peter O'Toole."

He looked puzzled. "I'm not?"

"No, I interviewed Peter O'Toole in England and I know him. You're not him." I was trying to be friendly, but I was making a mental note to decapitate whoever had the bright idea to send out a ringer on live television.

I sensed that the audience was growing uneasy with this exchange and the phony O'Toole seemed increasingly irritated by my attitude.

Then it dawned on me. "Wait a minute! You dyed your hair to look like your Lawrence character in the movie. That way people will know it's you when they see the picture, right?"

"Oh, *really?* I dyed it?" He was sarcastic and plainly unhappy with this line of questioning.

"Well, *didn't* you?" If I was going down, it wouldn't be without a fight.

"I'd rather not discuss that, Mr. Griffin." *Mr. Griffin.* Ouch.

"I'm sorry if I've offended you." I surrendered.

"Indeed, you have offended me, quite seriously."

I apologized again, then gamely tried to change the subject.

"Have you ever been to America before?"

"No."

"Is your family here with you?"

"Yes."

One-word answers. A disaster for something billed as a "talk" show.

So I dove into my notes and asked him ridiculous questions like "Do you have any hobbies?" and "What do you do for exercise?"

By this time he was furious and I knew that it was only a matter of time before he leaned across my desk and punched me in the face. I started to calculate how long it would take for me to make it to the nearest exit—then I had a flash of inspiration. I had the perfect question.

"Peter, you'd like to go home now, wouldn't you?"

"I would, yes."

"You'd probably like to go all the way back to London, wouldn't you?"

Suddenly, he was completely agreeable. "I certainly would."

"Well then," I said. "Thank you for coming, Peter. Goodbye."

And with that he walked off. As soon as he got backstage, he screamed (loud enough for the audience to hear), "He's a son of a bitch!" and stormed out of the studio.

Peter O'Toole's opinion of me was undoubtedly shared by a number of NBC executives (or "suits" as I've always called them) because Bob Shanks and I were quietly doing our part to undermine what remained of their notorious blacklist from the fifties. We booked people like Judy Holliday, Jack Gilford, and Phil Leeds, all of whom hadn't been on NBC's "air" in years.

In those days censorship took the form of a list of the following week's guests that had to be presented to the network. It made the rounds of the NBC executive offices and if any one of those names was black-penciled, they were off the show. We weren't told who was responsible for any given veto and, when we pressed for a reason, none was ever given. All we were told was that the person in question was "not a friend of the corporation."

If you've been paying attention so far, you've already figured out that this was just the kind of thing I'd never accept. People who tell me that I can't do something—without a good reason—are usually in for a fight. And there were two people that we really went to the mat for. One was Marc Connelly, a Pulitzer Prize–winning playwright who was once a member of the famed Algonquin Round Table. The other was a man named Ira Hirschmann, who'd written a powerful book about his exploits in Eastern Europe during World War II, where he successfully negotiated the freedom of thousands of Jews.

Marc Connelly was in his seventies by this time and posed less of a threat to national security than Arthur Treacher (who I often suspected was a spy for Cornwallis). We had Connelly on the program and he was a wonderful guest.

And I was just amazed when the network vetoed Ira Hirschmann. Not only was he a bona fide American hero, his travels in Eastern Europe had been at the behest of our *own* State Department. Suits. (We won that one too.)

But all of these were just minor bumps in the broadcasting road. The bottom line was numbers. Since *Password* was beating us soundly in the Nielsen ratings (a show that Betty White and I had demonstrated to all three networks as a favor to my old friend Mark Goodson—talk about sinking your own boat!), and since Johnny seemed finally to have found his footing, NBC decided that my numbers just weren't cutting it. We were canceled on April Fool's Day, 1963. Trying to put the best face on it, the network said, "Merv is just too sophisticated for daytime." Damned with faint praise . . .

In its wisdom, what the network hadn't anticipated was the public reaction to the decision. NBC received 160,000 letters of protest in only two weeks. At the time it was the largest amount of mail ever received in support of a canceled show. The nation's television critics also weighed in with column after column describing my show as "informative," "intelligent," "hysterically funny"—you get the idea.

But it was too late. NBC stuck to its guns, although they gave me a deal to develop my own shows as a sort of corporate consolation prize (*"What do we have for the contestants, Johnny?"*).

I don't spend a lot of time in life doing the "woulda, shoulda, coulda" routine. My philosophy has always been that when something's over, it's over. Turn the page.

But I must confess that I was more than a little pleased when the Emmy nominations came out later that year. I'd been nominated in the category of Outstanding Performance in a Variety or Musical Program or Series, along with Edie Adams, Danny Kaye, Andy Williams, and another newcomer, a young woman with a big voice.

No, not Streisand. It was the former president of my fan club, Carol Burnett. And *she* won. How perfect is that? (For the record, I should note that Robert Redford also came up short that year. *Don Knotts* beat him for Best Supporting Actor.)

Anyone who has ever been fired from a job knows how much it hurts. Now try imagining what it feels like to have the entire country in on that experience with you. It's not your gloating critics who make it the most difficult, it's your friends offering you endless amounts of sympathy that make you want to burrow right into the ground and pull the hole in after you. Instead, Julann and I decided to see Europe for the first time. We went to Paris, Rome, and the land of my forebears, Ireland.

Meanwhile, NBC, caught completely off guard by the over-whelmingly negative reaction to my cancellation, was now plying me with various offers to continue my relationship with the network. (Only in television can the equivalent of kicking someone out of bed be viewed as a "relationship.")

After we returned from Ireland, I agreed to appear in two summer stock plays, *The Moon Is Blue* and Neil Simon's *Come Blow Your Horn*. NBC was so desperate for a rapprochement, they even sent emis-saries out to plead with me in Bucks County, Pennsylvania, and War-ren, Ohio. Finally, I agreed to host a new game show I'd developed called *Word for Word*, provided that my company produced it.

It was during that year, 1963, that I also came up with an idea for a quiz show that I called *What's the Question?* But we'll talk about that a little later on.

That fall—exactly one day shy of a year since *The Merv Griffin Show* debuted on NBC—I found myself back at Rockefeller Center as the MC of my own . . . game show. In the not-yet-immortal words of Yogi Berra (who was also getting banged around a few miles to the north), it was "déjà vu all over again."

The premise of *Word for Word* was simple; contestants would at-tempt to make as many different words as they could out of one big "master word." It was anagrams with prizes. Since I've been a word and puzzle freak all my life (I still do four crossword puzzles a day), the idea for it came easily to me. And hosting it was even easier.

Of course, that was precisely the problem for me. It was like sleep-walking. Even though I was now wearing the producer's hat as well, this was essentially the same routine that I'd grown bored with on *Play Your Hunch* less than eighteen months before.

Enter Chet Collier.

Chet was a vice president of Group W, the broadcasting division of the giant Westinghouse Corporation that manufactured everything from washing machines to nuclear reactors. Group W owned television stations in five cities—Baltimore, Boston, Philadelphia, Pittsburgh, and San Francisco. A year earlier, using its five stations as the anchor, Group W had cobbled together a syndicate of over a hundred other stations from around the country—some network affiliates, some not—to carry a new talk show with Mike Douglas from Cleveland as the host. Thus the era of syndicating original programs (as opposed to *I Love Lucy* reruns) was effectively launched.

When Chet Collier came to see me in early 1965 about reviving *The Merv Griffin Show*, syndication was still in its infancy, an untested David to the three established network Goliaths. Although they'd had some success with Mike Douglas, and with another show by the first *Tonight Show* host, Steve Allen, it was still considered a risky venture, particularly if you had strong ties to a network (as I did). Still, the economics of owning your own show, as opposed to being a network employee, were a compelling argument for taking that risk.

Group W proposed that the new show would run ninety minutes, as opposed to the one-hour format we'd used on NBC. Moreover, I would have complete creative control over the show's content; the only suit I'd have to think about would be the one I wanted to wear on any given night.

If Group W could make *The Merv Griffin Show* fly again in syndication, it would be an unprecedented programming move, a phoenix rising from the network ash heap. Nobody had ever done it before.

That was all I needed to hear.

We made the deal in February; three months later, I stood in the wings of the Little Theater on 44th Street, next door to Sardi's, and listened as Arthur Treacher intoned what was to become my trademark introduction, "Look sharp! Here's the dear boy himself, *Merrrvyn!*"

I'd never forgotten the promise that I'd made to Arthur when we were on *The Tonight Show* together. Amazingly, neither had he.

His agent was flabbergasted when he called Arthur to tell him of my offer. Before the agent even said why he was calling, Arthur asked, "Did that dear little Griffin chap ring up?" More than three years had elapsed since our brief conversation, and we hadn't seen each other in the interim. Yet Arthur wasn't at all surprised to hear from me.

For my part, I had no doubt that Arthur's British reserve and dry wit would provide the perfect complement to my earnest enthusiasm. However, I was the *only* one who believed that Arthur was a good choice. He would turn seventy-one shortly after the new show was scheduled to debut; I would just be turning forty. Arthur was old enough to be my father. (In fact, he was born in 1894, eight years before my actual father.)

My wife, Chet Collier, and Bob Shanks (who once again had signed on as my producer)—everyone whose judgment I trusted—were all strenuously opposed to my choice of Arthur, a decision they thought of as "Griffin's Folly, a one-night joke."

I didn't care.

To this day, hiring Arthur remains one of my proudest—and smartest—career decisions. He was an instant hit with the audience, particularly among our younger viewers. Of course this flew in the face of the many research experts who predicted that Arthur would "skew" old; that is to say, his only appeal would be to viewers in his own age bracket. The numbers-crunchers were even more certain that young people couldn't relate to Arthur. As they saw it, someone who was alive when Queen Victoria was still on the throne would turn off the hip sixties kids in droves.

They couldn't have been more wrong. Each night after the show, legions of young people from our audience would literally follow Arthur down 44th Street.

Oh, Arthur could be irascible, and he often was, but that was part of his charm. I have two theories about why he was such a hit with the younger generation. The first is that Arthur wasn't a father figure to be rebelled against, he was a beloved *grandfather* figure. Big difference. Then there were his film roles. Arthur appeared in children's classics from two different eras: the Shirley Temple movies of the thirties and as the constable in *Mary Poppins*. The latter was his final big screen performance, released just a year before we started the new show. These roles connected him to young people in a meaningful way. This even included my son, Tony, who was five when he first met Arthur. It was a bit of a comedown for me to discover that "Constable Jones" was a much bigger star to my son than his dear old dad.

Early in every program we'd have our chat, then Arthur would move over to what he dubbed "Treacher's Corner," that section of the couch he had annexed as his own. On occasion, particularly when I was interviewing someone he found dull or pompous (Arthur was never fond of politicians—"Calvin Coolidge was my man," he'd sniff), I'd look over at Arthur, and he would have his back turned to me as an expression of disapproval. Other times his chin would begin sinking toward his chest, which meant he was starting to nod off.

One night I had on Dan Dailey, the veteran song-and-dance man turned actor. Apparently Arthur and Dan had crossed paths years earlier on the vaudeville circuit, because there was obviously a history between them. Midway through my interview with Dailey, I saw that Arthur was already dozing. So when Dailey said something about his old vaudeville days, I called out, "Did that ever happen to you, Arthur?" Arthur blinked several times and roused himself. Then, as if he were just seeing Dan Dailey for the first time, he said, "Oh *hullo*, Dan. Are you still wearing dresses?"

I cut quickly to a commercial.

Arthur wasn't the only one who could insult a guest. As was the case with Peter O'Toole on the NBC show, I also managed to irritate one or two people myself. During the sixties, my most memorable contretemps was with an unknown actor named Al Pacino. At the time he'd only done a few plays on Broadway and was hardly known outside of New York. I'd been told that he'd grown up in a rough neighborhood of the Bronx, so I innocently asked him, "How did you make it from the Bronx to Broadway?" It was a softball question with no hint of sarcasm on my part. But, for some reason, Pacino bristled at it. He stared at me, and then he finally said, "By subway." The audience laughed and I moved on, thinking little about it.

By the time Pacino broke big in *The Godfather*, a few years later, I'd honestly forgotten who he was or that he'd ever appeared on my show. So imagine how surprised I was to read that the hottest young actor in films had permanently sworn off doing all talk shows because "Merv Griffin once asked me the stupidest question." This year, after more than three decades of keeping his pledge and refusing to do a single talk show, Pacino finally consented to appear with David Letterman. The day of the taping, Dave called me, knowing the old story and wanting to hear my side of it. "You know, Dave," I deadpanned, "I really don't remember him on my show at all. Ask him if he ever worked under another name."

From the start, the second incarnation of *The Merv Griffin Show* was more freewheeling than its network predecessor. Part of this was the greater freedom that came with syndication; part of it was the additional thirty minutes that allowed us to keep going when things were getting interesting.

There were so many fascinating characters to talk with in those days—artists like Salvador Dali and Andy Warhol; writers like Gore Vidal, James Michener, Norman Mailer, and Truman Capote; actors ranging from legends such as Henry Fonda, Jimmy Stewart, and Bette Davis to "newcomers" like Richard Burton, Sean Connery, and Diane Keaton. Then there were the political figures of the era, many of whom only did my show: Robert Kennedy, Richard Nixon, Hubert Humphrey, Nelson Rockefeller, then Governor Ronald Reagan, Spiro Agnew (after his resignation), and, in one of his only talk show appearances, Dr. Martin Luther King, Jr.

My staff was always amazed that I would just ignore their notes and follow the thread of something that interested me. I asked Nelson Rockefeller how he'd first made his own personal money, as opposed to his family inheritance. He was taken aback; no one had ever asked him that question before. He thought about it for a long moment, then a smile crossed his face as he remembered: "I raised rabbits."

Because I didn't do my show to win a popularity contest, I wasn't afraid to tackle controversial subjects. During the Vietnam War, when the networks were under great pressure to present a united front in support of the war, I was the only one willing to give Cassius Clay (who'd just become Muhammad Ali) and Jane Fonda the opportunity to express their views. That doesn't mean that I agreed with everything they said or did—I didn't. But it seemed absurd to me that we were fighting to promote American-style freedom in a faraway corner of the world, while denying one of our most basic privileges—the freedom of speech—to our own citizens.

We were constantly out looking for new talent. Carson wouldn't do that. He'd always wait until someone was more established. I remember once saying to Bob Shanks, "How many times can I interview the *same* guests?" I told my staff that if it came down to booking a bigger name for the umpteenth time or taking a chance on someone new, they should always go with the new person.

I first heard about George Carlin when he arrived in New York in the early sixties. It seemed that George, who'd been a disc jockey in Boston, had run afoul of the powerful Boston prelate, Cardinal Cushing, and had to leave town somewhat precipitately.

The story goes that the Boston archdiocese sponsored a short nightly broadcast immediately preceding Carlin's slot that consisted of Cardinal Cushing reciting the rosary. One day, George arrived at the radio station and discovered that the cardinal was running long.

Now if you've ever seen a Carlin routine over the last forty years, you're aware that reverence is not his strong suit. To George, the sacred cows of organized religion simply meant more steak for him. You can probably guess what happened next. When it came time for him to do his show, George simply flipped a switch, cutting off the diocesan broadcast. Within moments, the light on the studio's private phone began flashing. As soon as Carlin had a record on the turntable, he picked up the urgently blinking line.

"Who cut off the Word of God?" thundered the voice on the other end of the phone.

It was His Eminence, demanding an explanation. Without speaking, George quietly placed the receiver back on its cradle. In that instant, he realized his career in Boston had just come to an end—he'd now cut off the most powerful man in the Catholic Church twice in as many minutes. Talk about being banned in Boston.

Shortly after we began the Group W show, I signed George to an exclusive agreement (similar to the one I'd had with Woody Allen on NBC), and he eventually made twenty-nine appearances on my show.

Another comedian who got his start with me was Richard Pryor. Just the other day, someone showed me a tape of his third appearance. Seated right beside me (in those early years it was our practice to have the first guest join me at the desk), Richard turns to me and says, "I just want to thank you, Merv. You've been really nice to me. You were the first one to have me on." I know it's hard to believe, but in those days he was such a sweet little kid, he wouldn't even say "hell" or "damn." Pryor's act was so clean-cut that Bill Cosby even called me once after seeing him on my show. "Hey, Merv," asked Cos, "are you sure that wasn't *me* you had on today?"

One of our bookers at the time, Paul Solomon, remembers a would-be comedienne named Lily Tomlin who took the train down from her home in Yonkers to audition for the show. She lived in a little bungalow right next to the railroad tracks, which was all she could afford.

Even then she had a unique personality. And she wrote all of her own material. On Paul's recommendation, I put her on television for the very first time. A year later she had signed to do *Laugh-In.*

Lily told me that everything changed for her after she did my show: "Cab drivers would yell at me, 'Hey, I saw you on *Merv* last night! You were really funny!' I might as well have been on the cover of *Time.*" By this point, my syndicated show, which had begun on only seventeen stations, was now carried by 155 stations in the United States and Canada.

As the number of stations carrying our show steadily increased, so did the interest in being on it. And I'm not just talking about celebrities. One of the more bizarre examples of this newfound attention occurred the time a strange man stepped off the elevator that opened to my office floor. He was carrying a wooden flute. Without speaking, the guy just began to play, right in the middle of our busy production office. I stopped to watch him, along with several members of my staff. How *was* he? Let's just say that if he'd been the Pied Piper, the mice would have been running for the nearest exit.

Anyway, after about five minutes of fluting, he finished. I said "Thank you" and he got back on the elevator. He never said a word, not even his name.

The next day we had a lock put on our elevator floor.

If there was one constant to *The Merv Griffin Show,* it was that we always managed to have fun.

There was the time when a young Neil Diamond, who'd been a championship fencer in school (I'll bet you didn't know *that*), tried to teach me how to fence on the air. After several scary parries and a thrust that came much too close for comfort, I shouted over to Arthur, "If you want the show *that* bad, you can have it!"

Zsa Zsa Gabor and Pamela Mason were the first two guests on a show that almost immediately turned into a gab and gossip fest. Nobody was spared, especially not their ex-husbands. The last guest out was the English actress and comedienne Hermione Gingold. When she entered, she was carrying a small dog under her arm.

"Why, Hermione," I said, unwittingly, "you've brought your little dog with you."

"Well, my dear," she said haughtily, "I thought that one more bitch certainly wouldn't matter."

There was a limit to what we could get away with even in syndication. I discovered what that limit was when the legendary burlesque queen, Gypsy Rose Lee, came on my show. Mort Lindsey, my whimsical orchestra leader, played her onstage with a strip number. Like a great racehorse, Gypsy hadn't lost the spark that made her famous. And this was a track she been around *many* times before. She started swinging her hips. Va-va-voom. Va-va-voom. The audience was egging her on. Without warning, Gypsy turned her back to the audience and—*va-va-voom*—she dropped her drawers.

If you were at home watching *The Merv Griffin Show* that day, I believe you saw a rerun of a show we did with Bishop Fulton J. Sheen . . .

My Catholic background often entered into my performance in a strange way. If there were nuns or priests in my audience, I almost couldn't do my show. They were the only people who intimidated me—not presidents, movie stars, or Nobel Prize winners. Just nuns and priests. If there were nuns seated in the third row, I'd tell my staff, "Don't be rude, but please ask them to move back a few rows." I just didn't feel free to be myself when I saw them watching me. I was afraid that if I inadvertently said something offensive, one of them might come up the aisle and rap my knuckles with a ruler.

Apropos of that, in 1966 *Time* magazine hit the stands with its now famous (or infamous, depending on your point of view) "Is God Dead?" cover story. The article featured a group of young theologians who described themselves as Christian atheists. Despite my nun-phobia, I invited one of the priests to appear on my show and explain his position. It was a scary moment. People in the audience were literally yelling, "Kill the bastard!" As I watched this poor guy's complexion turn increasingly pale as the crowd kept screaming threats at him, I remember thinking (somewhat devilishly, I admit), "I wonder who he's praying to *now?*"

As you might expect, one of my all-time favorite guests was my dear old friend, the incomparable Tallulah Bankhead. And Tallulah loved coming on my show because she felt that other interviewers often mocked her. She told me once, "My *dahling* Merv, you laugh with me, not *at* me."

By the mid-sixties, years of high living had taken their toll on Tallulah's health. In what would be her last appearance with me, I surprised her by booking two other guests who were emblematic of her life's passions: baseball and politics. Her heroes were Willie Mays and Harry Truman. I got Mays, but the former president was unavailable, so I persuaded his daughter, Margaret, to do the show in his stead. Tallulah was as gleeful as a young girl. She hugged Mays and greeted Margaret like a sister. When it was over there were tears in her eyes—and mine.

My beloved Tallulah died December 12, 1968. In character to the last, her final words were reported to be "codeine" and "bourbon."

The only appropriate way to honor the memory of Tallulah Bankhead is with laughter. Let me share with you my favorite Tallulah story, in loving remembrance of my wonderful friend.

It happened over Christmas one year, outside Bloomingdale's in New York City. Tallulah was walking past the store and one of the seasonal Salvation Army workers, a young girl, was shaking a tambourine to get people's attention for a donation. Tallulah stopped, studied the girl for a moment, then reached into her purse and gave her a hundred dollar bill. Recognizing her, the stunned girl could only say, "Oh Miss Bankhead, thank you *so* much!"

"That's all right, *dahling*," said Tallulah, gravely. "I know it's been a *terrible* year for you Spanish dancers."

She was one of a kind.

(Courtesy of Fred Wostbrock)

Three:
Play Your
Hunches

*L*egend has it that the word "quiz" was invented in a bar in Dublin, Ireland, in 1791. Maybe it's pure blarney, but it's a great story. It goes like this: A man named James Daly, who was the manager of the Dublin Theatre, was out drinking with his lads. Daly, full of ale and himself, boasted that he could invent a meaningless word that would become a permanent part of the English language within twenty-four hours.

The next day the letters "Q-U-I-Z" were scrawled on walls and buildings all around Dublin. Daly had hired a gang of street urchins, given them chalk, and set them loose on the unsuspecting city. That night, everyone in the bar was buzzing about this mysterious word, "quiz." What did it really mean? Nobody knew.

Over in the corner, Daly quietly collected his winnings and listened with amusement as everybody who wasn't in on the bet failed to guess the truth—that "quiz" was a nonsense word with no significance whatsoever. What Daly never anticipated was that in short order, the very act of trying to decipher the word's meaning would itself *become* the meaning. "Quiz" became synonymous with "puzzle" or "test."

As I've said, I've always loved puzzles and quizzes. One of my favorite radio shows growing up in San Mateo was an extremely popular program called *Doctor I.Q.*, where they went out into the audience and found people to answer the questions posed by a "mental doctor," who was also the show's host, James McClain. The show's signature line was, "I've got a lady in the balcony, doctor!" If someone got the right answer, Doctor I.Q. would shout out, "Give her ten silver dollars and a box of Mars Bars!"

Doctor I.Q. moved to television in 1953 with less success (although one of the doctor's assistants was a young navy veteran named Art Fleming), but it was part of the first wave of quiz and game shows that swept across America in the fifties.

Before we go any further, I think it's important to make the distinction between a "quiz show" and a "game show," since the two are often mistakenly believed to be the same thing. A quiz show tests the knowledge of a contestant for money; a game show (like *Play Your Hunch*) generally involves some kind of activity that results in a prize being awarded for the successful completion of a task. Panel shows like *What's My Line* or *To Tell the Truth* were yet a different animal. The celebrity panelists on these shows attempted to guess the identity or profession of the contestants. The only way the contestants could win any money was if the panelists guessed *incorrectly* and were therefore "stumped."

Confused? So were a lot of television viewers in the fifties, who saw average people like themselves winning ever-increasing sums of money and bigger and bigger prizes right there in their own living rooms.

By the mid-fifties, quiz shows had become a national obsession led by shows such as *The $64,000 Question, Twenty-One,* and *Dotto.* (For those of you too young to remember any of this, just think back to when *Who Wants to Be a Millionaire?* was on ABC four nights a week and you'll get the idea.)

A man named Herbert Stempel brought the whole quiz show phenomenon crashing down. Stempel was a graduate student at the City College of New York and, in 1956, he'd lost out to Charles Van Doren, a handsome Columbia University professor, on *Twenty-One.* The disgruntled Stempel revealed that Van Doren (whose matinee-idol looks were garnering big ratings) had actually been *given* the correct answers by the show's producers, in order to guarantee that he would return the following week.

Before Stempel blew the whistle, Van Doren had become so popular (he'd won $129,000—the equivalent of well over a million dollars today) that he was receiving hundreds of letters a week, including quite a few marriage proposals. NBC even gave him a contract to appear regularly on the *Today* show.

Desperate to save their shows and themselves, the producers tried to justify their deception with the sort of spin that would have been worthy of Richard Nixon. They argued that *everybody knew* (wink, wink) that these shows were "scripted," just like the great TV dramas found on *Studio One* or *Playhouse 90.* Providing answers to quiz show contestants was the same as giving a script to the actors before the show. Sure it was.

Needless to say, the public wasn't buying any of it. To sponsors whose livelihood depended on trusting viewers buying their products, this was a disaster. What if people began to doubt *them* too?

In a panic, the networks canceled every single one of their quiz shows, whether they were fixed or not. Most game shows survived, including *Play Your Hunch* (whew) and Johnny Carson's *Who Do You Trust?* Even so, we still got hundreds of letters from hypervigilant viewers who reported seeing strange "shadows" moving around in the background of our set. (*"Who knows what evil lurks in the hearts of men?"*)

The following year, Congress conducted hearings into the whole mess and Charles Van Doren was the star witness. Under oath he admitted that not only had he been given the right answers, the producers had even coached him as to what *facial expressions* would make him seem more believable while he was "struggling" with a difficult question.

The public was as fascinated with each new revelation as it had been with the quiz shows themselves. (I've always believed that "Hell hath no fury like an audience wronged.") Even thirteen-year-old Patty Duke, then starring on Broadway in *The Miracle Worker*, testified that her appearance on *The $64,000 Challenge* had been rigged as well. One of the New York tabloids trumpeted her confession with the headline, THEY EVEN FIXED THE KID!

President Eisenhower weighed in, calling the deception "a terrible thing to do to the American public." Finally, a law was passed in 1960 that made it "unlawful for any person, with intent to deceive the listening or viewing public . . . to supply to any contestant in a purportedly bona fide contest of intellectual knowledge or intellectual skill any special and secret assistance whereby the outcome of such contest will be in whole or in part prearranged or predetermined."

Of course, I watched all this play out with a great deal of interest, not to mention considerable relief that *Play Your Hunch* was a game show, not a quiz show. (I told you it was an important distinction.)

The only change that we were required to make was the addition of monitors whose job was to guarantee security. I was never quite sure what they actually *did*, since there were no real secrets to secure on our show. I used to tease them by saying that I wasn't really Merv Griffin, but an impostor who, in reality, could neither sing nor dance. They didn't think that was very funny.

Before I move on, I've got to tell you a story that connects *Play Your Hunch* to the quiz show scandals, in a very roundabout way. Do you remember the movie *Quiz Show* that was directed by Robert

Redford? Great film, wonderful performance by Ralph Fiennes as Charles Van Doren. Well, when the film was released, Redford naturally did a lot of promotion for it. During one of these interviews, he recalled having appeared on *Play Your Hunch*, not as a contestant, but as an actor who was pretending to be someone's twin brother. The players tried to guess if he or another actor was the real twin brother. He told the reporter that when he walked out, the audience booed him because he didn't really look like the guy's twin. (Probably the only time in his life that Robert Redford has ever been booed for his looks.)

Anyway, when the show was over, Redford contended that he went to collect the $75 that he'd been promised for his appearance ("My first payment in show biz," he explained to the reporter) and, instead of money, he was given a fishing rod from Abercrombie & Fitch that was valued at $75. Somehow, Redford tried to make a tenuous connection between what he considered to be his shabby treatment at the hands of *Play Your Hunch* and the whole quiz show scandal. He even went so far as to say that he called me personally to help him rectify this terrible injustice and that I turned him down.

It's a good anecdote, and since I enjoyed *Quiz Show*, I hope that it helped Redford sell some tickets to his movie. But, you've heard of "fish stories"? This is a fishing *rod* story.

Bob, if you're reading this, I can't dispute the fact that you may have gotten the shaft (so to speak), although truthfully I don't remember. What I'm certain of, however, is that I didn't refuse to help you. I *couldn't* have, since I had nothing to do with either prizes for the contestants or payments to the actors. *Play Your Hunch* was a Goodson-Todman production. I was merely the MC. Anyway, even if it *was* true, that hardly meant that our show was rigged.

So Bob, just to show you that there are no hard feelings, I'm sending you a check for $75. The next time you go fishing, maybe you can use it to buy bait. And, hey, I loved *A River Runs Through It* . . .

Many years later, sometime in the eighties, I was a guest on *Nightline* with Ted Koppel and the subject was game shows. As you may have noticed by now, I have trouble staying really serious for very long. It's just not me. Well, I must have gotten a little too silly for Ted, because he suddenly said to me, "You know, Merv, this is *not* a game show or your talk show. These are serious questions I'm asking you."

Looking straight into the camera (I was in a remote studio), I said, "I guess you've forgotten, Ted, that *you* started on my game show *Play Your Hunch*. You were part of one of the problems the players had to solve."

Glancing at the monitor, I saw Ted back in Washington, D.C., looking very embarrassed. In my ear, I heard him sputter, "Can we get on with this? Can we just get on with this, please?"

I thought to myself, Oh God, I've really done it now. I've ticked off Ted Koppel.

Aside from launching the careers of Robert Redford and Ted Koppel, *Play Your Hunch* also had the distinction of being the only program in game show history to run on all three networks. We started on CBS in 1958, and then moved to ABC the following year. After a hiatus of several months, we were picked up by NBC. The show ran there in daytime for another three years; I even hosted two prime-time versions in 1960 and 1962.

Now, as I said in the previous chapter, I'd grown increasingly bored with simply being an MC, although working with Mark Goodson gave me an invaluable education in how to develop and produce game shows. Trying to keep my enthusiasm up, he often used me as a substitute host on his other shows like *The Price Is Right* and *Beat the Clock*.

I often filled in for Bud Collyer on *To Tell the Truth*. I remember one show in particular, when my panel consisted of Tom Poston, Dina Merrill, Peggy Cass, and Johnny Carson. The guests were a Secret Service agent, a woman who was a mess boy on a Norwegian freighter, and an expert on the whooping crane. Honest.

After we moved to NBC, I finally got to provide my own input into the format of *Play Your Hunch*. Mark Goodson called me into his office and said, "Merv, you know all those ideas that you've had for years about how to loosen up the show—the ones that I've always told you that we couldn't do? Well, let's do 'em."

I learned several important lessons at the knee of Mark Goodson. One was that in order for a game or quiz show to succeed it has to be based on an interesting and easily understandable premise. Ideally, the person sitting at home will do better than the contestants.

There's nothing more satisfying to a viewer (and more likely to keep him tuning in) than to feel smarter than those "geniuses" who can't solve an obvious puzzle or answer even the simplest question.

Mark Goodson also taught me the importance of using precise verbiage in the structure of a show. By verbiage, he meant recurring phrases like "Will the real John Smith please stand up?" or "Enter and sign in, please." Goodson intuitively understood that viewers came to wait for these lines and that they provided a sense of continuity and comfort to the audience.

When the time came for me to develop *Word for Word*, I was more than ready to put what I'd learned into my own production. As I've told you, NBC was willing to put *Word for Word* on the air solely to keep me in the fold. It was a Faustian bargain, because they insisted that I host the show as well, not just produce it. Still, it gave me a chance to build up my company, so I saw it as a fair trade-off.

Word for Word was on the air for a year. It was canceled because it sank to a 36 share and NBC was horrified when it dropped that low. They told me that it was dragging down their whole lineup. To give you some idea of how drastically times have changed, today a 36 share (a "share" represents the percentage of all people watching television who are tuned in to a given program) would be more than *twice* the size of the audience for a top-rated program on any network.

Although NBC's cancellation of *Word for Word* was a disappointment, I didn't take it nearly as hard as I did when they canceled my talk show. By that point, I had come to understand how the networks really operated. No matter how popular you were, you would be canceled eventually. On the other hand, that also meant that the next wave of network executives (who lasted, on average, about eighteen months) could prove what creative thinkers they were by "rediscovering" you, conveniently ignoring the fact that their predecessors were the ones who made you disappear in the first place. Remember, in show business you invariably fail upward. (The most fun is when you're fired and hired by the *same* executive. That's like winning the lottery.)

Accordingly, I took the end of *Word for Word* philosophically. One door had closed and another was about to open. I told you before that I'd had an idea for a show called *What's the Question?* You'll probably recognize it under the name that I eventually decided to use—*Jeopardy!*

After Julann and I returned from Europe in 1963, we went to Michigan to see her family and give our young son, Tony, a chance to spend some time with his maternal grandparents. *Word for Word* was still three months away from going on the air, but I was already trying to think of ideas for other shows.

On the return flight to New York, as Tony slept, Julann and I talked about how the fallout from the quiz show investigations still clung to the networks like a radioactive cloud. No network wanted to take a chance on a format that had burned them so badly in the recent past. What if some crooked producer, despite the risks involved, decided to feed the answers to a contestant anyway? If it happened again, this time the people responsible would certainly go to jail— maybe even the network executive who put the show on the air.

Julann, who'll you remember has a wonderful sense of the absurd, made an offhand remark to the effect that "if everybody *knew* the contestants had the answers, nobody could accuse them of cheating." She was only kidding, but I immediately began pondering how that might actually work.

To give you a sense of how deeply preoccupied I was with this concept of answers instead of questions, when it came time for us to land at La Guardia I was barely paying attention; the stewardess had to remind me to buckle my seat belt. That may seem like a small thing to you, but in those days I was a white-knuckled flier, especially on takeoffs and landings. If I was *that* distracted, clearly this was an idea with great potential.

In *Poor Richard's Almanack*, Ben Franklin famously observed that there is "many a slip twixt cup and lip." In other words, a good idea is a pain in the ass to make happen.

It was almost a full year between Julann's casual remark about giving out the answers in advance to the first time Don Pardo ever said, "Now, let's play *Jeopardy!*" And during that year there were more than a few slips.

In developing this kind of show, you have to play it repeatedly in order to anticipate absolutely everything that might possibly go wrong. You can't wait until the program is actually on the air because by then it's much too late. For example, if there's a glitch in the rules that no one thought of, you can't sort it out while there's a studio audience sitting there expecting to see a show. Moreover, the contestants themselves have a funny attitude about rules that "evolve," especially when there's lots of money involved.

A. "Lawsuit."
Q. "What do you get when you change the rules in the middle of the game?"

During the year that it took to develop *Jeopardy!* the dining room of our Manhattan apartment was taken over by 3x5 cards, envelopes with abbreviations like "Hist." or "Lit." scrawled on the front, and bulletin boards covered with multicolored pushpins (Julann was convinced that the minute my back was turned, Tony would eat one of the pushpins, a not entirely unrealistic fear. He was an extremely adventurous child.)

After many months of playing the game at home with Julann and her sister, *What's the Question?* was ready for a more formal tryout. The normal routine in developing a show like this is to do a "run-through," where you get potential buyers (in this case, NBC) to come and watch the trial run.

I rented a small theater-style room in Radio City Music Hall, just up the block from NBC. We invited Bob Aaron, the vice president in charge of NBC's daytime programming, to join us for the run-through.

It was one of the funniest things I've ever done. I had all the categories on one giant board. And it wouldn't fit on the stage. I had to ask Bob Aaron to move farther and farther back to see it. Eventually, we put chairs next to the stage so that the board could extend out on top of them. It was "The Three Stooges Do a Game Show."

Bob Aaron, who loved the concept of the show, was immediately concerned with the practical aspects of shooting it for television. "Merv, how will we ever photograph this? It's way too big."

I learned early on that's it smart to admit what you can't do, and move on to the things you're good at. "I don't know, Bob. That's *your* business. All I know is that this is a good idea."

"I like it, Merv. I really do. But it's not aspect-ratio." (Translation: "It's too big to be photographed by a TV camera.)

That night I went home and began trying to figure out how to cut it down. Necessity being the mother of invention—and television—I came up with a plan to have three different rounds, thereby reducing the number of categories in each one. (It was about this time that another NBC executive, Ed Vane, told me that he also liked the premise but that it lacked enough "jeopardies"—situations where the contestants were at risk of failing. Not only was he right—I decided to deduct money for a wrong answer; that had never been done before—but he'd also inadvertently given me a perfect name for the show.)

Three months after that first run-through, we were ready for the final dress rehearsal, this time in front of NBC president Mort Werner, the man who would decide whether or not to put *Jeopardy!* on the air.

I personally carried the large poster board with envelopes glued on to it into the NBC boardroom. Inside the envelopes were index cards with the answers written on them. As the mock MC (this was the only time that I ever hosted *Jeopardy!*; I'd made it abundantly clear that this time *I* didn't come with the show), I guided our two volunteer contestants through the three rounds, now called "Jeopardy," "Double Jeopardy" and "Final Jeopardy."

When "Final Jeopardy" was over, I was beaming. The contestants had both played beautifully and the game had worked smoothly, no hitches at all.

I looked over at Mort Werner and he said, "I didn't get one."

At first I didn't understand what he meant. "You didn't get one *what*?" I was genuinely confused.

"I didn't get one *question*," he said, somewhat irritated at having to make that admission. "It's too tough, Merv."

I was taken aback. I hadn't expected this. It never occurred to me that a man who'd risen to the top of a major television network wouldn't have the breadth of knowledge to play the game. Before I could think of what to say, Werner's assistant, a young man named Grant Tinker leaned over and whispered to him (loud enough for me to hear), "Buy it."

Still abashed that he'd done so poorly, Werner said, "It's just too hard. I think it needs more work." But Grant Tinker didn't back down. "Buy it, Mort. It's a great idea."

Reluctantly, Werner agreed, although he told Grant that if it flopped, he'd be held responsible. We all shook hands and *Jeopardy!* was out of . . . *danger.* (Gotcha.)

All that remained was to find the perfect host. I'd seen Art Fleming on a TWA commercial and remembered that he'd been one of the assistants on *Doctor I.Q.* a decade earlier. Julann and I took him out to lunch and he regaled us with stories of his exploits in World War II (he was a decorated naval hero) and his colorful experiences in almost every aspect of show business. He'd started on Broadway at the age of four, and then he'd gone on to do radio, television, and motion pictures. He'd even been a carnival barker. On top of all this, he knew everything about everything. He was a walking encyclopedia of interesting and often obscure information.

When we finished lunch, Julann and I just looked at each other without saying anything. We both knew that we'd found our host.

The announcer's job was the final piece of the puzzle. I'd met Don Pardo when I was a substitute host on *The Price Is Right* and he was the show's announcer. I loved the intensity of his voice from the first time I heard him speak.

Jeopardy! went on the air for the first time at 11:30 A.M. on Monday, March 20, 1964. The first round of categories were "Television," "Women," "Fictional Characters," "Odds and Ends," "American History," and "Science." "Double Jeopardy" consisted of "U.S. Geography," "Sports," "The Funnies," "Words," "Opera," and "Famous Names."

The first "Final Jeopardy" answer, in the category of "Famous Quotes," was "Good night, sweet prince." The correct question was "Who is Hamlet?" (If you guessed, "Who was the artist formerly known as Hamlet?, shame on you.)

We'd been warned that our time slot was a potential graveyard since, opposite us, CBS was airing reruns of *The Dick Van Dyke Show*, which was in the middle of its phenomenally successful five-year prime time run.

Nobody, least of all the naysayers at NBC, expected the extent to which the public would eventually embrace *Jeopardy!* It got off to a slow start but built steadily, primarily through word-of-mouth.

We still hadn't convinced the suits, particularly the geniuses in the research department whose numbers told them that *Jeopardy!* was doomed unless we dumbed it down. Around the sixth week, I met with a deeply concerned man named Phil Klein, who was the head of NBC research (and later president of the network).

"Merv," he said, grimly, "Unless you make the questions easier, our surveys show that *Jeopardy!* will be off the air in two months. You've got to realize that the intelligence of most daytime television viewers is equivalent to that of an average thirteen-year-old."

I put on what I hoped was an equally grim expression and said solemnly, "I appreciate your coming in to see me, Phil. This is extremely valuable information. We'll get on it immediately."

Klein left and I never told a soul about his visit. We just went right on doing what we were doing. *Jeopardy!* ran on NBC for another eleven years, for a total of 2,753 episodes. I guess there are more smart thirteen-year-olds out there than the guys in research figured.

Four:
The Eye
and the Tiger

*A*lthough I wasn't invited to perform at Woodstock (my invitation got lost in the mail), the sixties ended for me, as they did for so many people, the day after that remarkable gathering at Max Yasgur's farm.

Yet unlike the hundreds of thousands of exhausted, mud-encrusted music fans who, on that Monday, August 18, 1969, were wending their way down the New York State Thruway en route to their normal lives, my great adventure was just about to begin.

That night, I would be taking the stage of the Cort Theater in midtown Manhattan to go head-to-head with the unbeaten, undisputed champion of late-night television, Johnny Carson.

It wasn't my idea.

I'd had a very successful talk show at Westinghouse for four years. I loved syndication because there was nobody looking over my shoulder with helpful "advice" about what I should be doing to improve on it.

In the meantime, Johnny had made *The Tonight Show* entirely his own. He'd already had a longer run than either Jack Paar or Steve Allen, and his position at NBC was more than secure—he could now write his own ticket. Carson's total domination of the 11:30 P.M. time slot made *The Tonight Show* the network's single largest profit center.

That fact wasn't lost on either of the other networks. Desperate to get in on this lucrative action, programming executives at both CBS and ABC huddled feverishly in their boardrooms and drew up their plans of attack.

In 1967, ABC fired the opening shot with *The Joey Bishop Show*, a talk show similar in format to *Tonight*. During its two-year run, it failed to make a significant dent in Carson's ratings and it's probably best remembered today for having introduced Regis Philbin (Bishop's announcer and sidekick) to a national audience.

CBS had mixed feelings about entering the fray. Its 11:30 P.M. programming had long consisted of running old movies that they already owned. But the advertising revenue from old reruns was negligible when compared to the golden eggs that Carson was hatching over at NBC. All CBS needed was its own goose.

Guess who they had in mind?

As I said, I was very happy at Westinghouse. The money was fine, I had complete creative freedom, and, although in most markets our show aired during the daytime, we reached as many viewers as *The Tonight Show* did at 11:30. It wasn't as glamorous as a network, but that didn't bother me at all. Truth to tell, if CBS hadn't approached me, it never would have occurred to me to move.

Their first overtures to me came in April of '69, through my attorney, Roy Blakeman, and my agent, Sol Leon. My immediate reaction was a firm "no way," but Roy and Sol persuaded me to let them at least *talk* to CBS and find out what they were offering. Everybody likes to be courted, so I gave them the go-ahead to have a meeting with Mike Dann, the CBS vice president in charge of programming.

Before they left my office for the short walk over to CBS, Roy and Sol asked me to consider what it would take for CBS to sign me.

I leaned back in my chair, and as I often do when I'm thinking, I rubbed my nose with my knuckles. After a moment, I said to them, "What do you think NBC is paying Johnny?"

Sol said, "I'm pretty sure it's in the neighborhood of forty thousand dollars a week."

"Good." I smiled slightly. "Now double that. So tell them I want eighty thousand dollars a week."

They stared at me in disbelief. Roy, who still hadn't learned that I knew what I was doing when it came to my own career, was exasperated. "Oh, come on now, Merv. Be realistic."

"It's eighty-four thousand dollars a week to move." My tone made it clear to them that there was no room for further discussion on this point. They rose to leave and it was obvious they felt that they were embarking on a fool's errand.

"Good luck, guys," I said, as they walked grimly out the door.

Roy and Sol may have been frustrated with me, but I was having fun. Since I had no real interest in going anywhere, I could make up some ridiculous number without worrying about the consequences. I turned my attention to preparing for that night's taping and figured that I'd heard the last from CBS.

Wrong. Within the hour, Roy and Sol were back in my office, looking a bit dazed. They were grinning, so at least I knew they hadn't been mugged. Maybe they'd blown off the meeting and gone out and gotten plastered. That would explain their silly demeanor.

"CBS said yes!" They said it—shouted it, really—in unison.

You know that old expression, "Be careful what you wish for, you may get it"? Well, I hadn't really wished for this—at least I didn't *think* I had. Now I was forced to deal with the reality of an offer that had enormous implications, not only for me, but for the nearly two hundred people who worked for Merv Griffin Productions as well. It wasn't just a question of moving to CBS; we'd also be under intense pressure to justify the network's investment in the show. In me.

One factor that worked to CBS's advantage (although they had no way of knowing it) was that my current contract was up for renewal and I'd heard nothing from Westinghouse. They thought they had me in their hip pocket, so they hadn't even bothered to negotiate with me. It's the oldest story in the world, in both romance and business. In the new relationship you're wonderful and wanted. In the old relationship, the phone never rings and you're eating TV dinners alone.

At a certain point, human nature takes over—and common sense goes out the window. If Westinghouse didn't appreciate me—*after all I'd done for them*—I was out of there.

Initially stung by my departure, Westinghouse rebounded quickly and gave the Little Theater to David Frost, a classy conversationalist whom they'd imported from England. He did an excellent job, but in only three months, more than a hundred Group W syndicate stations had dropped his show. The Midwest and the South just weren't ready to accept a refined British host on a daily basis. I told Westinghouse that this was likely to happen, but they weren't really in the mood to listen to me. No surprise there—nobody wants to hear what's wrong with a new relationship, especially not when that warning comes from the same guy who just walked out the door.

All of which explains how I found myself on the Cort Theater stage that muggy Monday night in 1969.

My first clue about what was to come in my relationship with CBS should have been the unpleasant experience of picking a new theater. When I found the Cort, the network was unwilling to let me negotiate the lease. My friends in the Shubert Organization were prepared to give me a sweetheart deal—$100,000 a year. The president of the network, Bob Wood, politely told me that I should stick to what they had hired me to do, which was to be "the talent." Their real estate department then proceeded to close the deal for two and a half times the price I'd been quoted. It should have been a major red flag, but I chose to ignore it. Like I said, sometimes common sense goes out the window.

The media buildup to opening night was tremendous. I gave dozens of interviews and grew hoarse from repeating the same sentence, countless times: *"No, Johnny and I are actually good friends."* *Newsweek* even did a cover story on me that asked the rhetorical question, "Is Merv Griffin the next king of late-night television?"

Led by my old Friday afternoon contract player, Woody Allen (whose first movie as a writer-director, *Take the Money and Run*, was just out in theaters), Bob Shanks and I put together a solid lineup for the premiere that also included Hedy Lamarr, Leslie Uggams, former JFK advisor Theodore Sorensen, and Moms Mabley (who brought the house down when she said people often compared her to Roy Rogers's beloved horse. "When I walk down the street I hear them shout, 'Hey, Trigger! Hey, Trigger!' " Then she paused, "At least that's what I *think* they say.").

At this point I need to tell you that in addition to nuns and priests, I also have a long-standing rule against putting family, friends, or staff members in the first six rows of any show that I do—although for an entirely different reason. Obligatory laughter or applause is just as disconcerting to a performer as open hostility.

So imagine my reaction when, following Arthur Treader's booming introduction, I bounded onstage only to encounter a sea of oddly familiar faces. No, they weren't relatives. They weren't friends either. And the only staff member within my line of sight was Bob Shanks, with whom I immediately locked eyes as if to say, "What is going *on* here?" As far back as I could see, every seat was filled with either a television critic or newspaper columnist. CBS had them brought to New York from around the country as a surprise "wedding gift" to me. Bad idea. By the time my first monologue was over, so was the honeymoon.

The next night, with no critics in the house (at least none who were paid), I began to recover my rhythm. I had a delightful visit from Max Yasgur, the upstate farmer whose property had just been overrun by five hundred thousand people during the largest three-day weekend in recorded history. Instead of railing against the free-loving, drug-taking, music-blaring hippie kids (as many of his neighbors had been doing on the news), Yasgur was surprisingly complimentary about how well behaved and friendly his guests had been.

Through the end of that first week, we ran even with *The Tonight Show* in the Nielsen ratings (in some key markets, we were actually ahead). But by the second week, I knew that CBS was already bailing out on its commitments to me and to the show.

Most significantly, I'd been promised that the show would air on almost all of CBS's affiliate stations. As a matter of simple mathematics, we had no chance of overtaking Carson if he was on a significantly greater number of stations than we were. When I received the network reports, I was stunned (and damned angry) to discover that the CBS version of *The Merv Griffin Show* was now being seen on slightly *fewer* stations than when we were on in syndication. Worse, *The Tonight Show* had a virtually insurmountable lead since it was being carried by 99 percent of the NBC affiliates. Sure enough, as soon as the publicity surrounding my debut faded, the ratings dropped and the late-night "war" was essentially over before it started.

Less than six months after CBS launched *The Merv Griffin Show* with tremendous fanfare, some of the affiliates had already thrown in the towel and moved the show to a safer harbor in the afternoon. I was very sympathetic to the local stations; they were getting clobbered and it wasn't their fault.

I remember giving an interview and being asked how I felt about "losing" the battle with Carson: "It's ridiculous for us to fight over small percentage points in the 11:30 slot," I said at the time, "when there's a much bigger audience—equivalent to the number of viewers that a prime-time program gets—who could be watching our show in the afternoon. People keep saying that the prestige is in the late-night spot. King Constantine has prestige, but he hasn't got Greece."

Whoever coined the expression "figures lie and liars figure," must have had the CBS research department in mind. All I can tell you is that it was responsible for the most serious injustice that I've ever seen in terms of so-called audience research. Curiously enough, it was done to me.

Here's what happened: CBS had hired an outside audience consultant to evaluate my show. Maybe you've participated in one of these sessions—they get thirty or forty people (sometimes paying them a nominal fee) and put them in a room where they watch the program to be evaluated. Everyone is given a button to press or a dial to twist—it varies—and this supposedly gauges their level of interest and enthusiasm at each stage of the show.

The test for *The Merv Griffin Show* happened to take place early on a Friday evening and the woman in charge of the session had a hot date later that night. Eager to get out of there, she was quite vocal in expressing her own opinion about the quality of our show—she hated it. Apparently a negative evaluation was quicker to complete. If a program was *that* bad, why bother to go on?

Well, I must have had at least one fan in the room, because somebody blew the whistle on this whole farce. The woman was fired and as a direct result of that incident, the audience research firm went out of business. If I'd been skeptical about audience surveys before, I was now adamantly opposed to using them for anything at all. There's never a way to guarantee impartiality in the testing, no matter how many safeguards are in place.

I've got to say that some of those tests were good for a laugh. I remember one long report that boiled down to this conclusion: what *The Merv Griffin Show* needed was *less* Merv Griffin. (*Thanks, guys. I'll keep that in mind.*)

My time at CBS coincided with some very tumultuous events in America, particularly around the Vietnam War. Richard Nixon had just taken office and his "secret plan" to end the war apparently involved expanding it into Cambodia.

With respect to Vietnam, the network insisted that I balance my guests to include both sides of the debate. I got a memo that said, "In the past six weeks, thirty-four antiwar statements have been made on your show and only one pro-war statement, by John Wayne." I responded immediately: "Find me someone as famous as John Wayne who supports the war and I'll book *him*."

So when I booked radical activist Abbie Hoffman as a guest in the spring of 1970, it was no surprise to me that everything about that show came under intense scrutiny. A month before his appearance, Hoffman, a member of the notorious Chicago Seven, had been convicted of violating the Anti-Riot Act for his role in the antiwar

protests at the 1968 Democratic National Convention (his convic-
tion would later be overturned on appeal).

Hoffman walked out wearing a red, white, and blue shirt that resembled the American flag. The network censors, apoplectic at the
prospect that this apparel might violate the strict flag desecration
laws of several states, managed to electronically block out Hoffman's
torso for the duration of our thirty-five-minute interview. To viewers
at home, it appeared as if I were talking to a black box with legs.

CBS president Bob Wood taped a brief opening and closing segment for the show, where he personally explained to my puzzled audience what the hell was going on.

Later that week, I decided that turnabout was fair play. I arranged
with our crew to employ the same blocking technique on my monologue. When I walked out, the picture was normal and the audience at
home could see me clearly. But as I explained what CBS had done to
Hoffman, the black box slowly expanded until it covered much of the
screen. As the monologue continued, I had to get down on my hands
and knees in order to remain visible. "I have since talked with the
president of the network and in the future such censorship editing of
my show will *not* take place without my knowledge and consent."

By now the picture was reduced to only a small sliver of light and I
had disappeared entirely from view. Nonetheless, I kept right on
talking. "Furthermore, it has just been agreed that I am to be the *sole*
judge of censorship problems on my show if they should occur in the
future. In this regard, CBS has decided to go along with my ultima-
tum. I don't like to swing my weight around like this, but as host of
the show, I think I have some power (on the word "power" everything went completely black) to regulate and control what is to be
shown and what isn't. That's all I have to say. May I have the network
back, please?"

My relationship with CBS had now deteriorated to the point
where separation seemed like the only way to save our "marriage." I
was sick of constantly being under a corporate microscope in New
York, not to mention that the competition for guests between me,
Johnny, David Frost, and Dick Cavett (who'd replaced Joey Bishop
at ABC) had become absurd. Since we all taped at approximately the
same time, you might think that we couldn't duplicate guests on any
given night. Guess again. One frenetic evening, Jerry Lewis some-

how managed to do all *four* shows without telling any one of us about the others.

That was enough for me. I was out of there.

Invoking the spirit of Horatio Alger, I packed up my show and headed west to California. CBS was furious, particularly after they'd overspent so badly on the Cort Theater. I told the network that it had two alternatives: stand aside and let me go, or implement the brilliant recommendation of their own research department and do *The Merv Griffin Show* with a *lot* less Merv.

Muttering words like "kidnap" and "blackmail," CBS reluctantly capitulated. That September, we did our first show from Television City in Hollywood.

I may have won the war, but there were two painful casualties that resulted from those pitched battles with CBS. The first was Arthur Treacher, whom the network had resisted from day one. I'm not sure what I would have done if I'd ever had to tell Arthur that CBS wanted him out. I honestly think that I would have quit the show rather than break that wonderful man's heart. Fortunately, it never came to that. From the first moment that I'd mentioned to Arthur that I was thinking about relocating to California, he'd made it abundantly clear that he had no interest whatever in "living in a state that shakes." I never even considered looking for another sidekick. Arthur was, and will always be, irreplaceable to me.

Arthur passed away in 1975 at the age of eighty-one. In the last years of his life, he enjoyed tremendous success as a restaurateur, having launched a highly profitable chain of fish-and-chip eateries that bore his name. Arthur's final triumph as an entrepreneur was a fitting come-uppance to the corporate hacks who couldn't see beyond their own demographics. While CBS was busy studying its charts and graphs about how Arthur was "skewing too old," his fish-and-chip houses were packed every night. The old boy had the last laugh after all.

The other scalp that CBS insisted on belonged to Bob Shanks. They really wanted mine, but his was the only one available. Bob is a consummate gentleman who fully understood that my hands were tied by CBS. He graciously deferred to Saul Ilson and Ernie Chambers, the talented producers of *The Smothers Brothers Comedy Hour*, whom the network believed could "save" my show, presumably from me. Ironically, CBS had just fired the Smothers Brothers for what it viewed as their insubordination—they'd refused to tone down the political content of their show. (Bob Shanks went on to many other fine achievements, including creating the long-running ABC news-magazine, *20/20*, and authoring *The Cool Fire*, considered one of the definitive books on the television industry.)

Although I came to hold Ilson and Chambers in high regard (Ernie Chambers now produces television and film projects for my company; we've remained friends for over thirty years), it was initially difficult to figure out the network's reasoning in making me hire them. CBS executives had had nothing but problems with the Smothers Brothers over issues of creative control, and one would have thought they'd be extremely skittish about matching Tom and Dick's producers with yours truly. Maybe the answer is contained in the sentence before last: the words "network" and "reasoning" are mutually exclusive terms.

Our next-door neighbors at Television City included Carol Burnett, Jonathan Winters, and the unknown cast of a soon-to-debut comedy series called *All in the Family*.

A few months after their first show aired, I put the entire cast of *All in the Family* on my show—Carroll O'Connor, Jean Stapleton, Rob Reiner, and Sally Struthers. CBS president Bob Wood called me afterward to give me some "advice": "Merv, this is exactly the reason your show is having problems right now. Why would you book the cast of a show that we're canceling?"

I was flabbergasted. Not only was the head of the network telling me that he was going to pull the plug on this brilliantly innovative show before it had a chance to find an audience, he was even chastising me for promoting his own show!

"You've got to be kidding, Bob," I argued. "It's a *wonderful* show. Archie Bunker is somebody we all know—he's that obnoxious guy at work or the relative who embarrasses us in a restaurant. The point is that he makes us laugh at ourselves and we need that now."

"It's not getting the numbers, Merv. It's losing its time slot badly."

"Well, why don't you move it to another night? Give it a chance."

Which is what they eventually did (certainly not on my say-so), and Archie Bunker's chair is now sitting in the Smithsonian. Meatheads . . .

Following the move to the West Coast, I also decided to shake up our format. Probably the most significant change was the introduction of "theme" shows, where we devoted an entire program to one topic or person. Although it's the norm today (*Oprah* is almost an entirely theme-driven show), you have to remember that this was a brand-new idea back in 1970. Ernie Chambers and Saul Ilson overcame my initial skepticism about their concept (*"How the hell am I going to keep people interested in the same subject for ninety minutes?"*), and the first one we did was a salute to Charles Schulz and his beloved *Peanuts* characters. It turned out to be a terrific show. After it was over, I said to Ernie and Saul, in mock seriousness, "I *told* you guys this was a great idea! I could have gone *three hours* with it!"

After that we did many more theme shows, some of which pushed the CBS envelope—and what a tiny envelope it was. We did programs on such highly incendiary topics as incest and pedophilia at a time when those words were barely even *spoken* on network television. Indeed, the only way we were even allowed to approach these controversial subjects was by including a psychiatrist or therapist on the panel, so that they fell under the heading of "medical" shows.

One of the most fascinating shows that I ever did featured a rare interview with the world's first surgically successful transsexual, Christine Jorgensen. She spoke eloquently about her historic operation in Denmark, and, based on the mail that we received, I know that a lot of people (including me) were greatly impressed by her dignity and sincerity.

One of the most satisfying aspects of doing my show was that I was sometimes able to open a window for people that allowed them to reexamine their own prejudices. I never preached; that wasn't my job. Instead I found experts on a wide range of subjects and gave them a platform to discuss and debate their points of view. It was still possible to have a genuine *talk* show in those days, before the pressure of ratings reduced them to little more than promotional vehicles for movies, books, and pet causes. Today it's impossible to explore a subject with any seriousness (or even thoughtful humor) when time constraints limit the guest to a few sound bites and the film clip he brought with him. But I digress.

Johnny Carson used to love poking fun at my theme shows. In his monologue he'd often say something like, "Make sure you watch

Merv tonight. He's got one of his provocative themes. Six Lithuanian proctologists who want to be nuns." His audience roared and it was always great publicity for us. If I never told you this before, let me say it now: Thanks, John.

Johnny could certainly afford to be charitable because, as I said, we were no real threat to him. Format changes were fine, new and different guests made for interesting shows, but none of it made any long-term difference in our ratings. And now the clock was ticking on my future at CBS.

The network clock-watcher whose happy task it would be to pull the plug on my show was a diminutive man named Fred Silverman. He was the wunderkind who, at the age of thirty-three, was the youngest person ever to be solely responsible for a network's programming. Fittingly, Silverman had built his reputation at CBS on the strength of having revamped its Saturday morning cartoon schedule. He'd clearly learned a lot from the experience—as head of programming, he combined the temperament of the Tasmanian Devil with the decision-making skills of Daffy Duck.

Because Silverman had experienced tremendous career success at a relatively young age, he was a very difficult man to work with. When you're that young and in charge, you think you know *everything*.

One night, after I'd been in California for about a year, Freddy came to my dressing room prior to a taping. He wasn't much on pleasantries. "Merv, your show is in the tank. You're losing stations right and left. Here's what we're going to do. Remember *Broadway Open House*? [It was a vaudeville-style late-night show from the very early fifties hosted by comics Morey Amsterdam and Jerry Lester and featuring a statuesque blond actress named Dagmar, one of television's first sex symbols.] That's the kind of show I want from you."

"Freddy," I said trying not to lose my temper (something I rarely do), "Jerry Lester, Morey Amsterdam, and Dagmar are all still alive. If that's the format you're looking for, why don't you just call *them?*"

"I'm *not* . . . this *isn't* . . . you can't *speak* to me that way . . ." Freddy tended to sputter when he got angry. Like a cartoon character.

"Read my contract," I said evenly. "I can and I just *did*. Now would you please leave? I have a show to do."

I turned my back to him, ignoring the standard *"you'll never work in this business again"* speech and the loud report of my dressing room door being slammed.

I never saw Fred Silverman again.

Remember my old friend Perry Lafferty, the director of *The Hazel Bishop Show*? Almost twenty years later, he was now the CBS West Coast vice president in charge of programming. Although he nominally reported to Fred Silverman, Perry was an independent and highly respected executive (he'd later become president of the network) who kept his own counsel. Because we'd known each other for so long, I often found myself in Perry's office railing against all the terrible things *"your network"* and *"your boss"* were doing to me. As I vented, Perry would pick up the small baton he kept on his desk and literally conduct the crescendos and diminuendos of my wrath, until both of us started cracking up.

By late 1971, it was clear to everyone involved that the relationship between Merv Griffin and CBS was beyond repair. All that remained was for one of us to make the first move and end it. But there was still one contractual wrinkle that complicated the situation. According to our agreement, if I was the one to initiate the break, CBS was off the hook financially. However, if at the end of two years (which was December 3), the network hadn't exercised its option to renew my show for an additional six months, it owed me a one-time severance payment of $250,000.

It was against this backdrop that I'd been quietly talking with a man named Al Krivin, the president of Metromedia Broadcasting, who I knew from my days with Westinghouse. Back then Al was the person responsible for bringing *The Merv Griffin Show* to the influential Metromedia group of stations. Our strong showing on Channel 5, Metromedia's flagship station in New York City, had been enormously helpful in building momentum for our national roll-out.

Unbeknownst to CBS, Al Krivin had given me a firm commitment that if I were ever to leave the network, *The Merv Griffin Show* could go back into syndication with Metromedia immediately.

As the renewal date approached, I didn't know what CBS intended to do. If they elected to renew me, I was going to quit. There was no way that I could do another six months on that network. Life is too precious ever to be spent with the Freddy Silvermans of the world.

By keeping quiet and continuing to do my show as if I had no thought of leaving, there was a good chance that CBS simply wouldn't pick up my option. I'd be free to go back into syndication, which I loved, and they'd have to send me on my way with a handsome check.

If, on the other hand, word somehow got back to the network about my discussions with Metromedia (which, while entirely legal, would embarrass CBS publicly for having been outmaneuvered), it was quite likely that they would renew my show just for spite, not to mention $250,000.

December 3 fell on a Friday. Of course, there had been no word from the network all week. Late that afternoon, Bob Wood, accompanied by an entourage of CBS executives, arrived at my studio. Freddy Silverman was conspicuously missing from the group.

It was hard to know what his absence meant, although if I *wasn't* being renewed, I'd have thought that Freddy would have wanted the pleasure of delivering that news in person. I'd find out soon enough.

"How are you, Bob?"

"Fine, Merv. Just fine. How are Julann and Tony?"

"They're great, Bob. Thanks. I'll give Julann your best."

"Please do that, Merv."

There was a brief pause. This was clearly it.

"Merv, I stopped by because, as I'm sure you know, it's time for us to renew your option. We love working with you, Merv. You're a helluva broadcaster."

My heart sank. Damn, they were going to do it. Six more months.

"That's why I wanted to see you in person, Merv. I wanted to wish you well, because I know you've got great things ahead of you in this business."

Wish me well? Great things? My God, he was letting me go!

I looked down at my shoes, as if totally dejected. In truth, I was afraid that if I looked directly at Wood I'd start grinning, which wouldn't have been very smart right then.

"Bob, you've been very supportive of me from the beginning and I know that. I've been in show business a long time and I know the ropes. This goes with the territory. I'm just sorry that our crew here," I waved my hand at all the production people who were standing around the studio, pretending not to listen, "will all lose their jobs. That's the tough part."

Everyone nodded somberly and, out of the corner of my eye, I saw several crew members looking stricken.

I extended my hand. "Thank you, Bob. I really appreciate your coming here in person."

As soon as Wood and his traveling party exited the studio, I called my attorney in New York. "Roy, they didn't renew. I want you to send them the letter about payment of the penalty clause and then call Al Krivin. Tell him I said that I'll see him Monday. He'll understand."

I made one more call, to the publicist who handled all my dealings with the media. I told him to arrange a Sunday press conference at my house so that I could announce the deal with Metromedia. (My favorite question would come from a reporter who asked if I had any plans for my final show on CBS. "We'll be doing one last theme show," I said, as she scribbled earnestly in her notebook. "We're calling it "A Salute to Freddy Silverman—Ninety Minutes of Silence.")

The headline in Monday's *Hollywood Reporter* blared the news: "Merv Moves to Metromedia."

Had I written it, it would have read, "The Eye Blinked."

As soon as the news broke, I felt like a great weight had been removed from my shoulders. (Unfortunately, it needed to come off in a few other places as well. Two years of stress had taken their toll—I'd gained more than thirty pounds.)

Despite everything, I have a lot of warm memories from those CBS years. Most of them involve the new talent that we were able to introduce to a national audience—a young Diane Keaton, who giggled and blushed no matter what question I asked her; an opera singer named Madeline Kahn who also happened to be a very funny comedienne; Sonny & Cher, who did so well guest-hosting my show that CBS gave them their own prime-time variety hour, after initially declaring that I was crazy for letting "two old rock and roll singers" fill in for me.

Jerry Stiller and Anne Meara guested frequently with me on CBS (they actually got their first break on my NBC show), and they used to bring their little five-year-old son, Ben, along with them. Standing in the wings, he'd watch, wide-eyed, as his parents did their stand-up routines and the audience laughed hysterically. I guess I was cheaper than a baby-sitter . . .

Obviously, CBS no longer wanted me as a tenant at Television City (although they did make me serve out my contract to its final day, February 15), so we took over the venerable Hollywood Palace Theater on Vine Street, just steps away from its famed intersection with Hollywood Boulevard. It was a seamless transition from CBS; all of my nervous production staff made the move along with me.

As we depart the story of *The Merv Griffin Show* on CBS, let me make one observation about the network today. The Silverman years are now only a dim memory. He went on the become programming chief at the other two networks and nearly sank NBC with *Supertrain*, described by one critic as an "atomic-powered *Love Boat* on rails." CBS is now run by Les Moonves. Even before coming to the network, Les was responsible for developing terrific shows like *Friends* and *E.R.* And he's taken CBS back into ratings contention with quality programs like *CSI: Crime Scene Investigation* and *Everybody Loves Raymond*. It's nice to see the "Tiffany Network" finally back in the hands of someone who appreciates it.

The fifth and final incarnation of *The Merv Griffin Show* had its premiere broadcast on March 13, 1972. My guests were Dinah Shore, Dionne Warwick, Milton Berle, Angie Dickinson, Steve Lawrence, and Dom DeLuise.

What I recall most about that first night was watching the tape afterward and noticing that I'd stopped blinking.

In my last few months at CBS, my staff had become aware that I'd started blinking quite a bit during many of my interviews. They also said that it was happening even while I was singing. When I reviewed the show tapes, I saw that they were right. And I knew why.

Throughout my career as a host and interviewer, I've observed that whenever my guests blinked too much, it meant that they were either lying or, at a minimum, deeply uncomfortable. All of my efforts to appear cheerful on camera during those difficult times at CBS had apparently been pointless. I wasn't "delighted to be here tonight," and it showed.

But now that I was back on my own turf again, I didn't have to pretend anymore. I honestly *was* delighted to be just exactly where I was.

Over more than two decades on the air, there were many "firsts" on *The Merv Griffin Show*, many of which I've already told you about. Inevitably, there were also a number of poignant "lasts" as well. One of these was the final television appearance of Groucho Marx. It never should have happened.

We were doing a tribute to the late comic genius Ernie Kovacs. His widow, Edie Adams, had invited Groucho to participate, along with Milton Berle and Mickey Rooney. This was one of the few times where I regretted my rule about not spending any time with a guest prior to the taping. Had I talked with Groucho earlier, I would have gently tried to persuade him not to do the show that night. Unfortunately, the first time I saw him was when he shuffled slowly out onstage.

At eighty-five, Groucho was a fragile shell of his once vibrant self. A series of small strokes had dulled his razor-sharp intelligence, and the caustic wit that had skewered so many victims was now gone. There was also a sadness in his eyes I'd never seen before.

Although he was sporting his trademark beret and brandishing an unlit cigar, Groucho seemed dazed, as if he wasn't quite certain where he was (although he still knew enough to ogle Edie). Every time I tried to direct a question to him, he deflected it by rolling his eyes and waving his cigar in the air. I quickly realized that there wasn't going to be any "interview" with Groucho, so I focused on my other guests until, mercifully, the clock ran out.

He died the following year. Ironically, it wasn't until after he was gone that Groucho's magnificent wit had its final encore. When his children went through his papers, they found a letter from their father with mock "instructions" for his funeral and interment. His last request was that he be "buried on top of Marilyn Monroe."

In the mid-seventies, Rosalind Russell also made one of her final public appearances on my show, as part of a salute to Josh Logan, the man who directed her in *Picnic*. For some time, Roz had been fighting bravely against breast cancer and crippling arthritis, so it wasn't until the last minute that we knew for sure if she'd even show up.

Although I wasn't in the Green Room to witness it personally, Paul Solomon, who booked Roz on the show, told me later that she'd arrived early that day, ahead of the other guests. Paul said that she regaled the staff with stories about what a "miserable son of a bitch" Josh Logan *really* was.

While she was talking, Jimmy Stewart, one of the other participants in the Logan tribute, walked into the Green Room. Roz, who had trouble getting up, waited as he came over and bent down to kiss her on the cheek.

"Jimmy, you look so good!" she enthused. "What work have you had done?"

Stewart straightened up and looked at Roz with a befuddled look, not unlike Elwood P. Dowd studying a six-foot-tall invisible rabbit.

"Well, ah, Roz . . ." said Jimmy slowly, in his famous drawl. "Ya know that I . . . that is, I *haven't* . . . it's just *me*, Roz."

"Oh come on, Jimmy, don't try and kid me. Look at your face. Look at your hair. You *know* you've had work done. Don't get me wrong, sweetie, it looks *great*."

The timely arrival of the makeup girl saved Jimmy from further embarrassment.

Moments later, Josh Logan walked in.

"Josh," gushed Roz, as my staff tried not to laugh, "what have you had *done?* He did a fabulous job! You *must* give me his name."

Of course, I knew none of this during the taping. But I do remember thinking to myself, Gee, Roz must be feeling better because she's really *on* tonight. The funny thing is that both Jimmy and Josh seem a little uncomfortable whenever she's speaking. I wonder why that is?

Unquestionably, the saddest "last" for me was the final interview I ever did with one of my favorite guests—and very dear friend—Totie Fields. To this day, people stop me on the street or write me letters about Totie. She was so loved.

It was the summer of 1978. Totie's diabetic condition had worsened dramatically. Having already lost a leg to amputation, she'd just spent several weeks in the hospital, where the doctors had made a final valiant effort to save her life. In the end, they were only able to buy her a little more time.

When I talked to her in the hospital, Totie made me promise to have her on my show as soon as she was released. She wanted to bring her doctors on the show too, as a way of expressing her appreciation for all they'd tried to do. Of course I agreed. It was the hardest show I've ever done. We finished taping and everybody had tears in their eyes. Still, I'd never been more grateful for having my job than I was that day. We've all said to someone, "Is there *anything* I can do for you?" when there really wasn't. I was able to give my sweet friend a last gift that she truly wanted. How lucky is that?

Less than two weeks later, before the show had a chance to air, Totie was gone. I taped a new opening, informing the audience that it had been Totie's final wish to do this program. Because of that, I explained, it was only appropriate for us to go ahead and air it. And we did.

There's one more "last" I need to tell you about. And it was very nearly mine.

When we first moved the show to California, I'd made an arrangement to tape at Caesars Palace in Las Vegas for eight weeks out of the year. We started doing this while I was still on CBS, and continued the practice after coming over to Metromedia.

Tickets for a taping of *The Merv Griffin Show* were among the toughest to get in town. People from all over the country planned their vacations to coincide with the weeks we were at Caesars.

The demand for tickets was so great that on the day of the show, the line would start at the front door, wend its way around the entire casino floor, and then move outside past the swimming pool. On any given day there were literally thousands of people trying to get in, many of whom had to be turned away when we ran out of seats. The hotel had to hire extra security to protect the slot machines and guard against fights breaking out. It was some kind of scene.

Each morning our crew came in at 4:00 A.M. in order to install a specially constructed ramp that extended from the stage out into the house. During the show, I used it to get closer to the huge audience.

Okay, now that I've given you the backstory, here's what happened. On this particular show, my guests were those two Las Vegas icons, Siegfried & Roy. They'd been on before and their tiger act was always a big hit with my audience.

The final part of Siegfried & Roy's act involved a beautiful Bengal. When it was over, they left the stage to great applause and I cut to a commercial. During the brief break, I walked out on the ramp and began to chat with the audience. Offstage, just out of my field of vision, the tiger somehow managed to get away from his handler. The audience saw it before I did. There was a collective intake of breath and, as I turned to look, I saw the tiger trotting toward me. Before I could move, this sleek, eight-hundred-pound animal was right beside me. To my great relief (sort of), he didn't leap for my throat or into the audience.

What he *did* do was sit right down on my foot.

I kept talking, quietly. "Now ladies and gentlemen, if I were you I wouldn't make any sudden moves. Everything is going to be okay. He's a trained animal. He just likes me." There was a brief murmur of nervous laughter, then the packed house fell silent again.

On the other hand, there was a *lot* of commotion behind me. I could hear Siegfried and Roy backstage, screaming German epithets at the handler. It sounded like a bad episode of *Hogan's Heroes*. At the same time, the stalwart members of my band suddenly remembered something very important they all had to do. In my dressing room. With the door locked.

The women sitting closest to the stage had the strangest reaction. They immediately grabbed their purses off the edge of the ramp. Gosh, that's the *first* thing a tiger will go for—the credit cards.

Meanwhile, the Bengal seemed to have fixed his gaze on a little girl who was seated only a few feet away from us.

Oh God, I thought. I've got to get his attention back on me.

I don't know how I was able to come up with it right at that moment, but I suddenly recalled something that Tippi Hedren once told me about tigers.

Tippi (Melanie Griffith's mother, for those problem spellers who think *The Birds* was David Crosby's first band) has been deeply involved for a long time in rescuing tigers and other jungle cats from abusive situations. To this day she still maintains her home on the property of an animal reserve in Southern California.

Once, as a guest on my show, Tippi brought with her a very young tiger cub who played adorably on top of my desk. She decided on the spot to name him Merv.

Going for the laugh, I asked her, "What will you do if Merv ever gets mad at you?"

Tippi said, "Oofa."

"I beg your pardon?"

"Oofa. O-O-F-A. It's a sound that's very soothing to tigers."

We'd soon see if Tippi was right. Softly, I spoke the magic word into the microphone.

"Oofa."

Still sitting on my foot, the tiger looked around, wondering where the sound was coming from.

"Oofa," I repeated. "Oofa, oofa, oofa."

The audience had no clue what I was doing. But the tiger did. By now, he'd figured out that I was talking to him, and he was staring up at me with what I could only hope was a friendly expression. At least he was no longer looking at the little girl.

"Oofa."

He began to purr.

"Oofa. Oofa."

The handler was next to us now. Very gently, he got my new friend up off my foot and led him backstage.

I looked out at the audience. You could feel the tension leaking out of the room, like a balloon slowly deflating.

I held the microphone up. There was only one thing left to say.

"Oofa."

Five:
The End of the
Beginning

"*Now it's on to Chicago and let's win there.*"

Those were the last public words spoken by Senator Robert F. Kennedy, shortly before his assassination at the Ambassador Hotel in Los Angeles, early on the morning of June 5, 1968.

My dear friend Rosemary Clooney had spent months campaigning around the country for Kennedy, as his presidential campaign moved toward California and its crucial winner-take-all primary election.

On that night, she was in Los Angeles to celebrate Kennedy's anticipated victory along with several thousand other supporters gathered in the second-floor Embassy Room of the Ambassador.

Rosie arrived early that evening, accompanied by two of her five children. The Embassy Room was packed to capacity; a second room had to be opened up on the floor below to handle the throngs of people who couldn't fit inside. At one point during the evening, as the election returns trickled in from around the state, Rosie went down to the overflow room and sang a few songs to pacify the anxious crowd.

Shortly before midnight, Robert Kennedy took the stage to claim victory. Rosie and her kids were in a roped-off VIP area adjacent to the stage. Although Kennedy was speaking less than hundred feet away, they had to watch him on a television monitor because the podium was around a corner, just out of their line of sight. A red carpet had been laid down at the base of the stairs, so that Kennedy would pass through the VIP area when he exited the stage. The plan was for him to continue downstairs to thank his supporters in the overflow room.

It never happened. When he finished speaking, someone said, "This way, Senator," and Kennedy was led off from the opposite side of the stage to meet with reporters in a nearby banquet room. That room could be reached by cutting through the hotel kitchen.

Unaware of this detour, Rosie continued to wait with her young son and daughter in the crowded VIP area, expecting Kennedy to pass by at any moment.

Suddenly, a woman in the ballroom climbed up on a chair and began screaming, "Blood! Blood!" Pandemonium broke out as people ran wildly toward the exits. Rosie clutched her two children, then dropped to her knees in tearful prayer. Moments later, her worst fears were confirmed: Kennedy had been shot. He died twenty-six hours later.

Like much of the nation, Rosemary Clooney had tremendous difficulty coming to terms with the death of Robert Kennedy. But for Rosie, the loss was so devastating that she found herself unable to recover from it. She began drinking and using drugs in order to dull the pain. A few months later, she had to be hospitalized for what we euphemistically used to call "exhaustion." The truth was that Rosie fell apart completely. She was unable to perform and only barely able to function.

Earlier that year I'd interviewed Bobby Kennedy and I understood Rosie's anguish. Of all the political figures I had ever met, he struck me as the most sincere. I found him to be an extraordinarily compassionate man who seemed to follow his conscience instead of the polls.

After Rosie's release from the hospital, she isolated herself from her friends. After several *years* of trying to see her and being rebuffed, I'd lost patience with the situation. I kept calling her home until I finally got her on the phone.

"What the hell are you *doing*, Rosie?" I was yelling. "Are you going to sit in that house and mope for the rest of your life?"

Surprised by my tone (in twenty years of friendship, she'd never heard me raise my voice), Rosie said, "That's not fair, Merv."

I didn't back down. "It *is* fair, Rosie. Somebody's got to tell you this. You've got to get off your ass and get out of that house."

"Merv, I don't know . . ." She was wavering.

"Come on, Rosie. Do my show. I promise you, you'll be great."

A few weeks later, she finally agreed. She came on with songwriters Alan and Marilyn Bergman and was predictably sensational. Fittingly, she sang their hauntingly beautiful "What Are You Doing the Rest of Your Life?" The audience went wild, showering her with love and applause.

Rosie told me that because of that one appearance, she gained the strength to start singing in public again. Not long after that, Bing Crosby asked her to join him on tour.

I was traveling in Europe earlier this year when I got word that

Rosie had succumbed to lung cancer. The news hit me hard. During the two months I was abroad I had stayed in frequent contact with her husband, Dante, who told me the doctors believed that she would pull through. What a loss. Rosie was one of the great ladies of show business and an even greater lady in life. I will miss her deeply.

In addition to providing Rosemary Clooney with the opportunity to end her self-imposed retirement, my show in the seventies often made news for other reasons. Spiro Agnew gave me his first in-depth interview after resigning the vice presidency. Watergate Judge John J. Sirica chose my show as his first posttrial forum only because his daughter was a big fan of mine. I brought the Maharishi Mahesh Yogi into the living rooms of millions of Americans for the first time. His appearance generated over one hundred thousand calls and resulted in forty thousand new practitioners of Transcendental Meditation (including yours truly).

At the same time, I continued to develop new programs through my production company. By 1975, *Jeopardy!* was in its eleventh year on NBC and still going strong. But the new head of NBC's daytime programming, a hard-driving woman named Lin Bolen (on whom Faye Dunaway supposedly based her portrayal of a ruthless television executive in the movie *Network*), decided to move *Jeopardy!* out of its noontime slot, where it had been enormously successful for most of its run.

Although I had many bitter fights with this difficult woman, I developed a grudging respect for her talent and determination. She wanted to put her own stamp on NBC's daytime lineup, and if that meant throwing out a few babies along with the bathwater, well so be it.

Bolen first moved *Jeopardy!* to the morning, immediately costing us the college students who had been our most loyal viewers. Even in a weaker time slot, it still managed to beat its chief competition, *The $10,000 Pyramid* on CBS. Then she shifted it again, this time to the afternoon slot opposite *Let's Make a Deal* and *As the World Turns*. Soon after this last move, *Jeopardy!* was canceled, allegedly for "low ratings." This is the programming equivalent of killing your parents and then complaining about being an orphan.

I subsequently learned that Bolen's real goal was to get rid of Art Fleming. She believed that he was too old to attract young female viewers and she knew that I wouldn't replace him. Her only alternative was to pull the rug out from under the show itself.

After that, you'd think I would have had enough of game shows . . .

Wheel of Fortune came about as the result of a game that my sister and I used to play in the back of the car during those endless summer vacations that kids never want to go on. My parents would take us all the way to the Carlsbad Caverns to see the bats fly out or something equally exciting. There was no air conditioning in those days; people would hang a bag of water out in front of the car in order to keep cool. It was *so* hot driving through the desert, and we'd be sitting in the back, bored out of our minds.

To pass the time, we used to play a game called Hangman (kind of a violent name, when you stop to think about it) where one person selects a word or name. Blanks corresponding to the number of letters in the word are drawn on a sheet of paper, and if the other person doesn't guess the right letter, he has to sketch in various body parts, starting with the head. The object is to fill in all the blanks before getting "hanged." Barbara and I would usually guess the names of movie stars—"Franchot Tone" was a particularly good one.

One day during a production meeting in the mid-seventies, I told my staff about my childhood memories of playing Hangman. They all thought it had great potential as a game show, but that it needed a gimmick or "hook" in order to succeed on television.

That's when I remembered the wheel.

When I was a kid our church had an annual bazaar and there was always a wheel that spun around with prizes written on the spokes. If you were lucky enough to hold a ticket with the right number on it, you won. During all those years that I did *The Merv Griffin Show* at Caesars Palace, surrounded by blackjack and crap tables, it was always the big spinning wheel that I was drawn to. It drove me crazy. I could never win on it, but I still loved to play.

Wanting to find out everything that I could about how the casino wheels operated, I sent the president of Merv Griffin Enterprises, Murray Schwartz, to Las Vegas. There I arranged for him to meet with a powerful Caesars Palace executive named Ash Resnick.

Ash was a tough customer; you didn't mess with him. He insisted on collecting all the casino's markers (debts) personally—*render unto*

Caesars what is owed—and he never returned empty-handed. His car had been machine-gunned more than once; luckily for him, never while he was in it. Acid had been poured in his swimming pool. Like most of the top Caesars Palace executives, Ash owned a remote control device that allowed him to start his car in the morning from a safe distance away.

Let's just say Ash didn't have a lot of friends.

Strangely enough, I was one of them. He used to come see my show when I was taping at Caesars, and we'd swap stories about the old days, when Vegas was a wide-open town run by men named Siegel, Lansky, and Luciano. I found him to be a colorful and likable character. On the other hand, *I* didn't owe him any money.

Murray asked Ash lots of questions about the big gaming wheels—how they were constructed, how often the various numbers hit, how fast the wheel spun—everything he could think of. Then he brought all that information back to our production staff. In late 1974, that data, in combination with the basic rules of Hangman, led to the invention of the *Wheel*.

As the host for the pilot (which had the awful working title of *Shopper's Bazaar*), we used Edd "Kookie" Byrnes, the comb-carrying teen idol from the old *77 Sunset Strip* TV series of the early sixties.

It's funny how history—and television—has a way of repeating itself. Remember when NBC canceled the original *Merv Griffin Show* and gave me a deal to produce *Word for Word* as a consolation prize? Well, it was happening again. *Jeopardy!* went off NBC after eleven years and 2,753 episodes on Friday, January 3, 1975. *Wheel of Fortune* made its debut the following Monday.

The first host of *Wheel of Fortune* was Chuck Woolery, who remained with the show for six seasons, from 1975 to 1981. The original "letter-turner" was a young woman named Susan Stafford, whose previous television experience was as the co-host of a local talk show in Los Angeles.

Both Chuck and Susie did a fine job, and *Wheel* did well enough on NBC, although it never approached the kind of ratings success that *Jeopardy!* achieved in its heyday.

In 1981, Chuck decided to leave *Wheel of Fortune*, en route to making his *Love Connection*. The following year, Susie Stafford left show business entirely, choosing instead to do wonderful work as a caregiver for cancer patients.

My first job was to find a new host. And I thought I knew the perfect guy.

Pat Sajak did the weather on KNBC, the NBC station in Los Angeles. At that point, Pat's only television experience was as a weatherman, with four years at KNBC and five more at his previous job with a Nashville station.

Pat's sense of humor was . . . well, *odd.* I used to watch him every day, just to see what he'd do next. Because the weather was always the same in L.A.—74 degrees and sunny—Pat figured that he had to do some unusual things to keep people's attention. I remember once he came out wearing a small bandage on his right cheek. He went over to the weather board, did the forecast—74 *degrees and sunny*—and then cut to a commercial. When they came back on, he was wearing the bandage on the other cheek. I don't know how many people caught it, but *I* did. He was hilarious.

So I brought him into NBC. The new vice president of daytime programming (who'd replaced Lin Bolen) said, "You've got to be kidding. He's a weatherman, for Christ sake. And not even a *network* weatherman. He's *local.*" He said the word "local" with absolute contempt in his voice.

I just sat there and let him rant. By now I was used to it at the network.

"No way, Merv. He's not acceptable to us. Find someone else."

I got up to leave. "No problem. I'll just stop taping *Wheel of Fortune* until Pat Sajak is the host."

One down, one to go.

When Susan Stafford left the show, the production staff brought me in a big stack of 8 x 10 glossies representing dozens of candidates to take her place. They were all beautiful girls—models, actresses, beauty contest winners. There was no way for me to go through that many photos without having the faces blur together.

So I said, "Okay, here's what we'll do. You guys narrow it down to ten and spread their glossies out on top of my desk. I'll come back into the room and point to the one I want."

After about an hour, they were ready for me. I went back in to the office and walked over to my desk. Then—and I *swear* this is true—I looked at the ten photographs for no more than ten seconds, before pointing to the picture of a young blonde. I picked up the photo and turned it over. She had an unusual name.

"Vanna White. She's the one. Call her in."

Many months later, when the nation was in the fevered grip of "Vannamania," the press wanted to know how I'd discovered her. I gave them two answers. The first was a toss-off line designed only to garner a quick laugh:

Q. Why did you hire Vanna?
A. Because she knew the whole alphabet.

To those reporters not satisfied with my flip response, I gave an honest answer—and it *sounded* like a joke:

Q. Why did you hire Vanna?
A. Because she has a large head.

The truth is that what made me choose her photo over all the others is that, relative to the size of her body, Vanna has a large head. Don't laugh. Many of the great Hollywood stars—Joan Crawford, Bette Davis, even Marilyn Monroe—had outsize heads. For some reason the camera compensates for the disparity by making their features stand out, thus causing them to appear more attractive on-screen.

About a week after an article containing my "head theory" appeared in print, Vanna called me.

"Merv, can I come in and see you?" She sounded a little strange.

I said, "Of course. Is anything wrong?"

"No, I just have something I want to talk to you about." She often asked me for personal advice, so I told her to come on over.

As soon as she came into my office, I could tell that something *was* wrong. Vanna is exactly the same person off camera as she is on. Sweet, upbeat, always smiling. But not today.

"What's the matter, Vanna?" I asked, as she shifted uncomfortably on the couch in my office. I came around from behind my desk and sat down in a chair opposite her.

"It's hard for me to put into words." She was looking down at her shoes (for the record, size 7½ pumps that were part of her new line of Vanna footwear), rather than directly at me.

I was beginning to worry that this was really serious.

"Whatever it is, you can tell me. What's bothering you?"

She looked up at me with the beautiful brown eyes that had recently graced the cover of *Newsweek*. "Is my head too big for my body?"

I was so relieved that she was okay that I started to smile. Then I quickly caught myself, realizing that if she was genuinely concerned about this, she could probably find some doctor who would shrink her head. *"A little off the top, please."*

Reaching over and taking her hand, I gently explained to her about Marilyn, Bette, and Joan. And if that wasn't enough to convince her, I told her that *my* hat size was 7⅞.

She left my office smiling—like I said, in real life she's exactly the same wonderful girl you see on the show. Well, maybe there's one difference. Off camera, she talks a lot more . . .

Finding good hosts was a never-ending challenge for me. When the syndicated nighttime version of *Wheel* debuted in 1983, I needed a substitute for Pat on the daytime show since he couldn't do both. Being a big tennis fan, I had what I thought was an inspired idea. I taped an audition with Jimmy Connors, who, at the time, was the number one tennis player in the world. He was terrific, but the network wouldn't let me use him because NBC Sports wanted him as a commentator. Every news organization in the world tried to get their hands on that audition tape, but I refused to release it because it wouldn't have been fair to Jimmy.

If you've noticed anything about me by now, it's that I don't like to be told that something can't be done. When I have an idea that I'm passionate about, I'm like a dog with a bone—I won't let go.

I still had an old bone to pick with NBC about its shabby treatment of *Jeopardy!* In 1978, I used the leverage of *Wheel of Fortune* to get *Jeopardy!* another shot on the network. I brought back Art Fleming (take that, Lin), moved the show to Los Angeles, and redesigned the format, adding a fourth round called "Super Jeopardy!"

That version of the show lasted only five months. This time it wasn't the network's fault. It was mine. The original *Jeopardy!* had a far more loyal audience than even I realized, and they didn't like anyone messing with its basic structure. It took me six more years, but with a lot of help from a nonsinging family named King, I eventually got *Jeopardy!* back on the air.

Roger King is the greatest salesman I've ever met. He could sell sand in the Sahara, ice in Antarctica, coal in Newcastle. He's so good, he could open a kosher delicatessen in Baghdad and get Saddam to cut the ribbon.

Roger and his brother Michael are the benevolent despots who rule King World, the most powerful television syndication company in the known universe. Big, brawling Irishmen, the King brothers are to New Jersey what the Kennedys are to Massachusetts. But unlike Joe Kennedy's clan, their field of battle is electronic, not electoral.

The family patriarch, the late Charlie King, started his broadcasting career in radio in the thirties and forties, not as a performer, but as a producer and advertising salesman. The elder King was successful enough to buy a good house in Hunterdon County, which is in the horse country of western New Jersey.

It was there that he and his wife, Lucille, began raising their large brood, which eventually numbered six—four boys and two girls.

In 1952, the same year that I left the safety of the Freddy Martin Orchestra to explore the uncharted waters of Hollywood, Charlie King set sail on his own venture into the unknown. Unfortunately for King and his young family, their trip had been forced on them by the rapidly declining fortunes of the radio business.

As television quickly eclipsed radio in the competition for advertising dollars, Charlie's business had foundered. The programs he produced were canceled and the future for commercial sales in radio was bleak. The King family had to sell its home and move into a small apartment.

Not yet forty years old, Charlie King was forced to reinvent himself as an entrepreneur (which I've always said is the French word for "hustler"). Employing the salesmanship skills that he would later bequeath to his son, King tried his hand at a variety of new ventures, many of them outlandish.

He began selling everything from fire alarms to home freezers packed with a year's worth of food. Seizing on the public's newfound fascination with golf in the Eisenhower era, he even attempted to launch a chain of driving ranges, but was ultimately unsuccessful in that enterprise as well.

Still hoping to mount a comeback in broadcasting, Charlie took a job working for a company called Official Films, which owned the distribution rights to the once popular "Little Rascals" pictures of the thirties. By then dated (and filled with racial images that, even by fifties standards, were hard to watch), the "Little Rascals" series no longer had much commercial value. Official Films decided not to continue its distribution contract with the series owner, Clinton Pictures.

Charlie, whose net worth consisted of little more than the six dollars he had on him, met with the executives at Clinton Pictures and offered them $300,000 for the exclusive rights to the "Little Rascals."

Before they signed an agreement, the Clinton people discovered that King had been bluffing about his "assets." Making the sales pitch of his life, he persuaded them not to tear up the contract, but instead to give him the rights for one day in order to come up with at least part of the money.

That same day, Charlie talked his way into WPIX television in New York (a Westinghouse station, by the way) and made an agreement for them to air the "Little Rascals" series exclusively in the New York area. He left the station with a $50,000 check in his pocket. A new television syndication company, King World, was now up and running.

King World did a steady, if unspectacular, business through the fifties and mid-sixties. In addition to the "Rascals," they distributed a number of cartoon programs and *The Joe Pyne Show*, an early forerunner to Jerry Springer.

By the end of the sixties, King World was in trouble. Pyne was dead and the "Little Rascals" had fallen victim to the emerging civil rights movement. Stations were not renewing their contracts because of the negative stereotypes contained in the films.

Before he could reinvent himself and his company again, Charlie King suffered a fatal heart attack in 1972. He was only fifty-nine.

A decade later, Murray Schwartz happened to be in New York on business. Running early for a dinner meeting, Murray stopped into the St. Regis Hotel to have a drink. Sitting at the bar was one of Charlie King's sons, Bob, who was having an animated conversation with a friend. Bob and his brothers Roger and Michael were now running the family business.

Alone at the bar, Murray couldn't help but overhear what Bob

King was saying to his friend. He was bemoaning King World's hard times.

"We know everybody in the goddamn television business and all we've got to sell is the 'Little Rascals,' " said King. "If I had a show like *Wheel of Fortune*, then it would be a whole different ball game."

Murray went over and introduced himself, giving Bob his business card. He said, "Show up next week in Merv's office with a $50,000 check and the syndication rights are yours."

Bob looked at Murray in disbelief. It was as if he'd just met Santa Claus on Christmas morning.

The following week, Bob King flew out to Los Angeles, pulled a crumpled $50,000 check out of his pocket, and, his hand shaking, gave it to me.

As all this was happening, the FCC regulations regarding local stations had also changed. A new rule now guaranteed prime-time access for all local stations. This meant that the seven to eight o'clock hour, immediately prior to the start of the network's prime-time lineup, was now reserved for the local stations' exclusive use. The networks could no longer program during that hour. The rule was designed to increase the production of original programs at the local level, but the practical effect was to open up a highly desirable time slot for the national syndicators. *Family Feud* was the first game show to successfully use the prime access rule.

Roger King, the family's brilliant salesman, grabbed the *Wheel* and ran with it. In a short time, he'd sold it to fifty-nine stations. Within a year it was the number one show in syndication, reaching 99 percent of the national television audience.

With the phenomenal success of *Wheel of Fortune* in syndication, it was the perfect time for me to dig up that old *Jeopardy!* bone and try again.

I returned to the original format (I can take a hint), but I knew that it was finally time to look for another host. My friend Lucille Ball was a big fan of daytime television. Her favorite game show in the seventies had been a program called *High Rollers*. Lucy loved that show and its host, a Canadian fellow named Alex Trebek. When I told her that I was intending to bring back *Jeopardy!* with a new host, she suggested that I give Alex an audition.

Thanks, Lucy.

We did a new pilot for *Jeopardy!* in 1984 and I turned it over to Roger King, the P.T. Barnum of syndication. It quickly became the number two show in syndication, right behind the *Wheel*. The rest, as they say, is history.

While Roger King was out selling *Wheel* and *Jeopardy!*, I was celebrating my twentieth year behind the desk of *the Merv Griffin Show*. I still found myself looking forward to each new show with what a friend dubbed my "evergreen enthusiasm."

"Who was the most interesting guest you ever interviewed?"

I've been asked that countless times and, frankly, I always thought it was a ridiculous question. By definition, the answer is entirely subjective. Not to mention that the very word "interesting" is the ultimate dodge. There's no value judgment in it. The Pope can be described as an "interesting" man. So can Osama bin Laden. You see my point.

All of this is a roundabout way of saying that I *am* going to tell you who I think my most interesting guest was. I don't need a job in television anymore, so I can say whatever the hell I want, right? God, I'm starting to feel like Rosie O'Donnell . . .

Okay, *okay*. It was Orson Welles.

What an awesome character. The first time we ever booked him, in 1976, my staff worked for two weeks to prepare detailed questions about everything from the Mercury Theater radio broadcast of *War of the Worlds* that caused a nationwide panic, to *Citizen Kane*, which he co-wrote, directed, and starred in at the unbelievable age of twenty-six.

Paul Solomon was the person responsible for researching this voluminous amount of material, as well as for developing questions about Welles's use of Marlene Dietrich in his magic act (he sawed her in half) and his tempestuous marriage to Rita Hayworth.

On the day of the taping, Paul called Orson to conduct the standard pre-interview done with every guest on every talk show. It isn't a rehearsal, but it gives the guest a sense of the topics to be covered and it's also a chance for him to volunteer good stories that the staff might have missed.

Paul was excited to speak with the great Mr. Welles, about whom he'd become something of an expert in the preceding weeks. He began by telling Orson about some of the film clips that he'd found to use during the ninety-minute show (he was to be my sole guest).

Before Paul Solomon could even say "rosebud," Orson exploded, his stentorian voice booming through the phone, forcing Paul to hold the receiver away from his ear.

"Fuck you! Fuck You! *Fuck* you! No goddamned trips down Memory Lane!" And he slammed down the phone.

Poor Paul. He broke the news to Bob Murphy, my producer. Bob is my oldest friend; we first met in sixth grade. Bob joined the marines after high school and was sent to the Pacific, where he served with distinction during World War II.

After the war, Bob graduated from the University of San Francisco and took a job in the real estate business. Although he was a success in real estate, I'd always had it in the back of my mind that as soon as the opportunity arose, I would ask him to come work with me.

That was finally possible in the mid-sixties when I was developing game shows in New York. I called Bob, who was going through a rough divorce at the time, and offered him a job. He accepted and moved east with only a suitcase.

From the time he started with me (on *Jeopardy!*), Bob held almost every position in my company, including interviewer, booker, associate producer, and, finally, producer on *The Merv Griffin Show*. The obvious assumption is that he got those jobs because he was my oldest friend. Well, maybe he got in the door because of that, but the truth is that Bob earned each promotion through talent, hard work, and a marvelous ability to win the respect and affection of everyone he worked with. To this day, I've never heard a negative word spoken about him by anybody. And how about this: in more than thirty years of working closely together, we never had a single fight. Not one. That has to be some kind of record.

Two hours before the cameras would start to roll, Bob came into my office and explained the dismal state of affairs. The good news was that we had Orson Welles for ninety minutes. The bad news was that we had nothing to talk about.

I don't mean to sound immodest (well, maybe just a little), but this is exactly the kind of situation I thrive on. Bob Murphy used to get terribly frustrated with me when a show would go exactly like we'd planned and afterward I would complain to him about how bored I'd been.

"You're just not happy unless you have something to fix, are you, chief?" Bob would say this with just a hint of sarcasm. But he was right.

On that first night with Orson, I had to throw away all my notes and wing it. I asked him about everything under the sun—politics, current events, art, cinema (other than his own work), literature, travel—and it was an extraordinary interview. I quickly discovered that he was conversant on any topic I could think of. We developed an immediate rapport that only deepened over time.

Briefly alluding to his childhood, Orson did reveal something to me in our first conversation that I've thought a lot about over the years.

"I was very lucky," he told me, "because I had parents who took me to the theater when I could hardly sit on a lap. As a child I had an adult vocabulary because I stayed up late at night and listened to grown-ups. You see, I was a kind of third-rate musical wunderkind, playing piano and violin, and I conducted too."

Orson and I had several things in common that contributed to our becoming friends. Each of us was the younger child, with only one older sibling (he had a brother, Richard). We were both piano prodigies at a very early age, which required that we spend a lot of time entertaining and impressing adults. I think there's something about the experience of being a child in an adult environment that changes you fundamentally—not always for the better. There's a certain loneliness that develops; a sense that you don't quite belong in either world. This was certainly true of many child actors. Look at Judy Garland or Mickey Rooney.

Ultimately, I think that both Orson and I were fortunate to have grown up the way we did. Yet only someone who's gone through it himself can really understand what it's like. Although we were different in so many ways, I believe that our friendship grew, in no small part, out of our similarities.

Over the course of the next nine years I did close to fifty interviews with Orson, each one more fascinating than the last.

I enjoyed our conversations so much that I broke my cardinal rule about never socializing with a guest. One day I met Orson for lunch at Ma Maison, where he dined daily on a little piece of grilled sole. On that diet, I couldn't understand how he had remained so overweight. I'd always thought that there were very few calories in fish.

On my way back from lunch, I passed by Pink's hot dog restaurant, an old Hollywood landmark. Wait a minute, I thought to myself. Could that be *Orson's* car parked out front? We'd only finished lunch twenty minutes before. Slowing down to get a better look, I saw Orson's chauffeur emerge carrying a tray piled high with at least a dozen hot dogs. He was headed straight for the car.

At least now I could stop blaming the fish . . .

One of my favorite moments with Orson was the time that I invited his old Mercury Theater collaborator John Houseman to appear with him as a guest. At this late stage in his career, Houseman, a distinguished film and theater actor, had recently become familiar to an entirely new audience as the imperious law professor on the television series *The Paper Chase*.

Bringing them together was an extremely risky thing to do, because after a highly public row in a London restaurant, Welles and Houseman, once close friends, hadn't even *spoken* in twenty-three years. By this point, I felt secure enough in my friendship with Orson to take the chance that it would all work out. And, what the hell, if they started shouting at each other on camera, it would make for an *interesting* show.

I needn't have worried. Orson positioned himself offstage and when it came time for Houseman's introduction (he was the first guest; we'd kept them separated before the show, so they still hadn't seen each other), he heard his old friend's voice describe him glowingly as "brilliant, talented, and inspiring." Both men walked out at the same time from opposite sides of the stage. Meeting in the middle, they embraced each other warmly and the show took off from there.

Although we touched on their estrangement during the conversation, the significance of their rapprochement was lost on most of the audience. But not on me. I looked over at Orson several times during the taping and I could tell that he was truly enjoying himself. Perhaps there would now be an exception to the rule—"no trips down Memory Lane" unless accompanied by an old and very dear friend.

Sadly, that on-camera reunion with Houseman was a one-time only event. They never spoke again.

My final interview with Orson Welles was taped on October 8, 1985. Shortly before the show, he rapped on my dressing room door with his cane. The door was at the bottom of a flight of stairs leading up to the dressing room itself. Orson didn't want to go up the stairs, because by this time he had terrible varicose veins and could barely walk. So I came downstairs and he was standing there, looking quite ill.

Although I was greatly concerned by his haggard appearance, I tried not to let on how worried I was.

"Hi, Orson. What's up?"

He said, "Tonight, I feel like talking."

"I'm sorry. What exactly have we been *doing* all this time?" I was joking, but when I looked into his eyes, I could tell that he wasn't. He wasn't mad. In fact, just the opposite.

"Merv, I mean it. I feel expansive tonight. You know all those silly, gossipy little questions you've been trying to ask me for years about Rita and Marlene? Well, go ahead and ask them. Ask me anything you want."

I was taken aback. "*Anything* I want? Even about the making of *Citizen Kane*?" This was the most taboo subject of all.

"Ask me." And he turned and walked slowly toward the Green Room.

It was far and away the most candid discussion we ever had. I'm convinced that it was the most honest and insightful interview he ever gave.

We talked about everything and everyone—Rita Hayworth ("one of the dearest and sweetest women that ever lived"), Marlene Dietrich ("the most loyal friend that anyone could ever ask for"), *Citizen Kane, War of the Worlds, The Magnificent Ambersons*—no subject was off limits.

At one point in the interview, we somehow got onto the subject of birthdays. Orson had turned seventy earlier that year and I asked him about age.

For the first time that night, he sounded tired. "De Gaulle, of course, said the truth about it. Old age is a shipwreck."

"But you *feel* wonderful, don't you?" It was more than just a polite question.

"Oh *sure*." And Orson rolled his eyes skyward.

Moments later, the rogue in him returned and he was back on the subject of birthdays: "I used to pretend it was my birthday whenever I took a girl out to dinner. And then I'd have the waiter bring a cake in, and sing 'Happy Birthday.' I'd use that as an excuse to extend the evening. One night, a friend of mine, Ty Power, God rest him, whose birthday was on May 5th, one day before mine—saw a waiter singing 'Happy Birthday' to me while I sat next to a pretty girl. But it was *February*. I got the dirtiest look I've ever had in my life."

The audience howled and I remember thinking, Why did it take us fifty shows before we got to do *this?*

Orson went home right after the show. Two hours later he died.

I've looked at that tape so many times. I honestly believe that when I asked him how he felt and Orson rolled his eyes skyward, God chose that moment to say, "Time to come home."

I'd known President and Mrs. Reagan since their days in Hollywood. Ronnie (as I used to call him back in the days when that was allowed) and I had crossed paths many times, although we didn't become close friends until after he and Nancy appeared on my show while he was Governor of California.

In the spring of 1983, I visited them in the White House for the first time. It was on a Saturday, so they were in their private quarters when I arrived shortly after 11:00 A.M. I rode up the tiny elevator that went directly to the residence. Although it wasn't my first time inside the White House (I'd attended a state dinner during the Ford administration), this would be the first time that I'd ever seen the First Family's private living quarters.

When the elevator door opened, they were both waiting there to greet me. Since we would be having lunch in the residence, they were dressed informally in California ranch-style clothes.

Uncertain of the protocol, I'd chosen to wear my best dark suit. When I saw how casually they were attired, I blurted out, "Oh, that's just great. Here I am dressed like Herbert Hoover and you two look like Roy Rogers and Dale Evans."

I got them laughing right off the bat, which I was hoping to do. I had arrived on a very difficult day. Later that afternoon they would travel out to Andrews Air Force Base for the arrival of the plane bearing the bodies of sixteen Americans who had been killed in the bombing of our embassy in Beirut.

While the president was momentarily busy elsewhere, Nancy took me on a brief tour of the presidential residence. We looked into each of the historic rooms, finally stopping at a small bedroom that she wanted to show me. Nancy had been redoing all the bathrooms, putting in new copper piping because the old plumbing was so corroded.

So there we were—the First Lady of the United States (or FLOTUS as she was referred to in the White House schedule) and me—down on our hands and knees under the sink in this little bathroom. I suddenly realized that somebody else was in the room. When I looked up, I saw that it was the president, standing in the doorway with an amused look on his face, as if to say, "What are you two up to *now?*"

As all three of us continued the tour, I heard band music coming from somewhere outside. I asked the president if he knew what piece they were playing.

He looked at me quizzically. "You know, Merv, I couldn't really tell you."

I feigned incredulity. "You don't *know?* Gosh, if it was *my* garden, I'd certainly know what the band was playing."

Both of them were smiling now. Nancy walked over to a nearby window and opened it. The music came drifting up. It was some kind of march. Trying to hear better, all three of us stuck our heads out the window. At that moment, the daily tour of the White House was passing by immediately below us. It was a funny scene, made funnier by the fact that not *one* of the hundred people on the tour happened to look up. If anyone had, they never would have believed it. We stopped by the president's study and I immediately noticed the numerous jelly bean jars scattered throughout the room. It was a kaleidoscope of candy—jars of yellow, jars of green, jars of purple, jars of orange. There was even a jar containing red, white, and blue beans, layered in a patriotic pattern.

I said to the president, "You really *do* love jelly beans, don't you?"

He walked over to his desk and opened the top drawer. Inside was a big bag of peanut brittle. "Actually, Merv, *this* is what I really enjoy. But don't tell anyone, will you? Everybody sends me jars of jelly beans because someone once wrote a story that said I liked them. I wouldn't want people to think that I didn't appreciate their gifts."

"And *I* wouldn't want all that peanut brittle arriving in the mail," said Nancy, dryly.

Exactly five months later, I returned to the White House, this time with a camera crew in tow. I'd been granted permission to conduct the first talk show interviews ever broadcast from the first family's private quarters. The President would be my sole guest for the first forty-five minutes, then Nancy would join us for the final fifteen minutes.

I was allowed to use the Lincoln Bedroom as a place to review my notes. (No matter what anyone tells you, I never jumped on the bed.) Rereading the notes that my staff had prepared, I started to shake my head. These were questions that Sam Donaldson should be asking, not me. I wasn't a hard news reporter, nor did I want the job.

The problem was that all of my questions had been sent to presidential assistant Mike Deaver weeks in advance. And there wasn't enough time to make any last-minute changes with Mike—the interview was scheduled to start in twenty minutes.

It was one of those moments where you just say to yourself, "Go for it." What Orson Welles had done to me, I was about to do to Ronald Reagan. I put aside sheaves of carefully prepared research material, as well as the approved list of questions, and pulled out a blank 4x6 index card. Sitting on Abe's narrow bed, I just began to write. The questions flowed out of me. I wanted to know what life in the White House was really like. As interested as I was in world events, I knew that I was in a unique position to pose the sorts of questions that most reporters couldn't get away with.

When we sat down, the only copy of the questions was in my hand. The president must have been puzzled when midway through our forty-five-minute interview, I had yet to ask him any of the questions he'd been told to expect.

When I look back on that interview, one question—and one very personal answer—stands out in my mind.

"After the assassination attempt on your life, Mr. President, did your personal priorities change?"

President Reagan paused before responding. This was definitely off the script, and he was clearly thinking about how he felt. Finally, he was ready to answer.

"Well, no. I can't really say [that they did]. I think I had them pretty well in line. But Merv, I had to feel—as I learned later how close it was—I had to realize that any time I've got left, I owe to Him."

As he said, "I owe to Him," the president cast his eyes skyward, just as Orson had done.

Nancy joined us shortly after that and lightened the mood considerably when she described one of her most embarrassing moments in the White House.

"Does anything ever go wrong, Nancy?" I asked. "Has there ever been a terrible moment for you here?"

"I had a meeting up here with a lady and it was a fairly serious meeting," replied Mrs. Reagan. "She and I and Jim Rosebush, who's my chief of staff, were all here."

"The president is laughing already," I interjected. "It must be terrible."

"He knows the story," said the First Lady, her eyes twinkling. "So we finished the meeting. Now I had on a skirt and a blouse. Jim had turned to go to the elevator, thank goodness. I stood up and I had my hand out to say, 'Thank you and goodbye.' As I stood, and she stood with her hand out, my skirt just went right down to the floor. And I was standing there with my *blouse* on. I was yelling to Jim, 'Don't turn around! Don't turn around!' The poor woman was standing there with her arm out and the only thing I could think of to say was, 'Well, I'm sure this is a meeting you'll never forget.' "

President Reagan will be remembered as one of the greatest chief executives in our nation's history. With his gentle good humor, unflagging optimism, and clear-eyed vision of a better America, he restored our national pride.

Yet for all of Ronald Reagan's accomplishments as a leader, I think it is his humanity that I admire most. He is one of the kindest, most compassionate people that I've ever met. But more than anything, his love for his beautiful Nancy is astonishing to behold. I've never known two people who love each other so deeply. I am honored by, and grateful for, their friendship.

I first heard Whitney Houston sing at a small New York nightclub over on Tenth Avenue. She was just a kid, only twenty-one years old at the time. A recording executive I knew had called me and said, "Merv, there's this fantastic girl singer—actually she's a model, but she's trying to have a singing career. She's giving a little performance tonight and I'd really like you to come see her. She'd be terrific on your show."

The club wasn't crowded, so my first reaction was that she probably wasn't any good. But then she started to sing.

I thought, "That's a *model?* Models don't have voices like that." My God, she was unbelievable—the voice of an angel.

I went backstage after her set and we were introduced. Cutting through the preliminaries, I said, "Whitney, I'm doing my show at the Vivian Beaumont Theater in Lincoln Center all this week and I want to have you on tomorrow night."

Bear in mind, I never did this. Even if I liked someone, I made it a rule to leave the actual booking to my staff. Every once in a while I'd pass on a conversation that I'd had with someone about coming on the show, but I almost never invited someone to appear on a specific night.

Whitney couldn't believe it. "You're kidding. *Really?*"

"Really," I said, feeling like Ziegfeld.

Ah, the advantage of celebrity. You could say something utterly incredible like, "I want to have you on my show tomorrow night," and people had to take you seriously.

Since the taping was less than twenty-four hours away, I asked a practical question. "Do you have any arrangements?"

"Well, I've done an album with Clive Davis that hasn't been released yet." Then she said, "By the way, Mr. Griffin. I think you know my mother—Cissy Houston."

"*She's* your mother?" I'd known Cissy for years. She was a great session singer who'd sung backup for the Supremes and Aretha Franklin. Not to mention that her sister—Whitney's aunt—was Dionne Warwick. This girl had quite a pedigree.

There were over a thousand people in the audience to see Whitney Houston's first television appearance. They weren't disappointed; she brought the house down. For an encore, I called her back out to sing a duet with her mother, whom she'd brought along for "luck." Like she needed it.

Comedians were always my favorite guests, particularly when it was someone new that later scored big.

In 1981, Jerry Seinfeld made his television debut on *The Merv Griffin Show*, and it was obvious to everyone that he would have a huge career. He'd just turned twenty-seven, but he looked eighteen.

It's the dream of every young comic to be invited over to the couch for an interview when he finishes his act. It's something of a rite of passage, after which a comedian's career is taken more seriously. In show business parlance, this is called "paneling." For some, it takes a long time to wangle that invitation. Others never get one.

His very first time out, Jerry got to "panel." He was as funny chatting with me about his life as he was doing his routine for the audience. He talked about an experience that we've all had, taking tests in school:

> If you have an essay test, you can just put everything you know on there and maybe you'll hit it.
>
> I would get my paper back from the teacher and it would just say, *"vague."*
>
> And I thought that was a very vague thing to say, so I sent it back. I wrote underneath, *"unclear."*
>
> She returned it to me: *"ambiguous."*
>
> We are still corresponding to this day.

He had *everyone*—me, the audience, even the normally jaded crew—laughing hysterically.

> I had braces. I had glasses. I was a *very* good-looking kid. In fact, I said to my parents, "Let's not stop now. Let's get me a hearing aid and orthopedic shoes."

Here's a good one. You'll like this. It turns out that a certain sixteen-year-old girl from Long Island happened to be watching my show that afternoon. This girl also thought that Jerry was very talented. So talented, in fact, that she took down his entire act verbatim, then performed it herself at a local comedy club the very next night.

Shortly after that, someone (not Jerry's lawyer) was kind enough to explain to Miss Roseanne Teresa O'Donnell of Commack, New York, that you weren't supposed to use other people's material without their permission.

On the other hand, I was very flattered when Rosie told me (and every reporter who interviewed her) that she had modeled her talk show after mine. I was familiar with her stand-up act and I knew that she'd be a hit, even before she went on the air. She's a natural. I'd seen her walk into a room and people would just laugh at everything she'd say, even when she wasn't performing.

Over the years, Rosie has also come to me for both career and business advice, which I've been happy to give her. Even during her show's first season, we had discussions about how to know when it was the right time to leave, and of the importance of doing so on her own terms. I have nothing but admiration for the way Rosie has handled herself, both personally and professionally. We haven't heard the last from her, not by a long shot.

In ways that I wasn't aware of at the time, my show affected a lot of people's lives. Once I asked Arnold Klein, now one of the world's leading dermatologists, to talk about skin cancer. Americans were just starting to learn about the dangers of pursuing the perfect tan. And in a culture that idealized the beach, this information was hard for a lot of people to accept.

"All right," I said, challenging Klein to back up his claims, "you guys keep talking about melanomas. Let's hear you describe one in detail."

Following the broadcast, we got a huge amount of mail from viewers who said that Klein's description of what a melanoma looked like caused them to get a potentially life-saving checkup.

The extent of my show's impact really hit home to me when I was a guest on *Larry King Live*, ten years after *The Merv Griffin Show* had left the air.

Toward the end of the hour-long interview, Larry took a call from a woman in Philadelphia.

"Hello, I'd like to thank Mr. Griffin. He saved my life many years ago with one of his theme shows."

Larry leaned closer to his microphone, signaling his interest in what the caller had said. "What was it?"

"Rape." Now she was talking to me. "You had a woman on there who said it was time for women to start fighting back. A man broke into my house and I realized he did not have a weapon and I fought."

"You fought," I repeated incredulously.

"And I got him out and he did not rape me. And I have always wanted to thank you for this, always."

Larry and I just looked at each other, stunned, as she continued.

"You have no idea how much I appreciate what you did. I wish you'd come back on the air because I think you handled it so wonderfully, so professionally, so beautifully, that I remembered it and was able to think [clearly] while this man was there."

I'm rarely speechless, but I was so moved by her call that all I could think of to say was, "Thank you. I appreciate that. That's an amazing story."

What do I miss most about being on the air? Truthfully, the answer would have to be bringing out new talent. It became a hobby for me, and I just got very good at spotting people. Eventually you develop a kind of third eye. When I stop and look back at the list of people who got their start on my show over twenty-three years— Woody Allen, George Carlin, Richard Pryor and Lily Tomlin all the way up through Whitney Houston and Jerry Seinfeld—it's pretty gratifying.

In the final season of *Seinfeld*, Jerry paid me the ultimate compliment by building an entire episode of his brilliant show around the hysterical premise that Kramer and Jerry had discovered the old set from my show in a neighborhood dumpster. Titled (appropriately enough) "The Merv Griffin Show," the episode was later nominated for an Emmy.

When Jerry's producer called to tell me what their plans were, I was delighted. That kind of tongue-in-cheek parody is an honor when it comes from someone whose work you truly respect. I talked to the *Seinfeld* writers about the various elements of my set and provided them with a tape of my show's theme music. Since I wrote the theme, this was actually my only official connection to the episode (I'm still getting *Seinfeld* royalty checks).

As a treat for the writers, many of whom were too young to have seen Jerry when he was just starting out, I also sent along several videocassettes of his early appearances with me. I heard later that even Jerry got a kick out of watching them again.

SCENE: *Jerry and Kramer in an alley*

KRAMER: Jerry, this is the set from the old *Merv Griffin Show*! They must be throwing it out. This stuff belongs in the Smithsonian!

JERRY: Yeah, at least in the dumpster behind the Smithsonian.

KRAMER: Look at this. Boy, one minute Elliott Gould is sitting on you and the next thing—you're yesterday's trash.

JERRY: Come on, Kramer, get out of there.

KRAMER: No, no, no. You go on ahead. I'm not finished taking this in. Oh, Jerry look . . . Merv Griffin's cigar!

I don't smoke cigars. But what the hell, when you're the number one show on television, I think you're entitled to a little artistic license.

SCENE: *Kramer's apartment*

KRAMER: Hey, Jerry! Come in here a sec! Hey!

JERRY: Oh my God!

KRAMER: It's the Merv Griffin set.

JERRY: How did you get this in here?

KRAMER: Oh, you just bring it in sideways and hook it.

JERRY: So where are you gonna sleep?

KRAMER: Backstage.

ELAINE: Phew! This chair smells like garbage!

KRAMER: Oh, well a lot of the stars from the seventies—they were not as hygienic as they appeared on TV. You take *Mannix* for example . . .

By the mid-eighties, I'd been doing my show for more than two decades. Although I still loved coming to work every day, I was beginning to feel a little like that Peggy Lee song, "Is That All There Is." (Don't even get me *started* on that song. Jerry Leiber and Mike Stoller, who lived in the same Central Park West building that I did, offered me that song before they gave it to Peggy. Genius that I am,

I turned it down. "It's not quite *right* for me, fellas. It's half-singing and half-talking." Good move, Merv.)

Thus far in my career, I'd had my own radio show; I'd been a band singer with a number one hit record; I'd been under contract as an actor at a major studio and starred in a feature film; I'd MC'd a network game show; I was currently hosting the fourth major television talk show that bore my name; and I'd created the two most successful syndicated programs in broadcast history. Not a bad track record, to be sure. But after a lifetime spent reinventing myself, was I fresh out of ideas?

Not quite yet.

Six:
Do You Want
That in Cash,
Mr. Griffin?

*I*n the eighties, I became casual friends with the legendary (according to him) industrialist Armand Hammer and his third wife, Frances. The truth is that you never were just "friendly" with Armand. He had a remarkable way of using you socially without your being aware of it.

Armand and Frances were devoted fans of *Wheel of Fortune* (but not of *Jeopardy!* "Too tough," he said). They watched it every night, without fail. Even when they were traveling abroad, as they often did, they had the *Wheel* taped. I'm absolutely certain that he took some of those tapes to the old Soviet Union during one of his many treks there, because the show popped up later on Moscow television without any deal having been negotiated for them to air it (Roger King was really ticked off). Subsequently, the Soviets announced that *they* had invented *Судьба Колесо.*

Around this same time, Armand got me interested in Arabian horses from Poland, which were then considered top of the line. For several years, Armand would take me with him when he went to Scottsdale, Arizona, for the exciting Arabian auctions. I fell under the spell of these beautiful animals and found myself bidding too much for them.

Armand established the Armand Hammer Race (I wonder how he thought to call it that) at a Florida track with a $100,000 first prize, the largest purse in Arabian horse racing. At the same time, he formed Oxy Arabs as a division of his company, Occidental Petroleum, just to purchase horses for his own collection—shareholders be damned. Almost single-handedly, Armand created a public relations buzz that led to a skyrocketing market for Arabian horses.

It was a great time for everyone . . . until the bottom fell out.

In one night, the inflated prices that Armand had generated through his clever marketing campaign collapsed like Enron stock. The same horses that had been worth six figures the day before were suddenly valued at less than $3,000, and of course that included the ones I'd bought as well.

Such were the benefits of "friendship" with Armand Hammer.

It was with all of this in mind that I received a call from Armand in late 1985, informing me that he was coming to see me. He was eighty-seven years old and had become totally obsessed with his legacy. Recently, Armand had endowed the Armand Hammer United World College of the American West, in Las Vegas, New Mexico. Now he needed a way to maintain the funding for it after he was gone.

When he arrived at my office, Armand came directly to the point. He said that he wanted to buy 50 percent of Merv Griffin Enterprises, primarily to acquire the rights to *Wheel of Fortune* and *Jeopardy!* His idea was that their revenues would fund his college in perpetuity.

It was a clever plan. The problem (for him) was that I hadn't even thought about selling. But as you know by now, change is the one constant in my life. So I listened to his offer and I was floored. He was offering me $45 million—my profit after taxes would come out to around $36 million. Even that sum was an unheard of amount for a relatively small production company like mine.

But remember, this was *Armand.* Once my lawyers and financial team pulled back the curtain, there was only a tiny yapping dog. He didn't intend to put up a single dime of his own money. His scheme was to get a signed agreement from me, then turn around and have a bank finance the entire deal.

For the next meeting, Armand brought in Louis Nizer, the famously bombastic civil rights attorney to conduct the "negotiations." Not to be outdone, I flew in Bobby Schulman from London where he was attending the Wimbledon finals. Schulman was a brilliant tax attorney and a partner in Williams & Connolly, the powerful D.C. law firm headed by famed trial lawyer and Washington Redskins owner Edward Bennett Williams. He agreed to fly to Los Angeles for one day just to attend the meeting.

He didn't stay long. Bobby Schulman took one look at the proposed deal and said, "Mr. Hammer is putting up zero capital. The IRS will never accept this arrangement." Then he drove back to the airport, got on a plane, and returned to London. I almost went with him.

After that, the meeting deteriorated quickly into a shouting match, ending abruptly with Armand and Louis storming out.

Armand Hammer didn't speak to me again for nearly a year. When I finally sold my company (not to him), the deal was reported in all the newspapers. He eventually swallowed his pride and called to congratulate me, no doubt expecting that I would now endow a "Merv Griffin Chair" at his college. I thanked him for his call, but kept my hand on my wallet the entire time we were on the phone.

After the Armand Hammer fiasco, I didn't actively pursue another buyer for my company. Still, I had to admit that the dollar figures Armand was throwing around my office that day were hard to ignore.

One Saturday during the fall of 1985, Frank Biondi, the new president of Columbia Entertainment, which had just been acquired by the Coca-Cola Company, was playing tennis with my William Morris agent, Lou Weiss. In between sets, he told Lou that he would like to buy my production company and some of my real estate properties as well, including the block at Sunset and Vine where *The Merv Griffin Show* was taped.

Lou brought me the offer—which had no dollar figure attached to it yet—and I told him to tell Biondi that I was interested. Then I met with my top administrative team to weigh the pros and cons of going forward with a possible sale. Included in that group were the president of my company, Murray Schwartz, and Roy Blakeman, my longtime attorney in New York, and Bob Murphy, my producer and oldest friend.

It was to these three that I turned for advice with respect to the possible sale of my company. The real question was not *if* I should sell—I'd already crossed that Rubicon—or even how much I should ask for. The numbers being bandied about, even preliminarily, dwarfed what Armand had offered me less than a year before.

No, the question I had to answer for myself, at the age of sixty, was the same one that a new college graduate asks himself once the cap and gown come off: "What do I want to do with my life?" While I was trying to sort that out, I left for Rio de Janeiro on a long-planned vacation.

Some vacation. I spent much of the time on the phone to the United States monitoring the fast-breaking developments in our negotiations with Coca-Cola.

I love Brazilian jazz. Antonio Carlos Jobim—his nickname was Tom—was a great friend of mine. Sergio Mendes also had an apartment in Rio and the three of us had all-night musical parties. We'd sing and play music until the sun came up. Yet all the while the phone was constantly ringing with questions from my team about various points in the proposed deal.

My memories of that trip, of the surreal juxtaposition of pleasure and business, will always be accompanied by a Brazilian beat.

When I got back to the States, the contracts were ready for me to sign. I'd just sold my company for $200 million, with profit participation that would take it up to $250 million—and beyond. The deal also guaranteed that I would retain creative control of *Wheel of Fortune* and *Jeopardy!*, and it provided me with a seat on the creative board of directors of Columbia Entertainment under the leadership of Frank Biondi (who would later head Viacom and Universal) and Fay Vincent.

Less than a year earlier, I'd been dazed at the prospect of forty-five million dollars. Now this.

I was asked by the press to describe how it felt to be the beneficiary of one of the largest sales of all time.

"Well, my first job playing in public was at the Coconut Bar in Santa Cruz. Then I played the Cocoanut Grove with Freddy Martin. And I had a hit record with "I've Got a Lovely Bunch of Coconuts." So when they offered me all that money, all I could think of was, 'Gee, that's a helluva lot of coconuts.' "

That's how my mind works.

Sometimes when you look back at a pivotal time in your life there's a small incident, which at the time seemed totally insignificant, but subsequently stands out in your mind with neon clarity.

The date was Monday, May 5, 1986. I'd signed the contract with Coca-Cola several months earlier. As is always the case with deals of this size, it takes time for the money to actually change hands. I'd been told to expect it any day now.

The small incident that sticks out so clearly in my memory took place that afternoon. *The Merv Griffin Show* was taping at the Celebrity Theater that I owned (but had just sold) at Sunset and Vine in Hollywood. Although I hadn't decided it yet, this would prove to be the final year of my show's twenty-three-year run.

Instead of prepping for my guests (Marsha Mason, Valerie Perrine, and Elizabeth Peña), I was crouched down on the floor of my office, sleeves rolled up, a pair of dice in my hand. My staff and I were playing a board game, something we often did when I was testing out ideas for a new game show.

I'd just thrown the dice. They rolled off the board under my desk and I was crawling on my hands and knees to retrieve them.

Even if my life depended on the correct answer, I couldn't tell you the name of the board game we were playing that day. But I do remember that exact moment, as clearly as if I were looking at a photograph—that snapshot instant of being down on the floor, looking for . . . what?

Luck?

I looked up to see a man standing in the doorway of my office, clearing his throat.

"Uh, Merv?" It was Gary Lieberthal, then the boss of TV and syndication for Columbia Tri-Star Television. He wasn't used to seeing me on the floor, let alone having to talk to me down there.

"Oh, hey, Gary." I pretended that this was a perfectly normal way to carry on a conversation. "What's up?"

"I just stopped by to say congratulations. Welcome to the family."

He reached down and extended his hand. As we shook, I said, "Gee, thanks, Gary. Did you bring that case of Coke they promised me with the deal?"

Everybody laughed, except me. I could barely muster a smile.

As I got to my feet, I realized what Gary's visit actually *meant*. The deal was now official. In a single day, my net worth had just increased tenfold.

Even though the people around me were excited and happy, the news made me strangely uncomfortable. I actually felt a little embarrassed by the amount.

I walked Gary to the door and thanked him for his kindness in coming by. Then I called my accountant in New York, Gloria Redlich. At that time, Gloria had been with me for more than twenty-five years (it's now forty-two). She doesn't suffer fools well. Or technology.

I asked her if it was really true.

"It's too much money." She might have been talking about an overfull piggy bank. "It broke the meshuganah system."

"I don't understand," I said, waiting for her to continue. Long ago, I'd learned to be patient and let Gloria explain what she meant.

"The wire system at the bank broke down. They can't find the money."

"You mean they've *lost* a quarter of a billion dollars?" *Now* I was laughing. This was the most fun I'd had all day.

Gloria was unimpressed by my attempt at humor. She knew me too well. "It's too much. We don't even have adding machines that go that high. We're going to need all new machines . . ."

"Gloria," I said, soothingly. "You're absolutely right. I'll give the money *back*."

An hour later she called to tell me the wire transfer had finally come through. The money was now in my account.

There's a funny postscript to this story. A few days after the transfer went through, I flew down to Atlanta for the one hundredth anniversary celebration of the Coca-Cola Company, my new corporate parent. They'd rented out the huge new Omni Arena and it was filled to overflowing with more than twelve hundred members of the Coca-Cola "family" who had come in from all over the world for this spectacular gala.

Given the prominence of my deal, I was seated next to Fay Vincent, the chairman of Columbia Entertainment (and later commissioner of major league baseball).

The vice chairman and president of Coca-Cola, Don Keough, was at the microphone delivering a stemwinder of a speech.

"Ladies and gentlemen," he was practically shouting, "as you know we have just purchased Merv Griffin Enterprises, one of the greatest television companies in the world! It includes *The Merv Griffin Show*, *Wheel of Fortune*, and *Jeopardy!* The capacity crowd cheered.

The closed circuit camera came in tight on a shot of me. The entire arena could see my beaming smile on the giant screens overhead.

But Keough wasn't through. "And what a great buy it was! Three hundred and fifty million dollars!"

Knowing I was on camera, my expression didn't change. But I turned to Fay Vincent and, out of the corner of my mouth, whispered, "Oh, so that's what you were *really* prepared to pay."

Fay turned bright red. He looked like a giant tomato on the Jumbotron screens.

I knew that I had to let Fay off the hook. He's a terrific guy, and now he felt guilty. So I leaned over and said, "That's the *last* time I'm ever listening to Don Keough speak. Just by sitting here, I'm out a hundred million bucks."

We both roared.

When I got back to California, I thought, What now? Do I have a glass of champagne? Go out and buy a new pair of shoes? How about a shoe *store?*

I felt like my old *Play Your Hunch* buddy, Robert Redford, in the last reel of *The Candidate*. Redford spends the whole movie trying to get elected senator from California. When he's finally won his hard-fought election, he turns to the campaign manager and says, *"Now what do I do?"*

The first thing I did was to make gifts to my family members. To this day, that may have been the most fun I've ever had in my life.

My sister (who I think had the best sense of humor of anyone in our family) had the best reaction: "You just never think about anybody else, do you, Buddy? Do you have any *idea* how much more paperwork I'm going to have at tax time? Selfish, that's what you are."

After helping my family, the next step wasn't quite so clear-cut.

I began seeking advice from people who knew more about high finance than I did (which, at the time, was a pretty long list).

Arthur Laffer, the top economic advisor to President Reagan (remember the "Laffer Curve"?), was one of the first experts I called. He suggested the names of several of the most respected financial institutions in America, then was kind enough to set up interviews for me with their top people.

Quite by chance, at a social function, I happened to meet Lord Solomon, the ninety-year-old founder of the famous London banking house that bore his name. He'd read of my sale and offered his congratulations. I brazenly asked him what he thought I should do with my money.

"Young man," he said with a wink, "there will be a charge for that information."

The room grew quiet, like one of those old E.F. Hutton commercials (*When Lord Solomon talks, people listen*).

"There is *nothing*," he said, sounding for all the world like Arthur Treacher, "more secure than the government bonds of your country."

I had a life-changing decision to make. I could roll the money over into bonds and live the rest of my life completely free of any responsibilities. Or I could start again in a different kind of business life.

In the end it was a no-brainer. I wasn't ready to retire (I'm not sure that I'd even know *how* to do that), so I began to actively consider new ventures that might be of interest to me.

Let me tell you, they were a lot harder to find than the ones that didn't interest me. Everybody and his brother-in-law's best friend's neighbor's cousin brought me the "opportunity of a lifetime." If I lived a thousand lifetimes, I couldn't have pursued half of them, nor did I want to.

One of my favorite "opportunities" was the chance to buy Hebrew National Foods, the maker of a number of kosher products, including hot dogs. My son, Tony, who is very health-conscious, said, "Dad, *buy* it. Their hot dogs are pure beef. They don't put all those chemicals in them."

I turned it down, but I've always wondered if I made a mistake in doing so. Don't you think that "Merv Griffin's Hebrew National Foods" has a nice ring to it? Not to mention a new brand of "Orson Welles Kosher Franks" that would have served as a lasting tribute to my departed friend. Oh well, you know what they say about the road not taken . . .

One thing was certain. Whatever I decided to do with my newfound fortune, it would be done under the microscope of public scrutiny.

Right after my deal was announced, I was driving near my home in Beverly Hills. I had the radio tuned to the local all-news station and I heard the newsreader say, "Today *Forbes* magazine released its list of the four hundred wealthiest people in America. Coming up, we'll tell you the name of the richest Hollywood performer in history." And he went to a commercial. I thought to myself, Wow, Clint actually made the *Forbes* list. My buddy Clint Eastwood produced his own films, so I figured that it had finally paid off for him.

I drove along.

Coming back from the commercial, the newsreader picked up the story: "*Forbes* magazine has added Merv Griffin to its annual list of the four hundred richest Americans. Griffin, whose net worth is estimated to be in excess of $300 million, replaces Bob Hope as the wealthiest performer in Hollywood history."

His words had the strangest effect on me. At first they didn't register at all. Then I looked over at the next lane of traffic to see if someone in another car had heard it too. I know it's irrational, but I got really embarrassed. Was it my imagination or were people now looking at me differently?

It *was* my imagination, of course, but I still scrunched down in the driver's seat and hurried on to my destination. (By sheer coincidence, I was headed toward the Beverly Hilton, a hotel I would own the following year.)

The next day, I went out and bought a copy of *Forbes* magazine to see exactly what it said about me. Glancing further down the list, I read the name of a woman who, according to *Forbes*, had almost the same amount of money as I did. I put the magazine down and started laughing out loud, until there were tears running down my face.

She was dead.

And she had *been* dead for several years. So I called Malcolm Forbes, who had made several appearances on my show.

"Malcolm," I began, "you probably know that I'm on your list . . ."

"Yeah, Merv, aren't you excited?"

Not wanting to offend him, I attempted to be diplomatic. "You know, Malcolm, I don't really know if *excited* is the right word."

Malcolm was taken aback. I tried to keep my voice from revealing how ridiculous I thought his list was.

"What's wrong, Merv? Didn't we put enough in there about you?"

And I said, "Noooo, it's not *that* . . ."

"What? What is it then?" Forbes was genuinely puzzled.

"Well, you see, Malcolm, there's a lady on there, she's actually listed right below me, who's been dead for three years. The reason I know this is because I bought my house from her estate."

For a long moment there was total silence on the line, then Forbes recovered smoothly: "Well, Merv, all that proves is that even after you're dead, your money will *still* make money."

It's hard to believe now, in this era where an actor's salary is practically an extension of his name (*Tom Cruise, $25 million*), but there was a time when it wasn't a good idea for a performer to be thought of as having money.

That lesson was driven home to me very early in my career. In the mid-fifties, when I was still struggling financially, I took a walk in New York City with Jackie Gleason, who was already a big star. Everybody—cab drivers, construction workers, even policemen—all shouted, "Hey, Jackie!" as we walked by.

One day it appeared in the papers that Jackie had signed a new contract with CBS for the then unheard of sum of $12 million. From that point on, nobody yelled "Hey, Jackie!" anymore. People now thought he was unapproachable because he had so much money.

I think the public loses its connection with you if they view you as being really rich. So for the twenty-three years my show was on the air, I had made it a point to keep a very low profile about my investments.

Of course, all that changed immediately after Coca-Cola purchased my company. Although the deal provided me with what I've often called "a great American fortune," it also meant that my business dealings would now be exhaustively detailed in the media. I was just as likely to find my picture in *Barron's* or *Fortune* as I was to see it in *Variety* or *The Hollywood Reporter*.

That was only one of the considerations in my decision to end *The Merv Griffin Show*. Truthfully, I had become tired of the daily grind. Having to tape five shows per week, forty-five weeks out of the year, is a highly restrictive routine, even if you enjoy what you're doing—and I always had. For a guy who thrives on change, it was difficult for me to even comprehend the fact that I'd now been doing the same job for almost a quarter of a century. (It was especially hard to believe, since, like Jack Benny, I was only thirty-nine years old . . .)

With all of that, I might still have continued to do my show were it not for one crucial factor that tipped the scales. As Jack Paar memorably observed when he quit *The Tonight Show*, "There's nobody left to talk to."

I was finally bored with asking soap opera stars questions, when I really didn't care about their answers. They'd offer their heartfelt opinion on foreign policy and I'd be thinking, Oh, *please*. You're on *Days of Our Lives*.

Even though I was often going through the motions, I remained polite; it was the way I was raised. I still said, "Ahhhh," to my guests. (For the record, it was *never* "Ooooh." I know this revelation will upset some people, but the truth had to come out eventually. I feel better already.)

By September 5, 1986, when *The Merv Griffin Show* left the air, I'd done over fifty-five hundred shows and interviewed more than twenty-five *thousand* guests. Over twenty-three years, our show was in the thick of cultural and political change in America. Through several vastly different eras, we always tried to reflect that change honestly. Making news was never the idea, although we frequently did. My satisfaction came from conversing with intelligent people who had something important to say.

Peter Ustinov once paid me the ultimate compliment. He said, "Merv, doing your show is how I find out what I think about things."

Our show evolved right in front of the public. When I started out, the standard talk show rule was to put serious guests—authors, playwrights, political figures—in the last eight-minute segment. The networks referred to them disparagingly as "heavy furniture." If you wanted higher ratings, you were encouraged to keep those bookings to a minimum.

After only a short time on the air, I came to realize that the networks were wrong (I was shocked, *shocked*). The audience was far more interested in those guests than they were thought to be. If nothing else, I knew this by the sheer volume of mail that we received after a Gore Vidal or James Michener had appeared with me.

I began to move the "furniture" around based on what *I* thought worked, as opposed to some focus group report. Not only would we sometimes open with a scholar or politician, I even built entire programs around them. One of the best shows I've ever done was all writers: Michener, James Jones, and Irwin Shaw.

I interviewed Dr. Martin Luther King when few news programs, let alone talk shows, would have him on. Lord Bertrand Russell, the brilliant Nobel laureate, gave me his scathing appraisal of U.S. policy in Vietnam in 1965. I was called a traitor for even putting him on the air. When I ran into John Lennon on the beach at Cannes, I persuaded him to sit with me for the only talk show interview he ever gave while still a Beatle. I spoke with four presidents—Nixon, Ford,

Carter, and Reagan—before, during, or after their tenure in the White House. It was almost five. In 1969, when I was still at Group W, I was told that former President Dwight Eisenhower and his wife, Mamie, were fans of my show. I flew to Pennsylvania and met with General Eisenhower, as he preferred to be addressed. I asked him if I could bring a camera crew to their Gettysburg farm and do an entire show with both of them.

He immediately agreed, then asked to discuss money. He wanted his payment to go to charity. We usually paid minimum scale to our guests (a few hundred dollars), but this was hardly the usual situation. I asked him what kind of figure he had in mind. When he said, "I was thinking in the neighborhood of thirty thousand dollars," I swallowed hard but tried not to show my shock. I knew that that was a lot more toasters than Westinghouse would ever pay. I shook hands with the general and left his office, wondering where I was going to find the money to pay him. Sadly, I never had the chance. He suffered a fatal heart attack shortly afterward.

I had guests who could tell wonderful stories. And we had the luxury of being able to do twelve- to fourteen-minute segments with a single person. One of the biggest problems with talk shows today is that they've been reduced to a mind-numbing collection of sound bite interviews. This isn't the fault of Leno, Letterman, or anyone else; they're prisoners of commerce. With the invention of the remote control (if you're under the age of thirty, pretend you know what I'm talking about), sponsors now live in constant fear of channel-surfers.

For me, it all came down to the question that I've asked myself at every stage of my career: "Is it still fun?"

The answer meant that it was time for me to hang it up.

Taping the final episode of *The Merv Griffin Show* was a very emotional experience for me. I sat alone in the theater, where the audience had always been, and introduced clips that my staff had assembled into a two-hour retrospective.

After it was all over, I wasn't ready to go home. I asked my young assistant, Ronnie Ward, to drive, and we just got in the car and took off. I had no destination in mind—we simply drove. I remember that we stopped at a tennis tournament in one of the beach communities south of Los Angeles. Then we got back in the car and headed east.

We made it just across the California-Nevada border, finally ending up in the bustling new gambling town of Laughlin.

It wasn't only the end of my show that was making me restless. This was the first time in more than forty years that I wouldn't have a job to go to the next day. Granted, I didn't *need* a job anymore. But the reality was that I hadn't actually needed to work for a long time, at least not for the money.

I came to terms with something during that long car ride that I hadn't been willing to acknowledge before. My sense of self-worth, my identity, my reason for getting out of bed in the morning—they'd all become tied up with my career. Sure, my family and friends were important to me, but if I was being honest—and in that car I was— my personal life invariably came in second to my professional one.

Luckily for me, Ronnie Ward is a wonderful listener. By the time we made it back from Nevada, I was almost hoarse from talking. But I felt a lot better.

I'm sure that Ronnie had no idea what he was getting into when I asked him to drive me that day. He'd been with my company for four years, and although he was only in his twenties, I could already see that he had a great future ahead of him. When I completed the sale of my company to Coca-Cola, I made Ronnie my personal assistant, the first time in my career that I'd ever had one. Clearly I needed someone in that job I could rely on, whose intelligence and judgment I trusted completely. Even though he was young, I knew that Ronnie Ward was the only choice.

Let me tell you about Ronnie. Next to Bob Murphy, Ronnie Ward is probably the most loved person I know. He's everybody's son, son-in-law, brother, best friend.

Like me, Ronnie is a native Northern Californian. He comes from the town of Salinas where, as it happens, he lived across the street from the children of a family that I'd grown up with in San Mateo. (Neither of us realized this for many years, until one day it just popped out. We were talking about a childhood friend of Ronnie's who was coming to visit him, a fellow named Steve Holetz. I said, "You don't mean Robert's son, do you?" Ronnie couldn't believe it. He said, "How did you *know* that?" I've got to tell you that I don't think things like that are coincidental. It's the way that the universe has of letting you know that you're in the right place.)

Growing up, Ronnie worked several summers on an Alaskan fishing boat with his grandfather, a veteran sea captain. After graduating high school, he moved to Los Angeles with his family and took a job at a record store.

One of his co-workers was moonlighting as a security guard at TAV Studios, the facility where I taped my show and which, at the time, I still owned (it would eventually be part of the sale to Coca-Cola). Ronnie's friend, knowing that he needed extra income, asked him if he'd be interested in a night job as well.

At the age of nineteen, he was hired as a security guard at TAV. I didn't know him when he first came to work for me. With *Wheel of Fortune*, *Jeopardy!*, *The Merv Griffin Show*, and *Dance Fever*, I had more than two hundred employees. He went on to work in every department and became familiar with the entire company, eventually making it up to the third floor, where my office was. When my secretary became ill, Ronnie filled in for her temporarily.

When we were finalizing the Coca-Cola deal, Ronnie had lawyers standing nervously over his shoulder as he hunted and pecked his way through last-minute changes to a quarter-billion-dollar contract. I ended up hiring a new secretary, but Ronnie stayed on as my assistant.

After more than twenty years of working with him, I've now concluded that typing is the only skill that Ronnie lacks. He can handle any situation, from employee problems to business decisions. Nothing rattles him, not even Donald Trump.

Yet for all of his professional accomplishments, it is his two beautiful daughters who are Ronnie's pride and joy. No matter how hard he works, they always come first. As good as he is at his job, he's an even better father.

Ronnie Ward never seeks publicity or accolades. In fact, everything I've just told you will probably embarrass him. Sorry, Ronnie. They made me do it.

Hotels have always fascinated me. To understand why, we have to hark back to my days on the road with Freddy Martin when I traveled the whole country by bus. We played every single state in America—all forty-eight of them (and, *yes*, we did have electricity back then).

Every day was a different city or town. Every night was a different hotel. Many were good; some were fleabags and flophouses. A few of them were so bad that it was actually a relief if they turned out to have been overbooked. The lobby couches were invariably more comfortable than the beds.

I remember one ancient firetrap of a place in South Dakota. Next to every bed was an emergency kit with a rope inside. If the building went up in flames, you were supposed to use it to lower yourself out the window. The only problem was that the rope was so old, it disintegrated the moment you touched it. I decided that night to quit smoking, just in case.

On the road, my understanding and appreciation of hotels grew daily. I learned that a traveler's three basic needs are a fast check-in, speedy room service, and excellent water pressure.

Even back then, it struck me that the hotel business, done properly, is entertainment at its finest. The guests are like an audience. They want to enjoy themselves, leave happy, and be eager to return. That's exactly what show business is.

I've said it many times: hotels are talk shows with beds. It's the same principle—an exotic variety of people coming through the door, staying a short time, then departing; sometimes never to be heard from again (with the possible exception of Charo).

Now, you have to realize that in all the years of hosting my show, I almost never got to meet my audience personally. I saw them when I passed through the theater curtain and walked out onto that proscenium stage every night, but that was all. My only other contact was limited to those fans who waited patiently after the show for an autograph.

I started to think seriously about the hotel business. Maybe I'd finally have a chance to meet the audience.

At the gala opening of the Beverly Hilton Hotel in 1955 (the same year that another Southern California landmark, Disneyland, first opened its gates), Vice President Richard Nixon recalled a time when Wilshire Boulevard in Beverly Hills—now the site of a mammoth, modern hotel—was largely farm land. Conrad Hilton beamed with pride when he heard the new crown jewel of his burgeoning empire described as "the most sumptuous hotel in the world."

At the time, it was.

Thirty-two years later, that great lady of luxury hotels had become a fading dowager whose best days were a distant memory.

Against everybody's advice, I bought her.

Conrad's son, Barron Hilton, is one of my oldest friends. He started in the hotel business as an elevator operator in 1951; his father wanted him to work his way to the top—literally. By the late seventies, he had become chairman of the Hilton Hotels Corporation.

So when his son, Rick, who was brokering the deal, phoned me in 1987, I was quick to take his call.

Rick informed me that the Hilton Corporation was looking to sell the Beverly Hilton. Only half of the hotel was actually owned by Hilton. The other half belonged to the Prudential Insurance Company. I realized quickly that it was Prudential that wanted out.

I put down the phone and stared off into space. I'd always loved that hotel. Several years earlier it was the scene of one of the greatest nights of my life. The Beverly Hills Chamber of Commerce had honored me with its Will Rogers Memorial Award and the presentation had taken place at a black-tie dinner at the Beverly Hilton. They went all out to make it an extraordinary night for me, even recruiting the Freddy Martin Orchestra to perform. The International Ballroom was converted into a replica of the old Cocoanut Grove, where I'd sung with Freddy three decades before.

Unquestionably, the highlight of the evening for me was the surprise participation of Orson Welles. I know it's immodest, but I'm going to tell you a little of what he said that night—it will help you to understand why the Beverly Hilton became so special to me.

"The talk show," intoned Orson in that magnificent voice, "is the TV art form that is unique to TV. It was never as good on the radio. It obviously couldn't happen in the theater or anywhere else. It is pure television form. There are a few talk show giants. I'm here to salute my favorite. A good host must be considerate to his guests, and bring out their best. Merv's enthusiasm is genuine. A real actor is a re-actor—he knows how to genuinely listen. They tell me he's very rich and he deserves to be. He's very rich in friends and I am proud to be one of them. To be able to genuinely listen in front of all those millions of people, to bring out the best in people without endlessly trying to score off them, or to be funny; to be compassionate, to be amusing and amused, to be concerned and intelligently concerned;

all these are the definition of the classic talk show host and the best of all talk show hosts."

You've probably figured out by now that I'm an emotional guy. Maybe it's the Irish in me, but it doesn't take a lot to move me to tears. On the other hand, I'd made a career out of maintaining my composure in front of an audience, usually by cracking wise. So when I came to the microphone to accept my award, I said, "Wow. Orson Welles makes you feel immortal. I didn't know that I was *that* great . . ."

It was a magical night that ended with me singing "Tonight We Love" in front of the orchestra, as the guests swirled on the dance floor in front of me. *Déjà vu all over again.*

It was that memory (and many others like it) that excited me about the prospect of restoring the Beverly Hilton to her former glory. So, despite the entreaties of my advisors who assured me that it was the worst possible time to get into the hotel business, I decided to do it. I made the Hilton-Prudential ownership group a substantial offer and, soon after, I was told that they were ready to accept it.

Then, out of the blue, a consortium of Japanese investors came in and topped my offer by 20 percent.

My old friend Barron Hilton gave me the chance to match their bid. I thanked him, but said, "Let them have it, Barron. The revenues won't ever be enough to recoup that purchase price. I wouldn't have a prayer of keeping it profitable." I walked away.

This was in October of 1987. Before the deal could be completed, Wall Street suffered through "Black Monday" and the Dow dropped more than five hundred points. The Nikkei Index followed suit the next day. Overnight, the Japanese group lost a significant chunk of its capital, so they had no choice but to bail out of the Hilton deal.

Two days later Barron called again.

"Want to jump back in?" he asked, hopefully.

"Sure," I said. "At what price?"

He didn't hesitate. "We accept your original offer."

Sold.

The Hilton name, particularly in Europe and Asia, is very strong. So I'm sure that my first press conference after purchasing the hotel (which would continue to be affiliated with the Hilton Corporation;

I pay them a fee for the use of their name and reservation system) must have *thrilled* Barron.

"I only bought it because I was tired of waiting for room service," I joked to the assembled press corps. Then I became serious as I talked about my plans. "I'm going to break the Hilton cookie cutter mold. This is where the action is going to be." Fifteen years later I'm still telling them that. They can't believe the things I've done with the Beverly Hilton, because they do everything as inexpensively as possible.

I knew when I bought the aging grandame that she was badly in need of a facelift—in fact, her whole body needed work. It was going to take millions of dollars to do it the way I envisioned, but I didn't care. This was the fun part.

The first improvements I made were to the International Ballroom, the largest hotel event space in the city, with a sit-down capacity of more than thirteen hundred. My staff believed strongly that I should start with redoing the guest rooms, but I was adamant. I knew that refurbishing the ballroom would send an important signal, particularly to the entertainment community. They would see that I was serious about restoring the Beverly Hilton to its former grandeur. "Trust me," I told my skeptical staff, "everyone will want to use that room." And they did.

I love it when a great plan works. Business boomed immediately. First, producer George Schlatter announced that he would use the room to tape several big television specials. Then the Hollywood Foreign Press Association renewed its contract to hold the Golden Globe Awards show in the International Ballroom. That's when the improvements that we'd made to make the room more production-friendly really paid off. TBS (and later, NBC) signed a long-term agreement to televise the awards, which now run a strong second to the Oscars in popularity. The American Film Institute Life Achievement Awards made its own television deal, and I knew that we had built the perfect ballroom.

The Carousel Ball is a star-studded event organized by Barbara Davis and held every two years in the International Ballroom to raise money for the fight against juvenile diabetes. It was in a speech at the Carousel Ball that Sidney Poitier made the observation that "more money has been raised for charity in this ballroom than in any other in the world."

An entertaining little sidelight to all the renovations was the rug.

In my youth, I'd spent a lot of time in the elegant Fairmont Hotel in San Francisco. As we were redoing the International Ballroom, I remembered that the Fairmont lobby had a magnificent rug fashioned by Dorothy Draper, the legendary interior designer. Charcoal black and covered with red roses—people came from all over just to see it.

Trying to help my staff visualize what I was describing, I came across a paperback book on roses. The cover art depicted a large pink rose on a black background. I sent the book cover to world-renowned weavers in Ireland and asked them to give me a sketch of a carpet bedecked with giant pink roses.

They did and I commissioned them to design it. Those pink roses have now become emblematic of the Beverly Hilton; they've been seen the world over because of the many international television broadcasts that originate from the ballroom. The inaugural network telecast of the Golden Globes featured the carpet prominently in many shots.

Warren Cowan, my publicist for many years, phoned afterward and asked, "Did you see that show? It was unbelievable!"

I said, "Yes, but did you see that *rug?*"

After finishing the ballroom, I redid the restaurant inside and out, renaming it Griff's. Next, I flew in stone from Spain to surround the Olympic-size swimming pool. On the cabana rooms around the pool, I installed French doors and red and white striped awnings reminiscent of the famed ice cream parlor of my youth, Will Wright's. Then I bracketed the rooms with huge bougainvillea of all colors.

All through the massive renovation period, I kept thinking of something that my father told me when I was growing up: "Always remember, Buddy. Nothing but the best." My dad would really love the Beverly Hilton.

Soon after I purchased the hotel, the *National Enquirer* ran a story that effectively said, "Merv Griffin only bought the Hilton so he would have a place to work in for the rest of his life."

My reaction was "How rude. I have no *intention* of performing there. It's strictly an investment."

Sure, Merv. A few months later I found myself, microphone in hand, singing to a large crowd—in the Beverly Hilton. I had to admit (if only to myself) that the *Enquirer* had it right. I still enjoyed having a stage to perform on.

Little did I imagine that my next "stage" would be all the way across the country, in Atlantic City. I was about to co-star in an amusing little comedy called "The War at the Shore."

Seven: He Forgot to Buy the Beach

What can you say about Donald Trump that he hasn't already said about himself?

I'm going to surprise you—and probably him—with what I'm going to tell you next. Donald is a very gifted man. In some ways, I believe he is brilliant. I think that his buildings are magnificent additions to the New York City skyline.

But he is also a person of extremes. There's no in-between with Donald. He's either your best friend or your worst enemy. Sometimes he's both—in the same conversation. There are days when his genius sparks him to dizzying heights of creativity. Then there are other, darker days when it causes him to rage at the world for failing to recognize his greatness.

In this regard, Donald is not unlike most of the legendary New York City developers, going all the way back to Edward Browning in the twenties. Browning's flair for the dramatic caused him to drop bags of water out of a low-flying airplane in order to demonstrate how vulnerable Manhattan was to an aerial attack.

Robert Moses, the master builder responsible for most of New York's roadways and parks, was as volatile as he was brilliant. When he failed to get his way on a project through persuasion, he would often bully his opponents into submission by resorting to character assassination.

Browning, Robert Moses, Donald Trump—these are men of outsize egos and temperaments to match. It goes with the territory.

Down through the years, there is a public stance that's been shared by many of these giants of New York City real estate, one of grand public lives led amidst highly visible excess. This is no accident; it accomplishes precisely what they want. Everyone turns to them with major deals. Banks lend them large sums of money on the strength of their flamboyant reputations.

That said, I actually knew very little about Donald in 1988, when I was first approached about investing in Resorts International, a company whose principal assets were Resorts, an Atlantic City hotel-casino, and Paradise Island in the Bahamas. Also included in the package was the unfinished Taj Mahal, potentially the largest (and most expensive) hotel-casino ever built in Atlantic City.

Donald, who owned 80 percent of the Resorts voting stock, likes to say that I relished the idea of taking him on. The truth is a lot less dramatic. At the time, I'd heard his name and knew that he was a successful New York City builder, but that was about it. I had no real impression of him as a person, nor was I familiar with his regional reputation as a swashbuckling developer. He was—and is—far better known on the East Coast than on the West Coast.

Unlike Donald, I have a long history with Atlantic City. In July of 1949 (when Donald was three), I sang with Freddy Martin's orchestra on the Steel Pier. We played to more than 100,000 people over that Fourth of July weekend. It was quite a scene, not only for the size of the crowd, but also because every member of the orchestra took turns vomiting behind the bandstand. The night before we'd arrived in Atlantic City, our bus had stopped at a diner in Pennsylvania. Everybody but Jean Barry and me ate dinner at three o'clock in the morning. Food poisoning and fireworks—it wasn't a pretty combination.

I'm not claiming to be Sinatra or Springsteen, but my connection to the Garden State is pretty strong. In the sixties and early seventies, Julann and I lived in New Jersey, on a farm in the small town of Califon. Around that time I'd also begun investing in radio. First I purchased WMID, the number one station in Atlantic City. Then I built an FM station that broadcast in the same market. And on several occasions, I'd brought *The Merv Griffin Show* down to Atlantic City for a week of tapings at Caesars or at the Golden Nugget for Steve Wynn.

Remember too that since its earliest days, I'd spent a lot of time in a little gambling town in the Nevada desert called Las Vegas.

Let me paint a picture for you of what Vegas was like in the late forties and early fifties. The famed "Strip"—Las Vegas Boulevard— was a simple two-lane highway. I used to perform at the Hotel Last Frontier, which was purchased in 1951 by two brothers, Jake and Bill Kozloff.

I learned a lot about gambling from the Kozloff brothers. Jake Kozloff showed me the secret of the double-reds in roulette. Here it is: there are four double-reds on a roulette table. What that means is that two red numbers are adjacent to one another on the betting table. The four pairs are 9 and 12, 16 and 19, 18 and 21, and 27 and

30. If you place your bet on the line between them, you increase your chances of winning. The payoff is 17–1 instead of 35–1, but that's still pretty good.

Next door to the Last Frontier was Beldon Katleman's El Rancho Vegas. And that was it. Las Vegas started out as a two-lane town with two casinos. It stayed that way until a fellow named Siegel (It was either "Mr. Siegel" or, if you knew him well, "Benjamin." That other name was death in the desert.) built a flashy new casino much farther down the street called the Flamingo.

Years later, when I did my show from Caesars Palace, I gained valuable insight into gaming as a business from Cliff Perlman. Cliff, who owned Caesars, was gracious enough to share his genius for marketing with "the talent."

So between my history in New Jersey (and Atlantic City in particular), as well as my familiarity with the gaming business, I was certainly receptive when the new president of my company, Mike Nigris, first brought the Resorts proposition to me early in March of 1988.

The idea had reached Mike in an unusual way. It all started with a car dealer from upstate New York named Dale Scutti.

Do you remember the movie *Working Girl* with Melanie Griffith? She played a secretary who fantasized about breaking into the world of high finance. In her spare time, Melanie's character studied both the financial pages *and* the gossip columns. Her unorthodox reading habits allowed her to spot a business opportunity that everybody else had missed and, by the end of the film, she's scored her big deal (and Harrison Ford).

Dale Scutti did the same thing in real life that Melanie Griffith's character did on screen. His hobby was to carefully examine publicly traded companies, looking for undiscovered opportunities. The way a tout reads the *Racing Form*, Scutti scoured the stock pages. First, he'd spot a company that he thought was undervalued. Then he would back up his hunch with a lot of research. As a result, Scutti's tips were often pretty good.

Scutti was already a shareholder in Resorts, and he wasn't a happy man. Donald had previously made a low offer of $15 per share to acquire the stock that he didn't already own, thereby gaining full control of Resorts. There were several pending lawsuits challenging

Donald's lucrative management contract with Resorts and alleging that Donald's offer of $15 a share for Resort's Class A stock undervalued Resorts. Donald vigorously denied the allegations contained in the lawsuits. However, as part of a proposed settlement of the litigation, Donald raised his bid to $22.

Believing that $22 per share wasn't sufficient, and angry that he'd already lost money through what he perceived as Donald's cynical stock ploy, Dale Scutti hired a New York securities attorney, Morris Orens, to find another buyer for Resorts. He showed Orens all the work he'd done, and said, in effect, "Resorts isn't in Trump's pocket, even though he thinks it is. It's up for the taking and I know how to do it."

Here's where the story gets a little complicated, so stay with me. A year earlier, Orens was in his car listening to the news when he heard an item about the wealthiest performers in Hollywood. Sound familiar?

Orens contacted me about Resorts through the president of my company, Mike Nigris (who was formerly my accountant). The link between Orens and Nigris was a man named Ernie Barbella. Barbella was Mike's roommate in college, so they went back a long way. I'm still not entirely sure how Morris Orens knew Barbella; suffice it to say that he did.

Even though the idea to get involved with Resorts had come to me in a roundabout way, I was still intrigued about the possibility of getting into gaming. I could see that it was changing from a business that catered primarily to Las Vegas–style high rollers into something that I was very familiar with: mass market entertainment. Atlantic City had the potential to become a tourist town more like Branson, Missouri, than a gambling mecca like Las Vegas. (Of course, Las Vegas has now evolved into precisely that kind of tourist destination.) What interested me most was the marketing aspect of it, the chance to make a creative connection between gaming and entertainment.

I decided to take the plunge. At the time, I had no idea how high the diving board was or how little water there was in the pool.

On March 17, I was having a St. Patrick's Day tennis party at my home. I kept the television on all day because I wanted to follow what was going on. Suddenly, the news broke that I'd made a

$35 per share offer for Resorts stock. My friends at the party kept looking from the television screen back to me. They were used to seeing my face on the screen, but not in the context of a major financial story.

Across the country, in New York City, I'm told that when Donald was informed of my offer, he said, somewhat in disbelief, *"Merv Griffin? Is that the band singer?"*

The timing also threw him. Donald was fully expecting that on the very next day, the Delaware Chancery Court was going to approve his settlement with the shareholders of Resorts International, which would give him everything: Resorts and the still unfinished Taj Mahal in Atlantic City, and Paradise Island in the Bahamas. He had planned on walking away with lots of real estate and a considerable number of assets without a further fight.

Then, from out of left field, my $35 per share offer came in, rendering Donald's settlement offer moot. Now, instead of dealing with the court, he had to deal with me.

About a month later, when I was planning a trip to New York, I called Donald, introduced myself, and asked if I could stop by and see him while I was in town. He agreed and we set up a meeting for 2:30 P.M. on Wednesday, April 13, in his penthouse office on Fifth Avenue.

When I told them about the appointment, my lawyers and financial advisors were aghast. Every one of them tried to talk me out of it. "You *can't* meet him on his own turf," was the common refrain. "It's usually done on some neutral ground like a restaurant."

"What's the difference?" I was amused by everyone's apoplexy. "Just because he owns the furniture? I've got furniture of my own. I have no interest in his. I'm going there to make a deal."

Somehow the New York City tabloids, the *Post* and the *Daily News*, got wind of the meeting (I didn't tell them) and built it up into something on a par with the Reagan-Gorbachev summit. *"They're going to meet! They're going to meet!"*

When the day of the meeting arrived, I took the elevator all the way up to Donald's office. When I got out, I had to pass through a sea of very pretty secretaries who were pretending to be typing things or on the phone, all the while trying to catch a glimpse of me walking by. The overheated media hype had turned this into a scene out of *High Noon.*

I was led into something you don't really see much of in California, a glass penthouse. Donald walked out from behind his desk to greet me.

"How are you, Merv? Come here, I want to show you something." He immediately took me over to a window that allowed us to look down on New York's great lady, the landmark Plaza Hotel, recently purchased by Donald.

He said, "There it is. I own it. It's my greatest acquisition." All of this in the first thirty seconds after I'd walked into the room.

We started talking about the number of rooms in the Plaza, and I said, very quietly, "That certainly will house the lawyers it will take for you to fight me."

What the hell. Get it over with.

He laughed. "You *are* a son of a bitch aren't you?"

Grinning, I replied, "I'm a son of a bitch *band singer.*"

I enjoy negotiations. They're very similar to doing a talk show. As each unfolds, you see where you can make your move. The trick in both is to get into areas that are easy, wait until you see a little spark, then seize upon it. That's the secret to a good interview—and to making a deal. You might even call it an art.

Twenty-three years of interviewing came right into focus sitting across from Trump. After so many years, you learn to judge body language, and speech—and to gauge, immediately, just how far you can go. Donald was a case study in impatience. In his chair, he sat all scrunched up, as if it were a chore for him to remain still. Apparently it was. Periodically, he'd just get up and walk around his office. It was as if he had a blinking sign on his forehead that continually flashed, "URGENT! URGENT!" And sitting or standing, he never stopped talking. He talked for almost thirty minutes and all I did was nod or utter an occasional "Ahhh."

Finally, I said, "Donald, I appreciate everything you've said (most of it about the difficulties I'd face taking on a project this size, and how I didn't have the experience or political connections to pull it off), but I'm here to make a deal. If you want to do a deal, then let's do one. If not, tell me now and I'll go home."

He seemed taken aback. For the first time in half an hour he wasn't speaking.

So I continued. "The way I see it, you have big interest payments to make," pointing out the fact that he had already borrowed many millions of dollars to buy up the remaining Resorts stock. "I can wait. I'll go back to L.A., and if it takes two years, that doesn't matter to me. *I* don't have any interest payments."

Stone-faced, Donald said, "I want the Taj Mahal."

I smiled and put out my hand. "Okay, it's a deal."

Clearly surprised that I would agree so quickly, he shook my hand while studying my face to see if I was really serious.

Our hands remained clasped when he added, "And I want the Steel Pier too."

My expression didn't change. Keeping my eyes locked on his, I said, "Done."

Each of us got what he wanted. Donald wanted the Taj Mahal and I wanted Resorts and Paradise Island. Built in the early part of the century, Resorts Atlantic City had a storied history. Originally known as Haddon Hall, it became the first Atlantic City hotel-casino in the seventies, shortly after gaming was legalized there. The other major asset included in the deal was Paradise Island, the jewel of the Bahamas. It was a property that I was eagerly looking forward to owning.

Trump couldn't understand why I wasn't remotely interested in the Taj Mahal. Much later, after everything was over, I explained it to him: "Donald, that place had 'sleepless nights' written all over it. You're a much younger man—you should be the one to finish it."

In preparing to write this book, I reread Donald's account of our deal, published twelve years ago under the title *Trump: Surviving at the Top*. I laughed out loud while reading his book until I realized—it was a novel! It *had* to be. What other explanation could there be for Donald saying that he'd given me an "honest appraisal" of the hotel-casinos that I "seemed so desperately to covet"?

First of all, I think you know by now that I'm not the "desperate" type. It's just not in my nature. And let me tell you about what Donald means by "honest appraisal." Before our deal was final, he took me on a personally conducted tour of Resorts. We were walking down a corridor—Donald, me, and his phalanx of giant bodyguards. (It seemed to make him crazy when people said hello to me first. And I'd say, "Donald, they can't even *see you* behind those guys.")

With a straight face, Donald said, "You know, Merv, for about fifteen million dollars you could really do a job fixing up this place."

I thought to myself, He must think that I work for him. Only someone he's paying would believe that bullshit.

But I said nothing and we kept on walking. In my estimate, that corridor *alone* would take about $15 million to repair. (It turned out later I was right.)

As a negotiating ploy, Donald speculated publicly that I wouldn't be able to raise the additional financing necessary to close the deal. I couldn't let him get away with that. We flew in all the outside directors of Resorts and put them in a room with my team from Drexel Burnham Lambert, then the top investment banking firm on Wall Street. Afterward, they told Donald that he'd better not try that again because Griffin has all the financing he needs.

For a time it looked to the world like our deal might yet fall apart. All the attention on what the press was calling the "War at the Shore" had resulted in posturing on both sides.

I was never concerned. Lord knows I'd experienced this sort of gamesmanship throughout my career. The only way to handle it is to stay focused on the bigger picture. All the blustering and name-calling was only a sideshow. My family and friends got tremendously upset by the things Donald said about me.

I just treated it with humor. I told the press, "If he doesn't behave himself, I'm going to take the "T" off his name all over town."

Finally, on May 27, we reached a truce. I signed off on a joint press release with Donald announcing the basic terms of our deal: he would give up control of Resorts and I would purchase his shares. That would give me temporary ownership of the Taj Mahal, which he would immediately buy back from me.

Even though we had an agreement in principle, a myriad of legal and financial issues still had to be resolved before the deal could be finalized. To oversee that process I needed a person who, above all, had the patience of Job.

I first heard about Tom Gallagher through William French Smith. Bill had served as Attorney General in President Reagan's first term. After leaving Washington, he'd returned to his partnership in the prestigious California-based law firm of Gibson, Dunn & Crutcher. Right after I'd sold my company, I retained Bill and his firm to do some estate work for me.

Tom had joined Gibson, Dunn right out of Harvard Law School

and quickly become the firm's "fireman." If there was something really difficult or unusual the firm needed done, he was always the one who put his hand up and volunteered. In the late seventies, Tom agreed to open the firm's London office. Then, in the eighties, he was assigned to oversee the firm's extensive Middle East practice from its office in Riyadh.

After having been overseas for the better part of nine years, Tom moved back to the United States in 1987 to Gibson, Dunn & Crutcher's New York office. This was another challenge for "Fireman" Gallagher since Gibson, Dunn had always been a Los Angeles–based firm; New York City represented its last frontier.

The way Tom tells the story is that he was minding his own business in Manhattan when he got a call one day from Bill Smith.

"Merv Griffin is about to do something very large," said Bill, with characteristic understatement, "and I think he could use your help."

I called Tom my "conservative" lawyer. Not politically; he once worked in Washington as an aide to former California Senator John Tunney, a liberal Democrat. In terms of temperament, however, Tom is quite conservative—thoughtful, deliberate, unflappable. In other words, the perfect choice to do battle with Trump.

My other lawyer was Morris Orens, the attorney whom Dale Scutti had originally hired to find a "white knight" for Resorts. Orens and Gallagher were a study in contrasts. As high-strung as Tom was low-key, Morris became the "liberal" voice on my team, enthusiastically advocating the deal, even as Tom counseled caution.

The two of them in a room together put on quite a show. Tom, dressed conservatively in a dark suit, would sit at the conference table, methodically reviewing the pros and cons of various deal points, while Morris, chain-smoking and talking a mile a minute, would be pacing the room, urging me to damn the torpedoes and move full speed ahead.

In fact, the deal *did* move ahead through the summer months as Drexel Burnham commenced our funding. The plan was to sign the final contracts with Trump sometime after Labor Day.

Because gaming is a tightly regulated industry, one obstacle that remained was my becoming licensed by the New Jersey Casino Control Commission as a casino operator. Although this required an extensive background check and character references, I had no reason to expect that it would be anything more than a pro forma process.

I've always been proud of my reputation and I'd left Robert Q. Lewis and Freddy Silverman off my reference list. No problem, right?

Wrong. But the problem wasn't mine. It came from the last place I ever would have expected—my own team.

In mid-August I flew to New York from my ranch in Carmel Valley to participate in a series of East Coast financing meetings. I should have known it would be an ill-fated trip—nothing good ever comes from being in New York City during the sweltering heat of August.

The humidity hadn't deterred people from coming to our bond sale presentation at the Helmsley Palace hotel in midtown Manhattan (maybe it even helped; we used a lot of Leona's air-conditioning that day). Potential investors crowded into the meeting room to hear me, Mike Nigris, and Ken Moelis, managing director of Drexel Burnham, make our pitch for Resorts. It was a very successful presentation, resulting in major bond sales. In the next few months, similar gatherings in Boston and Atlantic City would complete our financing efforts.

After the Helmsley Palace meeting, I hosted a reception in my suite upstairs for the entire team, including my management group and the investment brokers from Drexel Burnham.

What happened next seemed like a harmless social faux pas on my part. Only later would I realize how serious it was.

I was working my way down the receiving line, thanking each person for his or her hard work on behalf of the Resorts project, when I reached a dark-haired man in his mid-forties whom I'd never met. I assumed he was either with Drexel or that he was one of the other attorneys working with Tom Gallagher in New York (indeed, after talking with Tom for months by phone, we'd only met face-to-face for the first time earlier that same day).

The man was introduced to me as Ernie Barbella. I said, "Hi, Ernie. Nice to see you. Who are you with?"

Ernie looked at me kind of funny. Thinking that I'd made a mistake in not knowing who he was, I quickly said, "I have to apologize, I'm meeting people for the first time. I'm sorry if I don't recognize you. I know I probably should."

Looking uncomfortable, Barbella said, "Well, I've been working with Mike Nigris on your bond sale. Mike and I went to school together."

"Oh, that's terrific," I replied. "I'm sorry I haven't met you before, Ernie." Then I moved on down the line.

This awkward exchange was witnessed by several people from Drexel Burnham who found it quite disturbing. For months, Ernie Barbella had been participating in the meetings that decided how the deal would be financed. He'd presented himself, with Mike Nigris's approval, as a key member of my team. So it came as something of a shock to Ken Moelis and the Drexel group that I had no idea who Ernie Barbella was.

Just before meeting Barbella, I'd welcomed a new member of the Griffin Group with whom I *was* familiar. Like Mike Nigris, thirty-year-old Larry Cohen had been with Paneth, Haber & Zimmerman, the accounting firm that had handled my business for many years. While there, he was integrally involved in the sale of my previous company to Coca-Cola. During the negotiations, Larry had so impressed the executives at Columbia Entertainment that they offered him a job after the sale was finalized. Larry had been at Columbia for two years when my bid to acquire Resorts was announced publicly. Mike Nigris, realizing that we would need to build up our infrastructure, recruited his former colleague to come aboard as chief financial officer of the Griffin Group. I was delighted to see Larry again and gave him a hug to welcome him back to the fold.

Now we come to the part of the story that I always refer to as "Trenton, we have a problem."

After the bond sale presentation, I had returned home to Carmel Valley. About a week after the New York event, I received a phone call from Ken Moelis of Drexel. The call was unusual both for its timing—Sunday afternoon—and because Ken, who was normally very upbeat, sounded ill-at-ease.

"Merv," he asked hesitantly, "have you done any background checks on the people who are coming into the company with you, specifically, Michael Nigris?"

"No, why?"

"I don't think he can pass muster with the New Jersey Gaming Commission."

I was stunned. "What are you talking about, Kenny? What's wrong with him?"

Ken wasn't comfortable making accusations. "I really can't say, Merv. Just check it out as soon as you can."

I called Tom Gallagher immediately. His wife, Mary, answered the phone. It was dinnertime in New York and I apologized for interrupting them on a Sunday evening. When I told him about Ken's cryptic call, he was silent for almost a full minute. I'd never heard Tom, who is such a positive person, sound so troubled.

We agreed that the next step was to do a LexisNexis search (a service that retrieves legal documents and news articles) as soon as possible. It didn't take long to discover some significant red flags. Nigris and Barbella had been involved in some questionable financial dealings, unrelated to Resorts or any of my business interests. Tom, whose initial shock had quickly given way to steely resolve, said firmly, "We've got a big problem. As soon as we pull all of the documentation together, you need to come back to New Jersey and meet with the Gaming Commission."

It took a week for Tom to gather the information that we would present to the investigating arm of the New Jersey Gaming Commission. During that week I had barely spoken to Mike Nigris and, of course, I didn't tell him that I'd be coming east again so soon after my last trip. I'm not a cloak-and-dagger guy by nature, so this was very difficult for me. Although he wasn't a close friend, Mike had been a trusted employee and advisor for a long time. I was extremely reluctant to believe that he would do anything wrong.

On Friday I flew to Atlantic City to meet with Tom and some of his colleagues from Gibson, Dunn. From public records, they'd pulled together some pretty damaging information, most of it concerning Mike's college roommate, the mysterious Mr. Barbella. It became clear that he had associations with people alleged to be members of the Gambino crime organization. We would later learn that Barbella, along with various friends and family members (and I'm using the term "family" in the broadest sense), had bought up blocks of Resorts International stock, based on inside knowledge of my intention to offer $35 per share.

Tom recommended that, first thing Monday morning, we should personally present this information to the Gaming Commission investigators in Trenton.

I didn't want to wait. "Tell them we'll be there on Sunday."

Not given to theatrics, Tom said, "Merv, is that really necessary? One more day won't make any real difference."

This was probably the only time where I believed that my instincts were even remotely superior to Tom's regarding a legal matter. Actually, this really wasn't about the law; it was now a question of convincing the Gaming Commission that I was even more concerned than they were with both the fact and the appearance of propriety. I understood that the dramatic gesture of calling a meeting on a Sunday morning would accurately convey how strongly I felt about fixing this situation immediately.

"No, we're going down on Sunday. Set it up, okay?"

The key issue at the meeting was what to do about Mike Nigris. Since the information we had developed was still preliminary, my lawyers believed that it was important not to rock the boat too early. They recommended that instead of firing Mike, I move him over to the other parts of my business, the Beverly Hilton, Teleview Racing Patrol, and my radio stations, at least for the time being while we continued to investigate.

Of course, I agreed to move Mike totally out of Resorts and I immediately informed the Commission of my action. The next problem was finding someone to see the deal through to completion and to oversee the casino business once it came into my hands. I needed a quick study, someone of impeccable integrity and tremendous ability who could hit the ground running.

I've said many times that I had to drag Tom Gallagher, kicking his feet and dragging his heels, into the gaming business. Poor Tom. When he left the Middle East, he had no idea that he'd soon find himself in a quagmire that would make the Saudi desert seem like an oasis of calm.

For the next few months we concentrated on getting all of the arrangements in place to complete the final purchase and the financing. The deal was scheduled to close in November 1988 in a very complicated series of transactions.

The last stage of any deal of this size consists of what are called "closing adjustments," which meant that my accountants had to sit down with Donald's accountants and hash out every tiny detail. Following that, there would be one last session to incorporate all those points. Out of that would come the language necessary to generate the final signature contracts.

In October, a few weeks prior to the closing adjustments, Tom and his team were reviewing all the files. It wasn't a simple process.

Trump's people were still in control of the company, and all the deeds and documents had to come from them.

Tom Pennington, one of our young lawyers, flagged something that he thought might be important. He said, "They've screwed up the legal description of the land next to the Steel Pier. They left out the beach in front of the Taj."

He asked Tom Gallagher what our side should do about it during the closing adjustments. His reaction was immediate: "We do nothing. Trump is going to try and squeeze everything he can out of the final adjustment. We're going to hold this back. Knowing Trump, we'll need it later." Tom called and asked me if I approved of his strategy. I was delighted that our team had discovered a valuable ace to hold in reserve. I told him to play it however he thought best.

At the closing adjustments, Donald's team tried to slip it in without a fight. They stuck in what's called a "quit claim deed" for the beach and, of course, Tom spotted it immediately. Innocently, Tom asked, "What's this?" One of Trump's lawyers replied, "Oh, that's just a formality. It's language covering the beach in front of the Taj."

Now, if you remember, I had specifically agreed to sell Donald the Taj Mahal and the Steel Pier during our meeting in his office. But he'd never asked to buy the beach. In his typically understated and gentlemanly way, Tom pointed that fact out to Donald's people. He could sense the panic starting to break out across the table as they realized that if this situation wasn't easily resolved, they would have to explain to Donald why this "detail" had been overlooked. They tried gamely to make the case for letting it slide: "Well, the beach *obviously* comes with the Pier," was the Trump party line. Tom was unmoved. He calmly restated our position, "It's not part of the sale. Of course, we're willing to discuss a fair price for it. What do you have in mind?"

At the final adjustment meeting, held in the conference room of Gibson, Dunn & Crutcher's New York office, we negotiated roughly $10 million more for the beach that Trump forgot to buy. Exiting the meeting, Donald shouted, "I've been out-lawyered!"

Want to hear a story about devotion to duty above and beyond the call?

The deal finally closed after midnight and Donald's people turned over the check for the Taj Mahal at 2:00 A.M. With the check in his pocket, the newest member of my team, Larry Cohen, spent the next five hours sleeping fitfully on a couch in Tom Gallagher's office.

Shortly before 8:00 A.M., Larry drove downtown to the bank and waited for someone to arrive. A dozen senior citizens were already lined up on the sidewalk, waiting to cash their monthly Social Security checks. He was struck by the surreal contrast. Their checks were for $400 or $500 at most, while Larry was about to deposit a check for $273 million. The interest alone was $50,000 a day. By arranging to deposit the check before the bank opened, Larry had managed to earn the company an additional day's interest. Ten thousand dollars for every hour spent on Tom's couch. That's dedication.

To celebrate the closing, and as a thank-you to all the bankers, lawyers, and my management team for their incredibly hard work, I threw a big dinner at the Rainbow Room in Manhattan. Of course, the evening had to have a beach theme—umbrellas, palm trees, drinks with parasols. We had T-shirts printed up and given out to everyone as a memento of what Tom Gallagher still calls "the deal from hell."

A single question was printed on the front: *"Where's the beach?"*

One of the major differences between Donald and me is I only buy things that I enjoy running. It has to be something that interests me on more than an investment basis or it wouldn't be any fun. Then you're only a trader. You're out there buying up companies you never see. The only contact you have with management is to scream at them to get profits up. And if they do, you turn around and sell it out from under them.

I had always wanted to take a hands-on role in marketing both Resorts Atlantic City and Paradise Island in the Bahamas. That was the challenge for me, and I was eager to get started. It wasn't going to be easy, especially not in Atlantic City.

Both Donald and I had invested in the gaming business right before the end of an economic boom. In the next few years, the entire country would suffer through the recession and the Gulf War, while Atlantic City would be particularly hard hit by several very harsh winters that greatly diminished tourism.

One morning in early 1989 I woke up and found myself responsible for $925 million worth of debt. When I bought Resorts, it had about $600 million of debt. Added to that was the $325 million in bonds that we used to finance the purchase. As the economy grew worse, it became clear that we would have trouble paying the interest on the bonds and would need to restructure the debt. I know this sounds crazy, but it didn't bother me. What were they going to do, put me in debtor's prison? It's a momentary shock to the system, and then you start to work through it.

Rolling up my sleeves, I went to work in the back of the house, meeting daily with my management team and planning ways to keep Resorts afloat. It had nothing to do with saving my own neck. But I felt a strong personal responsibility to the bondholders who had placed their confidence in me.

I told my team to figure out the best way to deal with both the debt and the hard economic realities created by the recession. They developed a business plan that restructured the whole company. Then we presented it to every bondholder. It was approved overwhelmingly, with over 95 percent of the bondholders voting to support the restructuring.

In 1989, Resorts was reorganized under Chapter 11 of the federal bankruptcy laws. We were the first company to propose the idea of a friendly "prepackaged" bankruptcy that didn't require a judge to settle disputes between the different parties. Everything was agreed upon in advance for the benefit of the investors.

It was all accomplished in seven months, which was something of a record in the world of finance. Some reorganization plans take years to implement and produce extensive litigation, in which case only the lawyers win. (We reorganized a second time in 1994. As part of our new plan, I traded my debt for equity. In other words, I gave the bondholders 78 percent of the company, while I retained 22 percent. Then I invested additional money to keep the company going. Donald mockingly called the second reorganization my "Chapter 22." Somehow he neglected to mention that in 1991 he did the same thing with his Atlantic City hotel-casinos, employing the same investor-friendly "prepackaged" bankruptcy technique that we had pioneered.)

With the restructuring complete, I could now give my full attention to the marketing aspects of the gaming business that had attracted me to Resorts in the first place.

Creative change had always been the hallmark of my television talk show. I approached the marketing of Resorts Atlantic City and Paradise Island with the same philosophy that had proven so successful during twenty-three seasons as a host. Other casino owners spent their time worrying about whether a high roller on a lucky streak should be eighty-sixed or if that day's take was going to meet projections. I focused on ideas that would bring more people through the door.

I employed the "Field of Dreams" approach, with a twist. Unlike Donald, I had no desire to build a fabulous new casino to attract customers. I knew that if I created an atmosphere of fun and excitement within my *existing* casinos, they would come.

It was an incredible time. We did so many innovative things that had never been done before in Atlantic City.

One of the first calls I made was to Warren Cowan, my longtime friend and the man who invented modern Hollywood publicity.

"Warren," I said teasingly, "you know a few Hollywood stars, don't you? How about persuading them to come—all expenses paid—to Resorts Atlantic City or Paradise Island, where they aren't seen very often?"

Warren immediately started recruiting people such as Burt Lancaster, Robert Wagner, John Forsythe, and Dinah Shore to participate in a number of big events. Resorts was the first hotel-casino in Atlantic City to have artists like LeRoy Neiman come and personally sign their reproductions. That was a huge draw, as were the best-selling authors who came in for autograph sessions. One summer I'd seen almost every woman on the beach reading the latest Sidney Sheldon novel, so I said to my promotions director, "Let's bring him back here. Those women would love to meet him. And it will get them off the sand and inside the hotel along with their high-rolling husbands."

Occasionally we'd do a private dinner party for a few hundred high rollers and their wives. I'd book singers like Tony Bennett or Roberta Peters, the great opera star, to come and perform in a very intimate setting.

I made some changes in the games themselves. I was the first to bring in a European-style roulette wheel (again with the wheels), which doesn't have a double-zero, thus creating more favorable odds for the bettor. We also experimented with double-deck blackjack and changing the odds at the craps tables.

A world-class buffet was something that had been done successfully in Las Vegas but never in Atlantic City. I thought it would also be a huge drawing card at Resorts.

I was right. It went through the roof. In fact, the Beverly Hills-themed buffet became such a phenomenon that it created its own problems. Just as there had been mobs of people lining up for hours when we brought *The Merv Griffin Show* to Las Vegas, the buffet lines were so long that they would snake all the way in and around the building. Unfortunately, that also meant that people were spending hours in the buffet line instead of gambling. Necessity being the mother of all good inventions, I came up with a solution. We instituted an appointment system whereby someone standing at a certain point in line was given a ticket that told him to come back at, say, 12:06 P.M. We had measured exactly how long it would take to get from various points in the line to the buffet itself. Overnight there were no lines, but both the buffet *and* the casino tables and slot machines were now packed simultaneously.

Synergy also came into play. I decided to hold contestant searches for *Wheel of Fortune* at Resorts. The response was so overwhelming that the highway into Atlantic City was literally jammed with cars. Based on the success of the *Wheel* search, I subsequently added an open call for *Jeopardy!* contestants as well. Not only did the publicity attract a lot of new people to Resorts, we also recruited some pretty good players for both shows.

I used to do all my own TV commercials. If you lived in the Northeast in the late eighties and early nineties, you probably saw them. For those of you who didn't, they showed me running around Resorts, doing every job in the hotel. I'd be answering the phones, delivering room service, or fluffing up the pillows. Johnny Carson used to kid me during his monologue by saying, "Merv puts two mints on your pillow every night. Unfortunately, he's been eating them too."

I think my favorite marketing task had to be creating new shows for the 1,500-seat Superstar Theater at Resorts. I wrote the story lines, picked the music, brought in the choreographers, and even came up with a crazy name for each revue—my favorite being "Wahoo Baby." In five years, we only got one bad newspaper review. More to the point, there was never an empty seat in the house.

All the other owners came over to see what we were doing at Resorts, because they'd never seen anything like it. And, of course, they copied us like crazy.

The events most people still associate with my time in Atlantic City were the live TV shows that I hosted from Resorts every New Year's Eve. Much of the country got its first look at Atlantic City through a television lens that showcased the excitement of an entire city ringing in the new year. During those shows, I did something that flabbergasted the other casino owners. I brought David Spatz, the top columnist for *The Press* of Atlantic City up on the roof of Resorts with me and I'd have the camera shoot the casino marquees up and down the Boardwalk. We'd show what was happening that night at Caesars, the Tropicana, and even at Trump Plaza. The newspapers were constantly editorializing about how I was promoting the entire city, not just Resorts. It just seemed like good sense to me. If more people were attracted to Atlantic City, we'd all do well. What's the old saying? "A rising tide lifts all boats."

It was for that very reason that I accepted Donald's invitation to participate in the grand opening of Resorts's spectacular new next-door neighbor, the Trump Taj Mahal. Donald had finally completed his Xanadu in the spring of 1990. The opening ceremony had been heavily promoted and was expected to attract top celebrities from Tom Cruise to Michael Jackson. In the end, Evander Holyfield, Michael Spinks, and I were the biggest names to show up.

The opening also took place shortly after Donald and Ivana had begun their highly public separation. Almost every day, Donald was pictured in the New York papers with a different beautiful woman on his arm.

As the program commenced, the MC made what was clearly a shocking announcement to the thousands of people in attendance: "And now, here to officially open the Trump Taj Mahal and introduce Mr. Trump, is his good friend Merv Griffin!"

There was a tremendous cheer from the throng when I stepped to the podium. Everyone knew what had occurred between us over the previous two years.

"Good evening, everybody, and welcome to the opening of the Taj Mahal, which I used to own, before I sold it to Donald."

I paused and looked over at Donald, who was smiling broadly.

"We've all gathered here tonight to see who Donald was going to bring with him." (That night it was fashion model Carol Alt, who looked stunning.)

The crowd erupted with laughter. Out of the corner of my eye, it appeared that Donald was still smiling, although perhaps not quite so broadly.

I then proceeded to praise Donald's vision as a developer and to welcome the Taj Mahal into the neighborhood. *A rising tide lifts all boats.*

Several years later I celebrated the fifteenth anniversary of Resorts as the first hotel-casino in Atlantic City. I invited Donald, but he must have had a conflict that day.

Even without Donald, it was a great event. For months, my marketing group had been stymied in trying to design a special attraction to mark the anniversary. They'd asked me to mull it over and I did. The following day, I called a meeting in the Resorts conference room and told the entire staff what I'd come up with: "We're going to give away money."

They looked at me blankly. A few registered expressions that indicated they thought I'd finally lost it.

"Hear me out," I said, knowing they had to (sometimes it's fun to be "Da Boss"). "From noon till ten P.M., we're going to give away a hundred fifty thousand dollars. Thousand-dollar bags to fifteen people every hour. They're going to be required to come into the casino two weeks in advance, write their name and address on a card, and throw it into a drum. Then we'll have a big party and fly in a lot of Hollywood celebrities to pick the winners."

On the day of the event, in the elevator going down to the casino floor, I said to my head of marketing, John Belisle, "Do you think this is going to work?"

Based on the number of people who'd filled out cards, he already knew the answer. Just before the doors opened, he looked at me and said, "You'll see."

Then the elevator opened to reveal an absolute mob scene. The place was so crowded, you couldn't see the slot machines or the gaming tables.

That day, the slot machines at Resorts had the largest one-day take recorded in the fifteen-year history of the casino. Ultimately we gave away less than half of the money originally set aside for the contest—only $72,000. That was because you had to be present to win and a lot of people simply didn't want to stay all day. Amazingly enough, many of the lucky winners decided to test their luck on the slot machines and wound up giving back much of their winnings.

I know this may sound disingenuous, but I truly felt sorry for those people who were gambling with money they couldn't afford to lose. The truth is that although I genuinely loved the marketing and entertainment aspects of gaming, it was that part of the business that always gnawed at me and I certainly don't miss.

Don't get me wrong, I think gaming is a terrific form of entertainment that most people can either take or leave alone. I'm proud of having been a part of the business. I'm also pleased to see that many of the casinos are now making an increased effort to identify problem gamblers and get them help. It's no different than requiring a bartender to stop serving someone who's obviously intoxicated. Okay, end of speech.

Since "He Forgot to Buy the Beach" and "Trenton, We Have a Problem" have all the elements of a two-act play, I thought you'd like to know what became of the principal actors after the curtain fell:

- Ernie Barbella pled guilty to insider trading in the Resorts stock.
- Michael Nigris remained with the Griffin Group through May of 1989. I've had no contact with him since he left my company. He was never charged with a crime, nor do I believe that he was guilty of one. He *was* guilty of horrible judgment in friends and of playing fast and loose with the facts. I felt sorry for his wife, Norma. She's a sweet woman.
- Larry Cohen moved up quickly through the ranks and in 1997 he became CEO of the Griffin Group. Larry is a straight-shooter with solid judgment, whose character is beyond reproach. If he has one flaw, it's that he's a rabid and unapologetic Yankees fan.
- Tom Gallagher went on to become one of the most powerful people in gaming, when he was named president and CEO of Park Place Entertainment in 2000. Ironically, the man who never wanted to be in gaming found himself running the world's largest casino gaming company with over $5 billion in annual revenues and assets that included Caesars Palace and the Flamingo in Las Vegas and Bally's Wild Wild West and the

Claridge in Atlantic City. I'll never forget receiving the call from Tom, telling me that he'd been given the top job in gaming. I was on the dais of a banquet where I was the guest of honor when Ronnie brought me the cell phone with Tom on the line. I looked at him with an expression of "Can't this wait?" But I knew that if Ronnie thought it was important enough to hand me the phone in the middle of the dinner, I'd probably want to take the call. When Tom told me his news, I burst out laughing. My reluctant warrior was now the general of the largest gaming empire on the planet.

As for me, when I took over Resorts Atlantic City in 1988, its annual cash flow was $16 million. Eight years later, it had quadrupled to $64 million. And that was all from the marketing. We brought innovative promotional ideas to gaming that made Resorts unlike any other casino in the world. It was a thrilling experience for me to take that hotel and turn it around.

As a result, I was able to sell my stock in Resorts (now known as Griffin Gaming and Entertainment), which had previously been trading at $12 per share, for over $20 a share to South African developer Sol Kerzner.

Kerzner was looking to establish a foothold in the North American gaming industry. Initially, Sol had only purchased Paradise Island, but I knew that he was also intrigued by the prospect of owning a hotel-casino in the United States. So in 1996, I merged Griffin Gaming into his Sun International Corporation, giving him control of Resorts Atlantic City.

Those bondholders who had maintained their holdings through the ups and downs, the snowy winters and the restructurings, got their money back. In the end, they even made a profit on their original investment. Not bad for a "band singer."

Sol Kerzner was not as successful with Resorts Atlantic City and ended up selling it a few years later (ironically to a group that included a former associate of Trump's) at a deep discount from the price that he'd paid for it.

I was more fortunate. I took my experience with Resorts and used it to become involved in Player's International. You probably remember Player's from its promotional spots with Telly "Who Loves Ya Baby" Savalas as its TV pitchman.

I invested money to help them launch riverboat casinos in Illinois, Missouri, and Louisiana. When I finally sold my Player's International stock in 2000, it brought me a nearly twentyfold return on my original investment.

The best gamblers know when to hold 'em and when to fold 'em. Casino owners don't always share that wisdom. (If and when I ever write another book, I'm thinking of calling it "The Art of Knowing When to Get Out." Catchy title, huh?)

Last, but certainly not least, in our cast of characters is Donald Trump.

Donald Trump is the Vince Lombardi of developers. For Donald, winning isn't everything; it is the *only* thing. What he doesn't understand is that you can only beat someone who chooses to play your game. I never did. Oh sure, we had the "War at the Shore" (largely an invention of the press), but in the end, he got the Taj Mahal and I got Resorts and Paradise Island. Each of us got what he wanted, which, in my book, is the definition of winning.

Donald has remained in the gaming business and I'm happy to report that he's doing well with his three Atlantic City properties. He too suffered through the tough economic times and, like me, he used the bankruptcy mechanisms to reorganize his businesses and get them back on their feet. I love that town, and Donald is an important part of its ongoing success.

People ask me all the time if I still see Donald. Of course I do. Then again, how can you miss him? I see him constantly on those McDonald's commercials with his arm around a giant furry, purple creature named "Grimace." You know the spots. Donald is showing him New York City and reminiscing about all the great deals he's made. You can see the Plaza Hotel out the window, just as I'd seen it when Donald tried to impress *me* with his deal-making ability.

I think the handwriting is on the wall. Grimace used to be best friends with Ronald McDonald, who, as you may have noticed, is conspicuously missing from those TV commercials. I have to believe that before too long the purple fellow will be getting a new best friend. After all, how could anyone beat a character named *Donald McDonald?*

Watch out, Ronald.

Eight:
Healthy, Wealthy,
and Wise

I knew my life was in trouble when my psychiatrist threw up on me.

When I met him in 1972, Dr. Martin Grotjahn was already one of the world's most respected psychiatrists. He was in his late sixties, a diminutive man with translucent skin who had studied under Freud himself. Grotjahn's accent was so thick that one of his patients, Danny Kaye, patterned his hysterically funny impression of a little old German man after him.

Dr. Grotjahn headed the psychiatry department at the University of Southern California, in addition to maintaining a private practice in Beverly Hills.

As it happens, this brilliant and worldly man harbored a lifelong desire that had gone unfulfilled—he'd always wanted to see the Grand Canyon. Somehow I discovered his secret wish and took it upon myself to grant it. I arranged to pick him up on a Saturday morning in my twin-engine Beechcraft (the first of many planes I would eventually own) and we flew to the South Rim of the Grand Canyon for lunch.

The little doctor was so excited. Not only would he finally see one of the great natural wonders of his adopted country, but for the first time in his sixty-nine years he would be going up in a private airplane.

We had a delightful meal at a restaurant overlooking the Grand Canyon, topped off with several glasses of wine. Grotjahn was like a child, taking in everything around him with new eyes.

When it was finally time to get back in the airplane and return to Los Angeles, Dr. Grotjahn said, "Merv, zis has been vonderful. Danke schoen."

I told him that he was very welcome. Then we climbed back in the Beechcraft and buckled into our seats. A few minutes after take-off, we hit an air pocket and the plane dropped suddenly. It was only a momentary bit of turbulence, but the doctor's skin turned from pale white to sickly green. I put my hand on his arm to steady him. Before I could say, "It's nothing to worry about," he threw up in my lap.

That plane ride was a perfect metaphor for my life at the time— wonderful highs, interspersed with gut-wrenching lows.

You'll remember that 1972 was also the year I finished my tumul-tuous ride on CBS. What I didn't tell you was that in the same year, my marriage was coming to an end.

After almost fifteen years together, Julann and I had grown apart. My career had required her to give up living the life she loved on our farm in New Jersey and move to Los Angeles, a place she'd never re-ally enjoyed. She came along, although for the first time in our mar-riage I sensed that Julann's decision was based more out of concern for Tony than it was on support for me. Since he was an only child just entering adolescence, we both knew how important we were in our son's life, both individually and as a couple.

Truthfully, the distance between us was based on more than just geography. Even if we'd stayed in New Jersey, our lives were headed in different directions. I was consumed by my show, particularly dur-ing those stressful two and a half years at CBS. At the same time, it was clear that Julann's intelligence and abilities weren't really being challenged in the traditional role of wife as homemaker-helpmate. Julann loved raising Tony, and she was a terrific mother, but she was no longer content with subsuming all her other interests into my career.

Which brings us back to Dr. Martin Grotjahn. In ten years of doing my show, I'd interviewed literally dozens of psychiatrists, psy-chologists, and psychotherapists. They'd ranged from traditional Freudians to the pioneer of primal screaming, Arthur Janov. Dr. Joyce Brothers was practically a regular.

The public Merv Griffin spent hour after hour talking to highly trained therapists about every conceivable emotional issue. The pri-vate Merv avoided them like the plague.

Maybe it was the way I was brought up. My parents taught me to "never complain, never explain." I truly believe it was this advice that provided me with the unshakable self-confidence I displayed at such a young age. Ironically, the same creed that served me so well in my professional life prevented me from sharing my personal problems with other people, particularly strangers.

Funny, isn't it? My job was getting people to be candid, even re-vealing, about their personal lives. Yet the idea of doing that for my-self seemed pointless to me.

That all changed on February 7, 1973, the day Julann served me with divorce papers. Although I had some inkling this was coming—

things had become increasingly cool between us over the last several months—it caught Tony, who was barely thirteen years old at the time, completely by surprise. His reaction was just what I feared it would be.

He looked at both of us in tears and asked, plaintively, "Why are you *doing* this to me?"

Both Julann and I were devastated. We knew that it would be a mistake to stay together for Tony, but neither of us could bear to see him so crushed. I also understood that since he would now be living with his mother and seeing me mainly on the weekends, he was very likely to feel that I had abandoned him too.

My concern for Tony was all it took to get me over my life-long aversion to therapy. I knew that I needed guidance in order to help him get through this tremendous upheaval in his life. By rationalizing that I was only doing this for Tony, I could pretend that *I* didn't need any help myself. Of course that wasn't true, but it was an agreed-upon fiction which allowed me to open up to Dr. Grotjahn without ever having to acknowledge there was anything troubling *me*.

When I made my first appointment with Grotjahn, he and I had never met before. So I had no way of knowing that he watched *The Merv Griffin Show* every single night.

That first session was a comedy of miscommunication. He thought that I'd made the appointment in order to ask him to appear on my show. Before I could even tell him why I was there, he announced that he never appeared on television because he felt that it would compromise the sanctity of his doctor-patient relationships. He explained that the mere fact of his appearance on a talk show might raise doubts about his trustworthiness with his many high-profile patients, thus undermining his ability to treat them effectively.

Then Dr. Grotjahn threw me another curve by saying that he strongly encouraged his students to watch my show because I was the perfect example of how to conduct a psychiatric session!

I wasn't exactly sure how to take that, but he assured me that he was quite serious. Apparently my interviewing style employed the technique of "indirection" that Grotjahn favored in treating his own patients. He told me that I seemed to be intuitively aware of how to put a guest at ease while still eliciting good answers. Instead of putting someone on the spot with a direct question, I would "go around und come in ze back door," as he put it.

To his great credit, after I'd been seeing him for several months, Dr. Grotjahn never even acknowledged the identity of any of his other patients to me.

Not that I didn't probe a bit. My weekly appointment immediately followed Cher's. I don't think she ever saw me, but on a couple of occasions I saw her coming out of his office as I was arriving.

I'd sit down and say something subtle like, "Doesn't Cher look great?" *Indirection.*

He just gazed at me beatifically like a Teutonic version of the High Lama played by Sam Jaffe in the film *Lost Horizon.*

"Ve shood talk about you und your son."

I told Dr. Grotjahn how difficult it had been for Tony, particularly at school. It's no mystery that kids at his age can be unbelievably cruel. One boy waved a copy of a tabloid newspaper right in front of Tony's face. On the cover was a picture of his mom and dad with a graphically designed rip right through the middle of the photo to indicate the dramatic "break" in our relationship.

Tony slugged the kid and wound up serving many hours of detention. That was only one of several similar incidents that happened to him during the school year. Tony never complained to me (he's a Griffin all right), but the school administrators were in regular touch with both Julann and me about what was going on with him at school.

Generally, Dr. Grotjahn spoke very little during our sessions together. As Freudians maddeningly do, he preferred to let his patient do all of the talking.

So it was something of a surprise when, in the fourth or fifth session, he interrupted me with the following observation: "Mr. Griffin, you haff a vonderful opportunity now. Zis will make you und your son much closer."

I asked him what he meant by that remarkable statement and he replied, "Vot do *you* tink I mean?"

The damnedest thing was that he was absolutely right. Even though Tony stopped living with me, we became closer than we'd ever been before. I looked forward to our time together on the weekends, and I protected it from any encroachments by my professional life. More than just father and son, we became best friends. And we've remained that close ever since.

I did a number of things to help me handle the stress of going through the divorce, some of them positive, some of them not.

On the plus side of the ledger, I bought the twin-engine Beechcraft that I used to take my psychiatrist to the Grand Canyon (and lose his lunch); I took flying lessons that eventually allowed me to pilot a plane myself, and which helped me to overcome my long-time fear of flying; and I bought a condominium in Pebble Beach that served as a weekend getaway spot for me and Tony.

I also employed a not-so-positive coping method: I tripled my cig-arette habit, going from one pack a day to three.

When Tony was a little boy, he'd say, "Daddy, I just saw it on TV. You're going to have cancer."

"Tony, don't talk like that."

"Well, you're going to die from the smoke. They just said it on tel-evision."

Well then it *had* to be true. He used to scare the hell out of me with comments like that. Not to mention his gift for making me feel guilty: "Does that mean we won't go to the park anymore?" He was a very outspoken child.

My mother, a smoker herself (who never quit and lived to age eighty-three), took a more subtle approach than my son. When I was still doing my show from New York, she'd call from California and say, "Buddy, I like your show very much. But I can't see the guests."

I'd say, "Mom, that's an old television. Go out and get a new one. I'll send you the money."

"No, dear. It's not that. You're blowing smoke right at people." It was true. I took home some show tapes and saw that she was right. There was a billowing cloud of smoke wafting across the set, right into my guests' faces.

Not so subtle was the head of Westinghouse. He called me one day when I was doing my show with Group W and said, "Merv, I'm on the board of the American Cancer Society and we think that you're committing public suicide every night."

"Hey, if you don't like my singing just say so."

I don't have an addictive personality, so it's never been that big a deal for me to quit. And I don't use patches or gum. I wake up one morning and say to myself, "I don't feel like smoking anymore."

Mark Twain had it right. He said, "It's not hard to quit smoking . . . I've done it a hundred times."

I've stopped for two, four, six years at a time. Once I quit for twelve years.

During 1972 and 1973, when I was leaving CBS and breaking up with Julann, I quit three separate times. Which led to a different problem. Every time I quit, I gained between twenty and thirty pounds.

Throughout my life, I've had to fight to keep from putting on weight. It's been an awful battle ever since I was a kid. I've already told you I weighed 240 pounds after high school and that I subsequently lost eighty pounds (or looking at it another way, one third of myself). What I didn't tell you was why.

All during adolescence I was teased, often cruelly, about my weight. I think that I had extra empathy for Tony's difficulties with his classmates because I'd never forgotten how awful it feels to be mocked and taunted by your peers. *"Fatty, fatty, two-by-four, can't get through the kitchen door . . ."*

When I unexpectedly became an overnight radio star at the age of twenty, I wasn't prepared for some of the attendant requirements of fame. It's one thing to have a show named after you, but it's quite another to discover that total strangers have opinions and expectations of you as well.

You'll recall that it was Bill Pabst who hired me at the radio station in San Francisco. Bill was a good guy who always treated me well. Not wanting to make me feel self-conscious, he never mentioned my weight or the annoying facial acne that still plagued me.

Bill concocted a plan to create an air of "mystery" around his new romantic singing sensation. He told me that they wouldn't make any publicity pictures of me available to either the press or the public.

"They'll be clamoring for you, Merv. The less we tell them, the more interested they'll be."

I thought it was a little strange that the station was responding to requests for pictures of me with a form letter that said, "Sorry, but we don't have any photos of Merv right now. As soon as we do, we'll get one right out to you."

I was young and very green, so I didn't think it my place to question the wisdom of Bill's plan.

This is how naive I was: it never occurred to me that there might be another reason why Bill didn't want to send out my picture. He knew that the minute they saw my face, people would just start laughing at his roly-poly romantic star.

One day, I was walking out of the studio when a woman came up the stairs and asked me where they did *The Merv Griffin Show*. Pointing to the studio I'd just exited, I said, "They do it in there. But I'm sorry, ma'am, there are no guests allowed. They don't have a studio audience."

At that moment one of the crew came out and passed by as we were talking. "Hey, Merv," he said casually.

The woman looked me up and down and said, "*You're* Merv?" Then she became hysterical with laughter. Security had to escort her from the building.

That hurt a lot. So I went on a drastic salad and steak diet. In four months I lost eighty pounds.

Since then I've spent my life losing those same eighty pounds and then gaining them back. Up forty, down forty. I've had more swings than the stock market.

There's an old Totie Fields joke that sums up my experience with diets: "I've been on a diet for the past two weeks. And you know what I've lost?"

"*No, what have you lost, Totie?*"

"I've lost two weeks."

One of the perks of hosting your own talk show is that publishers send you free books on a daily basis. You can meet almost any author you want (except maybe J.D. Salinger), provided you're willing to do it on camera.

Every popular diet doctor came on *The Merv Griffin Show*.

And I murdered several of them.

You think I'm kidding? Okay, let's recap: in the late sixties, I had on Dr. Irwin Stillman, chief proponent of the "Doctor's Quick Weight Loss Diet." His plan basically consisted of cottage cheese and water (they should have called it the "*Prison* Doctor's Quick Weight Loss Diet"). I remember him literally screaming at my audience, "Drink eight glasses of water every day!" Of course I tried his diet myself (I tried them all—I wanted to be a good host), and I spent weeks sloshing around the studio like the Atlantic Ocean with shoes.

Not long after he appeared on my show, Dr. Stillman died. I'm not sure what was listed as the official cause of death, but it doesn't matter. Trust me, he drowned.

Then I had on Jim Fixx, who wrote the best-seller *The Complete Book of Running*. He was single-handedly ("footedly"?) responsible for the jogging craze in America during the seventies. I started jogging and kept at it . . . until Fixx dropped dead of a heart attack while *jogging*.

The most frightening example of my diet doctor curse has to be Dr. Herman Tarnower, inventor of the "Scarsdale Diet," which limited you to 700 calories per day, largely from protein. Within a year of doing my show, his mistress, Jean Harris, shot him to death. I've always wondered . . . do you suppose there's any protein in lead?

The poor guy never had a chance. I should have testified at the trial and told them that, although Jean Harris pulled the trigger, she really didn't do it. I consider myself to blame.

I once lost fifty pounds on the Jenny Craig food plan (this was after I'd stopped doing my show, which is why she's alive today). All her foods seemed to start with a "p"—pancakes, pasta, peanut butter. My problem was that I just kept right on going through the rest of the alphabet until I got to shish kebabs, steaks, and sundaes.

In recent years, I've made a certain amount of peace with my fluctuating weight. I've even gotten to the point of being able to poke fun at it publicly. Here's one of the promotional spots I did for Resorts Atlantic City:

MR. GRIFFIN: Do you know why I lost all this weight? So I can really enjoy my beautiful, new Resorts—like the elegant and delicious Le Palais restauarant. Capriccio's pasta is better than anything in Rome, and my Beverly Hills buffet is the best value in town. A little dessert, then gotta see our show!

USHER: Seat for one, Mr. G?

MR. GRIFFIN: No, better make it two. I'll start the diet Monday.

I still try to lose. It's not great for your heart walking around carrying too much weight. But I've accepted the fact that I will always love food. And a hundred years from now, what are they going to say about me? "Merv was *fat?*" I don't think so. They're going to say, "Who the hell was that guy with Arthur Treacher?"

There was another way I learned to cope with the stress and anxiety of my split with Julann; a way which, at the time, was considered highly unusual.

When I bought my place in Pebble Beach I became very friendly with Clint Eastwood and his then wife, Maggie. Clint and I played tennis most weekends during the early seventies and we often included Tony in our doubles games.

One morning I called him to set up a match, and the maid, who didn't speak English well, answered the phone.

"I sorry," she said, "Mr. and Mrs. Eastwood doing their BM."

This same, rather bizarre conversation happened more than once until I finally said something to Clint.

"I don't mean to get her in trouble, but I think you should know that your maid is telling people every time you're in the bathroom. And she's awfully *specific* about what you're doing in there."

Clint looked at me blankly for a moment, then he threw back his head and guffawed.

"Not *BM*, Merv," he said, between gasps of laughter, "*TM*. Transcendental Meditation. You remember the Maharishi Mahesh Yogi from India? The one who taught it to the Beatles a few years back? Maggie and I do it for twenty minutes in the morning and twenty minutes at night. It's the greatest."

I was surprised that Clint, a low-key, somewhat conservative guy (despite his "Dirty Harry" image), would be involved in something so . . . well, *weird.*

But the more he talked about it, the more intrigued I became with the idea of trying it myself. He described how TM allowed him to focus his thoughts so completely that when he was directing a movie he could visualize an entire scene, down to the tiniest detail, then shoot it exactly that way later on.

Lord knows I needed something to help me focus. My separation and pending divorce from Julann had left my thinking scrambled and my life in a state of perpetual chaos. I still did my show every day, but

I knew that my interviews were beginning to show the effects of my personal turmoil.

I asked a friend in Carmel to recommend a meditation teacher. He gave me the name of David Rosencranz, who ran the TM center in Monterey. The results were amazing and almost instantaneous. My thinking became more orderly, my mind became calmer, and I was able to get a good night's sleep for the first time in months.

When you meditate, you slow down everything within your body. You empty your mind into nothingness, and thoughts will just occur to you—whatever you want to think about flows freely.

I was so thrilled with TM's effect on me that I subsequently invited the Maharishi (the title means "Great Sage") to be a guest on my show. Actress Ellen Corby (Grandma Walton) joined him and made a passionate pitch about the benefits of meditation. Within days, TM had gained tens of thousands of new practitioners all over the United States.

Two years later I did a second show on TM, this time with the Maharishi, Clint, and Burt Reynolds as my guests. Now if you've never seen him (more to the point, if you've never *heard* him), Maharishi Mahesh Yogi is a tiny man who always dresses in traditional white robes. He has a long, flowing beard and a distinctive, high-pitched laugh that I loved to provoke. On that show, after the Maharishi emitted a particularly long series of "hee-hee-hees," Burt turned to the audience and said, "Hey, he has the same laugh I do." People were laughing so hard that it took a full minute to restore order in the studio.

I liked the Maharishi, but I didn't understand a lot of the religious aspects of his movement. He traveled with many disciples, one of whom had the job of carrying a lambskin for him to sit on at all times. You also weren't permitted to touch the Maharishi. I had to resist the impulse to greet him with a handshake for fear of offending him.

I've used TM many times over the last thirty years, especially during stressful situations. Actually, I now find it to be even more effective as a preventive step, before a situation has the chance to *become* stressful.

Today every doctor I know recommends meditation for dealing with tension and anxiety. Indeed, the healing methods of Indian culture made popular in the books of Deepak Chopra, one of the Maharishi's closest disciples and students, are rooted in the same science that gave rise to Transcendental Meditation.

Meditation helped me in many ways, but it was no cure for the loneliness I felt after the breakup of my marriage. The hardest part was the stark contrast between my days and my nights. Every afternoon at 5:30, I'd sit down to talk with some of the world's most intelligent and fascinating people. Then the camera light would go off, the tape would stop rolling, and I'd be left sitting there wondering what I had in the refrigerator for dinner.

After fourteen years with Julann, it was a rough transition to make. I know that a lot of people go through being single again after many years of marriage, but there's an added dimension to it when you're in the public eye. Meeting someone isn't the problem; it's meeting someone you can open up to and trust that's really difficult. This goes back to that whole idea of people's preconceived expectations of you when you're famous. The reason so many actors marry other actors is because it allows them to avoid the problem entirely. Someone who's had similar experiences with fame is a) not impressed or intimidated by it and b) comfortable with its many ridiculous, and sometimes unpleasant, accoutrements.

Which brings me to Eva Gabor.

Eva was the youngest child of Vilmos and Jolie Gabor. Born in Budapest shortly after the First World War, Eva, like her older sisters, Magda and Sari (known as Zsa Zsa), was constantly pushed toward fame and fortune (not necessarily in that order) by Mama Jolie, a frustrated actress. While still a teenager, Eva married Dr. Erik Drimmer, an osteopath who would later become the personal physician to Greta Garbo.

In the late thirties, Eva was the first of the three Gabor sisters to come to America, followed shortly after by Zsa Zsa and Magda, and eventually by Mama Jolie. I was never very clear about what became of papa, except that he remained in Hungary.

Although she had no formal training as an actress, Eva was put under contract at Paramount where she made a couple of forgettable films. Now divorced from Dr. Drimmer, she married a wealthy San Diego businessman named Charles Isaacs. That marriage lasted seven years during which time her career floundered. In 1950, Eva landed a major role in the Broadway production of *The Happy Time*, produced by Richard Rodgers and Oscar Hammerstein. This was also an apt title for Eva's life during the fifties even though she divorced and remarried twice more during the decade. Her career really took off after a successful run on Broadway. She was given her own radio show, where creative syntax quickly became an indelible part of Eva's public persona.

During this time her older sisters, Magda, and especially Zsa Zsa, were also becoming famous.

All these years later, it's hard to describe the phenomenon of the three glamorous Gabor girls and their ubiquitous mother. They burst onto the society pages and into the gossip columns so suddenly, and with such force, it was as if they'd been dropped out of the sky.

Let me try to translate the Gabor craze into more contemporary terms. Suppose Madonna had two sisters. Now suppose that their names were Jennifer Lopez and Britney Spears. Okay, now that you have that image in your mind, picture Elizabeth Taylor as their mother. From the standpoint of fame, that's how visible and popular the Gabors were in their heyday. They were glamour personified.

I told you before that my first memory of meeting Eva was when we both appeared on the Harpo Marx television special in 1961.

A year later, I asked Eva to be a guest on my afternoon show on NBC. She was booked for a Friday, the same day that Woody Allen made his weekly appearance with me.

On a whim, I asked Woody, "If you were writing a play, what part would you cast Eva in?"

Slowly giving her the once-over, Woody paused for maximum effect, and then said, "As my mother." Eva blushed bright red and hurled her purse at Woody's midsection. I kept them apart after that.

She made many other memorable visits to my show, ultimately appearing as a guest on all four versions: NBC, Westinghouse, CBS, and Metromedia. Throwing caution to the wind, I once asked Eva which of the Gabor girls was the oldest.

"Mama," she said, demurely.

When she achieved major stardom with the hit TV series *Green Acres*, I invited Eva and her co-star, Eddie Albert, to come on together. As it happened, one of the other guests on the panel was

Cleveland Amory, then the television critic for *TV Guide*. Amory hated *Green Acres*, and had said so in print. Eva and Eddie decided to give him their own review, telling Amory exactly what they thought of *him*.

Then there was the time Eva took questions from my audience. Not surprisingly, most of them were about romance or marriage. One woman asked her if it was proper to keep the ring after a broken engagement.

"No, darling, you should always give back the ring. But keep the stone."

My favorite Eva appearance happened when I was still doing my CBS show in New York. Eva was backstage, preparing to make her entrance, when the guy from Standards and Practices stopped her and insisted that she change into a less revealing dress. Her bosom, he said, was much too visible. She looked at him disdainfully, as though he were a peeping Tom, staring at her through a keyhole. Interposing himself between Eva and the stage, the insistent censor refused to let her go on. Eva ducked around him after she heard me introduce her. But before she could make it through the curtains, he reached in and shoved a handkerchief into her décolletage.

Of course, I saw none of this when it was happening, but as soon as she made her entrance, I said, on the air, "What's the matter with you?" A white cloth was sticking up from her breasts.

"It was that censor man, darling, he shtuffed this in me. He doesn't like my bosoms."

"That fool," I said, winking at the audience. Then I added, "Oh, come on. That's ridiculous. Just take it out."

She was happy to comply and we did the whole interview with her cleavage uncovered. Truth to tell, the dress wasn't nearly as revealing as others I'd seen her wear off-camera. Then I insisted she remain on the couch for the rest of the program, knowing that CBS would be helpless to edit her out of the entire show.

Eva and I got to be really good friends after her thirteen-year marriage to entrepreneur Richard Brown ended in 1973. That same year she met and married aviation executive Frank Jameson, who became her fifth and final husband.

In 1979, she called me out of the blue and asked, "Darling, do you do that show every day?"

I said, "Yes, I do it every day. Why?"

"Well my friends Al Rockwell [Willard Rockwell, Jr., chairman of the board of Rockwell International] and his wife, Constance, are going to fly all over Asia, and they've invited Frank and me. I told them that I wanted to invite you too."

They would be hop-scotching across Asia, stopping in the Philippines, South Korea, Japan, Taiwan, and Hong Kong, all places I'd never seen before. Since this was an important business trip for Rockwell, a large group of the company's executives had to be included. This necessitated using a converted 727, thus providing plenty of additional room for Eva and Frank (and possibly me) to tag along.

I thought, What the hell? You only live once. I arranged my taping schedule so I could get away, then I called Eva back and told her I was going.

"Darling, that is wonderful! These are *such* boring trips. We will pep it up together."

It was an amazing trip and if I were to give you all the details, it would fill an entire chapter. Let me tell you just one story that occurred on the very first leg of the trip, when we stopped to refuel on one of the Midway Islands in the Pacific.

Ever since the famous battle that took place there during World War II, the Midway Islands had served as a small naval outpost. The few thousand people living on Eastern, Sand, and Spit Islands (the three atolls collectively known as the Midways) are greatly outnumbered by the vast number of exotic birds, which are their chief residents. Indeed, some years after we landed there, the birds accomplished what the empire of Japan could not, and the navy finally surrendered. The Midways are now exclusively a wildlife preserve.

The most visible and certainly the most unusual bird living on the Midway Islands was the Laysan Albatross, commonly know as the gooney bird. Let me tell you, it's easy to see how it got its name. The gooney stands about three feet tall, with a seven-foot wingspan. It struts around a great deal, periodically emitting a mooing sound that makes you think of a small flying cow.

As the 727 was refueling, the pilot announced that a gooney bird had flown into one of the wings, causing a small dent. Obviously the bird suffered more than the plane, but just to be safe, we were all escorted to the officers club while the mechanics checked everything out.

When we got there, several hundred naval personnel and their wives were all sitting down, facing a large television screen.

Nobody turned around when we walked into the room, so I had time to look up at the screen and realize what they were watching.

"Eva," I whispered, "that's my show."

It turned out that gathering to watch *The Merv Griffin Show* was an important daily ritual for the men and women stationed on those remote islands. It was one of the ways they maintained a connection to home.

The show was almost over when we entered the room, so I decided to remain in the doorway until the closing credits came on. I'd motioned for Eva to stand outside in the hallway, just out of view.

When my theme music finished, the set was turned off and everyone stood up, preparing to leave.

"Well," I said from the back of the room, "how did you all like my show today?"

You'd have thought they were witnessing the Second Coming. Everyone began yelling, "It's him! It's him!"

"Wait a minute! *Wait* a minute!" I had to shout to be heard above the din. When they finally got quiet, I played my ace. Actually, it was more like my queen: "You think *this* is something? Ladies and gentlemen, please welcome Miss Eva Gabor!"

Like the pro that she was, Eva made a grand entrance. For a long moment everyone was so stunned that they didn't make a sound. They just stared at her, then back at me, as if the whole scene might be some sort of television-induced hallucination.

Then the entire room burst into deafening applause and cheers.

Smiling, Eva looked at me and said, "I *told* you we would pep things up, darling."

Eva and Frank Jameson were divorced in 1983. It may surprise you to learn that someone who had been married five times could still be heartbroken by a divorce, but Eva was truly crushed.

Understanding exactly what she was going through, I invited her up to my ranch in the mountains above Carmel Valley. It's an extraordinary spot with tremendous healing powers.

I gave Eva the use of one of the six guest cottages on the property and told her that she was welcome to stay on as long as she wished. Knowing how much she loved them, I had fresh roses delivered to her every day. Slowly, her natural effervescence began to reappear; what I always thought of as "La Joie de Eva." She later told our friends that being in Carmel during those dark days had almost certainly saved her life.

People always ask me if Eva was anything like the slightly off-center character she played on *Green Acres*. Let's see what you think.

We were at a party together at Zsa Zsa's house, chatting with an older man who seemed to know Eva quite well. When he walked away, I said, "Eva, that wasn't like you. We were talking with that man for ten minutes and you never introduced me. Who is he?"

She looked at me the way Lisa Douglas (Eva's character on *Green Acres*) used to look at Arnold the pig, vaguely with a kind of detached amusement. "Darling, I have *no* idea who that was."

At that moment Zsa Zsa came over and Eva asked her sister if she knew the name of the man we'd been talking to.

"Eva, that was *your* first husband." True story, I swear.

It wasn't long before I started to think of the ranch in Carmel as the home Eva and I shared. We began to take long trips together, especially after my show ended in 1986. No one was a better traveling companion than Eva. And always we returned to Carmel. There were two giant couches in the living room that came together in an L shape. Eva would get on one, I'd get on the other and we'd lie there for days at a time—laughing, sleeping, laughing, watching television, laughing, eating, and laughing some more. We almost never argued except when we watched *Wheel of Fortune*. She'd get furious because I knew all the answers in advance.

Eva used to say that we had the perfect relationship: "He has his place on the sofa, and I have mine."

She was fiercely protective of her friends. During the Trump battle, Mike Wallace came to Atlantic City and interviewed both Donald and me at Resorts. Eva, who had never met Trump, walked right up to him and said, "You awful man. You've said terrible things about my friends Barron Hilton and Marvin Davis." It was one of the rare times I've ever seen Donald speechless.

Once we took Eva's mother with us to Atlantic City. Like the former Miss Hungary that she was (a title she won long after becoming *Mrs.* Gabor), Mama Jolie refused to go out for the evening unless she was elegantly dressed and perfectly coiffed. She treated Atlantic City like it was Monte Carlo.

Eva and I were usually exhausted and asleep by 11:00 P.M., but that was when Mama was just getting started.

"You two are so boring," she sniffed. "Where is the little boy? Tell the little boy I wish him to take me gambling tonight." Poor Ronnie Ward, who was in his mid-twenties by then, had to stay up all night watching Jolie hold court in the casino.

Eva and I had so many marvelous experiences together. Getting to share my good fortune with her was one of the great joys of my life.

Larry King once asked me what it's like to be able to buy anything I see. My first response was to take a slow look around his set and say, "Well, I like this *studio*, Larry . . ." Then I got serious with him and said, "You can't ever think like that."

I think that's a result of how I earned my money. If you had to struggle for it, you know the value and the responsibility of money.

One of the reasons I've always been reluctant to talk too much about money is that the topic seems to attract some pretty strange people.

Ever since I was first included on Malcolm Forbes's ridiculous list more than fifteen years ago, I've received a steady stream of requests for financial assistance.

My heart truly goes out to the people who write to me about illness or personal tragedy. It's extremely hard to say no to some of their requests, particularly those involving children. But I do. I turn down everything that comes to me unsolicited, across the board.

Before you think that I'm some sort of Scrooge, let me explain why I do that. I believe strongly in charitable giving. But what I had to decide, as soon as I came into that "great American fortune," was how I could be most effective in helping others.

I quickly came to the conclusion that a scattershot approach to charitable giving was a terrible idea. If I simply reacted to whoever got my attention for a cause, no matter how needy, I'd be spread so thin that I would have time for absolutely nothing else. Moreover,

I'd inevitably wind up giving money to something that, on the surface, *seemed* worthy but was actually a scam.

That's why I've focused on just a few charities, primarily those involving children or people who are really suffering with life-and-death issues, such as in a hospice situation. I've given a great deal of money in support of groups like Childhelp USA or the Young Musicians Foundation.

And I do my homework. I ask to see their budgets before I get involved, because I really don't like to contribute to groups that are top-heavy with staff. Too much is eaten up by overhead and the people who are supposed to benefit wind up getting shortchanged.

Life isn't nearly as meaningful if you can't share your success with others. I now accept a few select invitiations to perform at charity functions. There's no pressure because I'm not getting paid and if they hate me, what are they going to do? "We didn't pay him. We can't throw him out."

Let me tell you about a recent one that was a classic. Dr. Arnold Klein is a longtime friend of mine and one of the country's leading dermatologists. He organized a major AIDS benefit in Laguna Beach where he lives, and I agreed to co-chair it, along with Elizabeth Taylor and Michael Jackson.

The evening was planned in two parts: a private dinner in an elegant Laguna Beach home for the highest donors, followed by a larger reception at a nearby art museum. The dinner was called for six and the reception was set to start two hours later, at eight o'clock.

I flew down to Orange County on my plane with my close friends Rose and Bill Narva. Until I sold it, Rose was the general manager of the Givenchy in Palm Springs. As an Admiral in the Navy, Bill served as the chief physician to the U.S. Congress for twenty-five years, while also treating every president from Lyndon Johnson to Ronald Reagan. Before we landed, I gave my prediction to the Narvas: Elizabeth and Michael would be at least two hours late.

When we arrived, I took Arnie Klein aside and said, "I've known Elizabeth forever and she's never on time. She was probably even a late baby."

We all sat down for dinner and, of course, there were two glaringly empty chairs at the head table. By 7:45 poor Arnie was sweating bullets and I realized that I had to do something. The guests had paid astronomical sums to dine with Elizabeth and Michael; we were now on dessert and they were nowhere in sight.

Arnie had hired a fellow to play piano in the background during the evening. With my friend Penny Marshall egging me on, I went over to the piano player, tapped him on the shoulder and said quietly, "Do you mind if I cut in?' I proceeded to do thirty minutes at the piano in order to distract the crowd from their irritation at my absent co-chairs. The Narvas said later that Arnie was both grateful and surprised, telling them, "I didn't even know that Merv played the piano."

Finally at 8:15 the door opened and Elizabeth and Michael made their entrance while I was still at the piano. Of course, I did what I've always done for guests—I introduced them: "Ladies and Gentlemen, they're here! Bonnie and Clyde have arrived." As I rose from the piano, everyone in the room stood up and applauded my brief interlude on the ivories.

Later on, during the reception at the museum, the press insisted on getting pictures of me together with Elizabeth and Michael. As the assembled paparazzi wildly snapped photos of the three of us together, I glanced outside and saw literally thousands of people milling in the streets, hoping to catch a glimpse of . . . *me?*

Some of my most embarrassing moments always seem to occur in the name of a good cause. In 1985, Prince Charles and Princess Diana were the guests of honor at a charity reception in Palm Beach at which I was the master of ceremonies. I had conducted the first American talk show interview with the Prince of Wales two years earlier and we'd gotten along famously. (I'd asked him about his education, knowing that the autocratic Prince Phillip had shipped him off to boarding school in Australia as a teenager. Charles's telling reply offered insight into the character of a man who may yet be king: "I was chucked into a pond and I either sank or I swam. At the age of sixteen, I was determined I wasn't going to sink." Ironically, "sink or swim" was the exact phrase that Diana herself would subsequently use in describing how she had been left to fend for herself in their troubled marriage.)

Eva and I had been invited to a small pre-reception function with about twenty other people, including Bob and Dolores Hope. As I moved through the receiving line, Eva was in front of me and Dolores Hope was immediately behind me. Shortly before I reached the prince and princess, a stud popped off my tuxedo shirt and fell inside the shirt itself. Dolores stuck her hand down my shirtfront and felt around for it. We arrived in front of Charles and Diana in that less-than-dignified but very funny way.

Prince Charles, ignoring the fact that a woman's arm was in my tuxedo shirt, greeted me warmly, "Diana," he said, turning to his beautiful young wife, "This is Merv Griffin."

"Oh yes," said the princess. "I know him."

"You do?" I said, disregarding the protocol that requires you not to ask questions of royalty, *"How* do you know me?"

"I've seen the tape of your interview with my husband many times," she said smiling in the shy, yet knowing way that had endeared her to millions.

It turned out that the heir to the British throne was just like any other talk show guest. He'd brought his interview tape home and showed it to his wife. A lot. I guess he liked it.

Oh, by the way, Dolores Hope eventually retrieved my errant stud. But wouldn't you know it, as soon as I sat down on the long dais for the formal dinner. I popped again, this time in front of the entire room. A true friend, Dolores again stuck her hand down my shirtfront, feeling around for the missing stud. Thank God, Bob missed all of this or I never would have heard the end of it. But His Royal Highness happened to look down the table just as Mrs. Hope was feeling me down for the second time that night. The expression on his face was mixture of curiosity and amusement. *Those Americans are truly odd.*

I mentioned before that one of my favorite charities is Childhelp USA, founded in 1959 by two amazing women, Sara O'Meara and Yvonne Fedderson. Two years ago I donated one of my hotel properties, The Wickenberg Inn and Dude Ranch in Arizona, to Childhelp as a home for abused children. It was a $10 million gift, the largest they had ever received.

I still cry when I think about the photograph of the little boy whose back was scarred with cigarette burns that spelled out the words "I'm a bad boy." It was that horrible image that inspired me to donate the Wickenburg Ranch. Along with the property, I also donated a herd of horses that Childhelp has been using as a form of "equine therapy" for emotionally withdrawn children. They've already had kids who hadn't spoken for months finally begin to smile and laugh again. For as long as I live, helping those kids is probably the most rewarding thing I'll ever do.

Nine:
Making the
Good Life Last

When it was first suggested to me that the title of this book be *Merv: Making the Good Life Last,* I just laughed. What the hell did *I* know about it? I told them to give the title to Shirley MacLaine. She'd only need to change it slightly and it would work perfectly for her: *Shirley: Making the Last Life Good.*

After thinking about it, I realized that there could be a few things I've learned along the way that might be worth sharing with people.

The best example I know of someone who made the good life last was my Uncle Elmer. He never stopped laughing.

For his eightieth birthday, I flew Elmer and five of his friends from Los Angeles up to San Francisco on my plane. Even at that age he continued to love—and still play—the game of tennis, so I got us all tickets for a John McEnroe match at the San Francisco Civic Auditorium. At eighty, Elmer remained a terrific athlete. He could slice a tennis ball with such backspin that it would land on the opposite court and then bounce back over the net before his opponent had a chance to swing at it.

As we were heading back to the airport, I said, "Elmer, you've had a wonderful night. There's just one question we all want to ask you. You're eighty years old now. Can you still *do* it?"

Elmer looked across at me as if I'd just broken wind. As always, he was fashionably dressed and distinguished-looking—a proper gentleman whose boorish nephew had just asked him something quite rude.

"Murv," he said, "that question is beneath you. I will not dignify it with an answer." He spoke as if he had adenoids, in a pinched, nasal tone. (In fact, he sounded remarkably like Arthur Treacher. Perhaps that's one of the reasons I was always so fond of Arthur.)

But I wouldn't let it go. Smiling at him as I would a recalcitrant guest on my show, I said, "Come on, Elmer. Tell us the truth. Can you still *do* it?"

There was a long pause and then a sigh. "Well," he said finally, with just a glint of wickedness in his blue eyes, "did you ever try to stuff a marshmallow into a piggy bank?"

Barely able to catch my breath between spasms of laughter, I managed to tell our driver to stop the limo right where we were, which happened to be on one of the busiest sections of Market Street in downtown San Francisco. Everybody fell out of the car and onto the sidewalk, laughing uncontrollably. It took one very unhappy traffic cop to finally get us back in the car and on our way home.

Long and loving relationships are what the good life is really all about. I've been blessed with more than I can count. There is the family I was born into—my parents, my sister (who earlier this year finally lost her five-year struggle with cancer and emphysema), and my uncles and aunts. There's also the family I begat (sounds biblical, doesn't it?): my son, Tony, and my two beloved grandchildren, Farah Christian Griffin and Donovan Mervyn Griffin. (I should mention that most of the actual *work* in this begatting process was done by my beautiful daughter-in-law, Tricia.)

Then there's my other "family"—the friends who've played crucial parts at (and on) each of the different stages of my life. I've already told you about two of my oldest friends, Bob Murphy, whom I've known since the sixth grade, and Jean Barry (now Jean Plant), who recruited me for Freddy Martin when I was twenty-two years old.

Bob is now retired and, with his wife, Lynne, lives only minutes from me at the Beverly Hilton, so I get to see him all the time. In the sixties, Jean married a marvelous fellow named Harold Plant and they were together until he passed away five years ago. Although I loved Harold, Jean still teases me about the fact that when she first told me they were getting married, I said, "Aw Jean, do you *have* to?"

Mort Lindsey, the orchestra leader on *The Merv Griffin Show* for twenty-two years, has been my friend for more than five decades. Mort has been the arranger and conductor for everybody from Judy Garland to Barbra Streisand (he won an Emmy for her Central Park concert special). His wife, the former Judy Johnson, is a wonderful singer who started on *Your Show of Shows* and had a hit record with "Joltin' Joe DiMaggio." Judy replaced Doris Day as Les Brown's vocalist when Doris went to Hollywood. The Lindseys are among my closest friends in the world. Indeed, we've seen a lot of the world together. My orchestra also provided me with another one of the great and lasting friendships of my life, the trumpet-playing wild man, Jack Sheldon. We still make appearances together and Jack's off-beat (and devastatingly funny) sense of humor never fails to put me on the floor.

In addition to the Lindseys, the other couple that has become like family to me is Bob and Audrey Loggia. Bob is a terrific actor who you'll immediately recognize from his roles in more than a hundred films, including *Big* (Remember him dancing with Tom Hanks on the giant keyboard?), *Scarface*, *Prizzi's Honor*, and *Jagged Edge*.

I met Bob on a fluke. During the Korean War, he was doing basic training in the army at Fort Dix, New Jersey, having previously graduated from the University of Missouri's School of Journalism. Bob was on a weekend pass when a friend of his from college said, "Why don't you come to the Roosevelt Hotel with me? Merv Griffin sings there with the Freddy Martin Orchestra. He and his girlfriend, Judy Balaban, have these great parties."

He picked a good weekend to drop by. I'd invited Harry Belafonte and Judy had brought along her good friend Grace Kelly, for whom she would later become a bridesmaid. Bob now describes his memory of that night as "like dying and going to heaven."

Bob and I didn't stay in touch after that night. I'd followed his career from a distance, but he never appeared on my show. About ten years ago, Warren Cowan brought us together for a charity event and from that day forward, Bob and I have become the closest of friends. The only thing that could ever come between us is my friendship with his wife, Audrey. Periodically Bob will see the two of us laughing together and growl, "Hey, Griffin. She's *my* wife. You'd better watch yourself." At which point Mr. Tough Guy will stick his tongue out and we all collapse in hysterics.

I'm a very lucky guy. My life is never boring. I think one of the most important aspects of the "good life" is always being excited about getting out of bed in the morning. And I've always had that.

It doesn't occur to a lot of people to say, "I am going to structure my professional life so that I'm having fun. I'm not ever going into a profession that doesn't make me happy."

It's never occurred to me to do anything else. Why would you? If you treat your personal life as the only time you're allowed to be happy, then you're consigning yourself to half a life spent in misery.

That's never made sense to me. I treat my professional life the same way I do my personal life. And I measure success the same way—by how much fun I'm having, and by how much fun I'm creating around me.

Kemmons Wilson, the founder of the Holiday Inn chain, was once a guest on my show and he said something that I later had transcribed because I thought it was worth remembering: "Success is not money. Success is being happy with what you're doing. I think you're extremely successful if you're happy doing what you want to do. Everybody thinks that when you get successful, and the money that comes with it, you have the 'end answer.' You don't. Money is the most unimportant thing in the world. You've got to live the way you want to live. For some people that's $25,000 a year, for some it's $50,000 a year. But anything above that is just a way of keeping score."

One of the most exciting periods of my life was when I was in "discussions" with Donald about buying Resorts. What I didn't tell you was that at the same time the Resorts deal was happening, I was also building a home in La Quinta, a small desert community thirty miles east of Palm Springs.

It's the most thrilling thing in the world to build your own home. In a way it's a form of artistic expression, because you get to infuse it with your own personality and vision. I was sixty-two years old when we broke ground. After working hard for forty-one years, this was something I'd waited my entire adult life to be able to do.

As you can probably guess, I was intimately involved in every aspect of the design and construction, down to the smallest details. There were to be five residences in the compound, a main house and four guest houses, all in a Moroccan-themed design. All the stone for the floors was brought in from Spain and we used French limestone for the entrance to the main house. By August of 1988, the main house was largely complete; the furniture had arrived and was being stored in the stable and garages.

About two weeks before I was due to move in, the contractor decided to test the electrical load. He fired up the electricity for everything—lights, kitchen appliances, air conditioning—all at once.

And my house burned to the ground.

At the exact moment this was happening, I was on the other side of the country giving testimony before the New Jersey Casino Control Commission. I'd spent much of the day in the witness chair, before returning to the apartment that I was using at Resorts. When I walked in, my nephew, Mike Eyre (who'd just become a vice president of my company), had CNN on. I glanced at the screen and saw live coverage of a fire in progress somewhere in California. *Gosh, doesn't California have a lot of fires during the summer?*

Then I recognized my four round Moroccan guest houses which, fortunately, were untouched.

In utter horror, I shouted, "That's my house!" The fire had completely razed the main house, and its ruins filled the screen. Amazingly, CNN had arrived before the local fire department.

It took an entire year to rebuild in La Quinta.

Now here's where the story really gets weird. Around the same time that the La Quinta house burned down, there was also a fire in the kitchen of the Popeye's chicken franchise on the Resorts pier. The fire spread to adjacent buildings, causing extensive damage and rendering the casino helicopter pad located on the pier unusable for many months.

Given the timing of the two fires—both occurring right in the middle of my battle with Trump—I started thinking, "Gee, this guy really plays rough." Joking aside, of course it was all just an unfortunate coincidence.

Let me take you for a tour around the property in your mind's eye. There are 240 acres, most of them covered by tamarisk or palm trees. Ducks float on the lake, a man-made body of water with a fountain in the center. Every few minutes it sends streams of water as high as fifty feet in the air.

Inside the main house, there are thirty-foot-high ceilings and the walls are decorated with the works of French Impressionists and Colorists. The stone floors are inlaid with green and white marble. There are twelve-foot-high French windows that open out onto the terraces and the lake.

Back outside and past the four round guest houses, all with interiors painted in different pastel hues, is the tile-covered stable, which, at any given time, houses over fifty of my horses. And beyond the stable is the five-eighth-mile racetrack with its thatch-topped viewing stand. The same people who built the track at Hollywood Park designed it for me.

As Eva always said (and mind you, for her this was *really* swearing): "Darling, you built a frigging palace."

Waking up to the early-morning desert sunlight is magical. At seven, my housekeeper, Marylou Martinez, delivers me a tray with oatmeal, coffee, and five newspapers—the *New York Times*, the *Los Angeles Times*, *USA Today*, the *Palm Springs Desert Sun*, and the *Wall Street Journal*. I do the crossword puzzles—*in ink*—in the first four papers. Then I scan the headlines in all of them, before going back to sleep for another hour and a half. The second sleep of the morning is the best one of the day. Try it some time; you'll see what I mean.

Then Marylou returns with breakfast, usually something like an egg white omelet with goat cheese, and more coffee. By 9:30 A.M. I move down to a swivel chair by the lake, where I start my business calls on a cordless phone.

No two days are alike. Just like when I did my show, I get to improvise my life. One day I may get up and say, "I wonder how my racehorses are doing?" Then I'll go down to the stable and work with the horses for a few hours. The next day, I might think, "How's that marketing plan coming for the hotels?" And I'll get my staff together by phone and start working on that.

I call it "planned spontaneity."

Now, in the summer months you really don't want to be in La Quinta. The temperature gets up as high as 125 degrees. It's so hot that you feel like you need sunblock even in the shade.

That's when I head north to my ranch in Carmel Valley. The property is actually 1,700 feet high in the sky, on a mesa covered with ancient oak trees. I bought it more than twenty-five years ago from the Crocker banking family of San Francisco, the same people who were kind enough to give me that awful job when I was a kid.

Like my home in La Quinta, the ranch is visually stunning to visitors, yet for very different reasons. The contrast between the desert vistas of La Quinta and the breathtaking views of the mountains and the ocean in Carmel Valley couldn't be more dramatic.

The property itself is spread over fifty-seven acres, including one acre of Sauvignon Blanc grapes that are bottled as part of my Mount Merveilleux private label. There are six buildings on the property, including a number of guest houses, one of which Eva used following her divorce (and before she moved into my house).

Janice and Bob Emmett have been with me in Carmel for nineteen years. Janice is the cook, and Bob supervises the property. I've told you that Eva and I would often come back from long trips and collapse onto our respective couches. By midday, Janice would put two TV trays in front of us and, like zombies, we'd sit up and eat lunch, then fall immediately back to sleep until dinnertime. Five hours later, like Pavlov's dogs, we'd answer the dinner bell (still never leaving our couches) and repeat the same routine. One weekend we slept through nine movies on television. But the food was great.

I think the only word for the ranch is "Shangri-la."

Sometime in the late seventies, not long after I purchased it, I invited an eclectic group up to Carmel for the weekend. It included Cary and Barbara Grant, Gary Morton and Lucille Ball, Arthur and Kathryn Murray, and Armand and Frances Hammer. Like the President of the United States, Armand traveled with a personal photographer, so I have some lovely, albeit Armand-centric, snapshots of that weekend.

For three days, Cary and Barbara strolled the grounds holding hands and taking in the different views, each one more spectacular than the last. Barely speaking to anyone else (except to remain unfailingly polite), they walked around as if they'd just been transported to another world.

At one point, I said, "Come on, Cary, we're going down the mountain to John and Monique's for lunch." (John Gardiner was one of my oldest and dearest friends. We'd first met when both of us were in our twenties and John was teaching tennis to Bing Crosby. He founded the Senator's Cup tennis tourneys that I played in and MC'd more than a dozen times. John passed away two years ago and it was a very tough loss.)

Cary looked at me with a mystified expression and said, "Why would you ever *leave* this place?"

You know me, particularly when it involves food. "Cary," I said, firmly. "We've *got* to go get something to eat. I promise you the ranch will be here when we get back."

Lucy was just the opposite of Cary. Natural beauty be damned, she wasn't going to miss her soap operas. She stayed in bed so much that, only half-jokingly, I asked Janice to go check on her to be sure she was all right. When she knocked on the door, Janice heard Lucy's familiar throaty voice shout, "Whoever it is, come back after *All My Children*!" Eventually she'd appear, carrying a bag of Scrabble tiles with her. Lucy was a killer Scrabble player who would virtually accost you until you agreed to play with her. She was really good at getting lots of points out of three- and (not surprisingly) four-letter words.

Can you picture it? There was Lucille Ball hunched intently over a Scrabble board, while Cary Grant wandered around draped in a large caftan, looking like a Tibetan holy man. Every time Cary passed by, Lucy looked up and said, "There goes the great High Lama. Hello Lama!" Meanwhile, Armand, trailed everywhere by his photographer, kept trying to thrust himself into the picture. It was quite a scene.

There's one more story connected to that weekend that I want to tell you. It involves my Carmel neighbor, Clint Eastwood. Now I'd known Clint long before we lived near each other. We first met back in the fifties when he was still putting fish oil in his hair to make a ducktail in the back. Cats followed him everywhere.

Anyway, Clint and I had a long tradition of playing tricks on each other (actually, *I* played the tricks and he just got mad), so that when Cary decided to come up for the weekend, I had a perfect opportunity to pull something on my old pal. As it happened, Clint was at his place up in Sun Valley that weekend, but I had the number there, so I called him on Friday afternoon.

"Hey, Clint. It's Merv. When are you coming back?"

"Tomorrow." Even off screen, he is a man of few words.

"Great," I replied. "Cary Grant is going to be here for the weekend and he'll be here for dinner tomorrow night. I want you and Sondra [he was living with Sondra Locke by then] to come over and join us."

Clint said, "Merv, Cary Grant is *not* going to be at your house for dinner."

Years of successful gags had made him understandably skeptical of me, as I knew he would be. I also knew how much he admired Cary Grant, whom he'd never met, so the hook was baited perfectly. "If he's not going to be here, why would I take the trouble to call you up in Sun Valley?"

"Because you're a sonofabitch and these are the kinds of gags a sonofabitch like you pulls."

Patiently, I said, "Clint, trust me. He *will* be here."

He was unconvinced. "I don't believe you, but I'll call you as soon as we get back."

The next day Clint called me. His voice dripping with sarcasm, he asked, "Is *Cary* having a good time?"

"He sure is. He and Barbara are out walking on the lawn right now. So are Lucy and Gary, Armand and Frances, and Arthur and Kathryn. Will you and Sondra be joining us for dinner tonight?"

Furious that I'd checkmated him, Clint growled, "I'm going to chance it, but if this is one of your jokes, Griffin . . ." He used his best "I'm-Dirty-Harry-and-you'd-better-not-mess-with-me" tone to let me know that I was flirting with real trouble if Cary suddenly "disappeared" from my living room.

When he got to the gate, which is a bit far from the ranch house, he asked *again* over the intercom, "Okay, Merv. Is Cary Grant really there?" For the umpteenth time (and loving every minute of his uncertainty) I said, "Yes, Clint. He's *here*. I'll buzz you in."

When Clint walked into the living room, Cary leapt up in that fabulously graceful way he had about him. Before Clint could speak, he said, "I'm so happy to meet you. I admire your work as an actor. And I admire you as a director. You're quite wonderful." Cary had a tremendous gift for putting people at ease.

Do you know what Clint's reaction was? He turned to the whole roomful of people, who had grown very quiet, and said, "He talks just like he does in the movies."

Everybody roared. It was one of the truly great nights.

*A*s a youngster, I'd always enjoyed watching movies about rich people cruising the seven seas in their yachts, having glamorous adventures in exotic ports of call. I dreamed of owning a yacht myself someday and of being able to take the people I loved around the world on adventures of our own.

My yearning to spend time on the high seas was somewhat ironic, given that I am also deathly afraid of the water. Remember when I went up to Camp Imelda on the Russian River to visit my sister, Barbara? That was where I first heard the song "Where or When." It was also where I nearly drowned.

I'd gone swimming with a bunch of other kids out to a raft in the middle of a lake. When we got out there, each of us took turns diving off. When my turn came, I hit the water and then came back up under the raft. I could hear voices above me shouting, "He didn't come up!" Several adults then dove in and started frantically looking for me. Fortunately they found me quickly. I was pulled out from under the raft, gasping for air.

To this day, I don't go swimming. Every house I've ever owned has had a pool, and Tony is an excellent swimmer. But not me. I love the water—as long as I'm on top of it.

My first experience captaining a ship came in the sixties, when my show really started to do well. For the first time in my life, I could afford to splurge a little.

One weekend, I chartered a yacht in New York. It was the sister ship to the *Honey Fitz*, the Kennedy clan's famous vessel. I took Julann and Tony, my mother, Julann's two sisters and their husbands, and George and Tad Vosburgh (George was a longtime friend who produced *Jeopardy!*). We cruised Long Island Sound, swimming (except for me) and dining, singing and laughing, overwhelmed by the Gatsbyesque quality of the whole experience.

It was every bit as wonderful as I had imagined it would be when I was a child. But I knew that to make the dream complete, I'd need my own boat.

Twenty years later, after selling my company to Coca-Cola, I was deluged by yacht brokers who somehow had gotten wind of my dream and knew that I could now afford to realize it. They inundated me with glossy brochures filled with photographs of yachts for sale. I just tossed them in the circular file until, one day, a picture caught my eye. I sat and stared at it for a long time. The next day I phoned the broker and arranged to fly to Fort Lauderdale where the yacht was docked. When I arrived, he walked me along the dock looking at various other possibilities, none of which appealed to me. Then we arrived at "her." She was, quite literally, my dreamboat. I boarded this 127-foot, three-story beauty and stood in the middle of the main salon. I swear I could hear the song "You're Mine You."

Turning to Ronnie Ward, who was with me as always, I said, "Do you think you can get all this furniture reupholstered and the interior recarpeted in one month?"

Ronnie, who never shrinks from a challenge, immediately replied, "Yes."

Away he went to meet upholsterers and drapemakers, and quickly the ship began to get a new face. I flew back to Los Angeles and went directly to the big design center in West Hollywood. The majority of materials I wanted couldn't be delivered immediately, but those they had in stock were almost as beautiful. I went on a four-day shopping spree for my new "girl."

My next step was to phone Tony, who was fishing near Key Largo with Trisha and their eight-month-old baby daughter (and my first grandchild), Farah.

"Tony, I want you to fly to Fort Lauderdale right away and meet someone. It's urgent." I told him nothing more.

Tony and his pal Guy Manos, the world champion skydiver, took off immediately in Guy's plane and got to Fort Lauderdale a little over an hour after our phone call. He met the broker, who rushed him to the boat without telling him why. When he got there, Tony called me from his cell phone and said, "Dad, what are you doing?"

"I bought it."

Even without the cell phone, I could hear him whooping and shouting all the way across the country.

The *Griff* was delivered to me in Atlantic City one month to the day after I'd first laid eyes on her. Ronnie, as usual, had done a flawless job in outfitting her for our maiden voyage.

I assembled a great British crew (the Brits are born to the water), headed by Captain Mike Mullin, a gifted sailor who had spent most of his life at sea. We cruised up the Atlantic Coast, stopping to visit Bob and Audrey Loggia at their summer home on Martha's Vineyard. The Loggias were also thrilled with my new acquisition and they would become the perfect traveling mates on all my future voyages. Over the course of the next seven years, we would make eleven trips together.

Days later, out in the middle of the Atlantic, I received a call informing me that Eva had died.

You know how you can hear something and it doesn't quite register? Like when President Kennedy was killed or Princess Diana died in a car crash, there are times when the brain simply can't process overwhelming information—it needs time to sort it out.

Eva's death was one of those times. My immediate reaction was identical to when I was told that my father had died suddenly of a heart attack. It must be a mistake. It *had* to be.

After a series of tortured ship-to-shore calls, I pieced together what had happened.

Eva had been in Baja California with her former stepdaughter, Mary Jameson, when she'd slipped and fallen in the bathtub. Although she was in pain, Eva refused treatment in Mexico, insisting on flying home to Los Angeles where she could see her own doctors at Cedars-Sinai Hospital. That much I had known before we even left port in Atlantic City. But I'd been assured that it was only a hip injury and that she might need surgery for that. There was never any suggestion it could be something more serious. Had there been, I never would have made the trip.

I need to explain why Eva wasn't with me on a voyage she surely would have loved.

Over the ten years since her divorce from Frank Jameson, Eva and I had been together far more often than we'd been apart. But there were periods of separation where we saw other people. Sadly, this was one of those times.

In my heart I know that we would have healed our relationship. We'd worked out our problems in the past because, no matter what, we never stopped loving each other.

I know that there's one more question you're probably asking, and I'll try to answer it as best I can.

More than anything else, the reason Eva and I never got married was because I couldn't forget something Julann said soon after our divorce: "I married my best friend and it was the end of a beautiful friendship."

Our other problems may have been worked out over time, but I was reluctant to make the same mistake twice.

Eva truly was my best friend. And, in the end, I lost her anyway.

The happiness of finally realizing my lifelong dream of owning a great boat was overwhelmed by the devastation I felt at the news of Eva's sudden death. We somberly returned to port, arriving back in Atlantic City on July 6, my seventieth birthday. The longer I live, the more I've come to understand that the composition of life is great joy and great despair, often in a single moment.

I flew back to Los Angeles for Eva's memorial service. Nancy Reagan came with me; I wouldn't have made it through that day without her. She's been a tremendously supportive and compassionate friend to me, not only in the immediate aftermath of Eva's death, but in the months and years that followed.

Since the president's illness worsened, Nancy has had the very lonely role of caregiver. She never complains, but I know it exacts an enormous toll on her. We talk almost every day and I periodically succeed in coaxing her out of the house for either lunch or dinner. Last year we saw the revival of *Kiss Me, Kate* in Los Angeles. It was the first time I'd seen her enjoy an evening out in such a long time. We also have the same birthday, so it's now become an annual tradition for us to share it together, usually with a quiet lunch at the Beverly Hilton.

Little more than a year after Eva's death, I was diagnosed with prostate cancer.

My first reaction was no reaction at all.

When I told my son, Tony, and Ronnie Ward, they both cried. I thought, "What the hell is the matter with them?" I wasn't even interested in it. I simply gave it none of my attention.

There's that old joke about denial being a river in Egypt, but this is the way I've always been about rough news. I don't dwell on anything. Give me a problem and I'll try my best to solve it. If I can't, I just go on to the next thing. Turn the page.

I asked my doctor, Skip Holden, if I was in any immediate danger. He said, "No, but . . ."

Before he could finish the sentence, I said, "Good, then I'm going out on my boat. I'll call you when I get back."

We took the *Griff* to the Mediterranean and I brought my chef along for the trip. I ate like a sonofabitch and thought, "I'll just force the damn thing out with a little crème brûlée." (It's too bad it didn't work. I'd be marketing it today as the world's tastiest pharmaceutical.)

The first stop on the trip was the Cannes Film Festival, which I'd never been to before. After the festival concluded (*Secrets & Lies* earned the top prize, the Palme d'Or, and the Coen brothers won the best directing award for *Fargo*), I called Bob and Audrey Loggia, who were staying at a friend's house in France. I invited them to join me on a month-long voyage along the Italian coast. They had their bags packed before we hung up the phone.

I also asked my friend Princess Elizabeth of Yugoslavia to join us, knowing that she needed a break from the extraordinary work she was doing in her war-torn homeland.

Elizabeth is the daughter of Prince Paul, the Prince Regent of Yugoslavia, and Princess Olga of Greece. On her father's side she is the great-great-granddaughter of Karageorge, who led the Serbs in their insurrection against the Turks in 1804. From her mother, she is a descendant of Catherine the Great. She is also the second cousin to Prince Charles and to Queen Sophie of Spain. Yet for much of her lifetime, Elizabeth has been a refugee from her ancestral homeland. As a three-year-old prior to World War II, she was sent to live in Africa for her safety. Eventually she was brought to America where she became a U.S. citizen.

As an adult, she started the Princess Elizabeth Foundation, whose mission has been to transport medical supplies, food, clothing, and blankets to refugee camps in her native country. Even before the fall of the communist government, she snuck in and out of the country dozens of times, often at great personal risk.

Before joining us on the boat, Elizabeth had been working secretly in Belgrade to buy prosthetic limbs for children who had been maimed by land mines.

She arrived exhausted, but ready for some well-earned rest. We cruised along the Italian coast for a month, starting in the northern villages and working our way down to Corsica and Sardinia. Tony, Tricia, and baby Farah flew in to join us on what became one of the most enjoyable trips I've ever had.

Although it couldn't cure my cancer, that voyage helped me begin the healing process after Eva's death. Out on the water that she loved so much, I remembered the joyous trips we'd made together and, for the first time in almost a year, I was able to smile again when I talked about her.

All good things come to an end, so after two months on the water, I flew back to face the music. Prior to my departure, Skip Holden had listed the various treatment options for prostate cancer, the so-called champagne of cancers (I kept waiting for the bubbles). These included both radiation and surgery. But before they'll do either, you're given a hormone pill so that your body has a chance to fight the cancer on its own. When I later mentioned this treatment on *Larry King Live*, I quipped, "Hey Larry, did you ever have a hormone?" The joke went right by him. (I've since joined Hom-onyms Anonymous. *"Hello, my name is Merv. Stop me before I pun again."*)

I told Skip that I was ready to start radiation and, in September of 1996, I began the five-day-a-week treatment as an outpatient at Cedars-Sinai. Every morning for seven weeks, Ronnie picked me up at 7:00 A.M. and drove me to the hospital. They pointed the radiation at me for five minutes and, bang, that was it. You're in and you're out. And I got weekends off.

After several weeks, I had occasional moments of exhaustion, so I took half-hour naps, like a little baby. Other than that, it was surprisingly easy.

I was lucky because they caught it early with a PSA (prostate specific antigen) screening. At my age, I was tested regularly. After the treatments were complete, I decided to share my story with the media, in part as an incentive for other men to get tested early.

I called Steve Coz, editor-in-chief of the *National Enquirer,* because I knew how he would handle it. Steve is a tough guy, but he's scrupulously honest. I called him and said, "Steve, I don't usually do this, but I've got a scoop for you." I told him what it was.

He was quiet for a moment. Then he said, "Will you tell that same story to my reporter?"

"Absolutely."

I figured that if I hadn't given the story to them first, it would have only been a matter of time before there were banner headlines in the supermarkets screaming, "Merv Griffin Dying of Cancer—Distraught Vanna Says, 'I Can't Turn Letters When My Heart Is Breaking.' "

The *Enquirer* printed a very fair and accurate piece. Within twenty-four hours all of the so-called mainstream media had picked it up and run with it. They don't like to admit it, but that happens a lot. As I recall, much of the original reporting on the Monica Lewinsky story was done by the *Enquirer,* a fact that even the *New York Times* was eventually forced to acknowledge.

Three years later Skip told me that my PSA level was again on the high side, but that it was nothing to worry about.

Because prostate cancer is so slow-growing, most experts believe that careful monitoring is all that's necessary in older men. The theory is that after a certain age you will die of something else before the cancer becomes lethal. (There's a happy thought.)

So, what did I do? I bought a new boat. Hey, it worked the last time.

I flew to Majorca to pick up the *Griff II*, having sold the first *Griff* just the week before. She was another beauty—165 feet long, four stories high, with a crew of fourteen. Over the next three years I made many trips with her, including another two months spent cruising along the coasts of Spain, France, and Italy. I confess that after that last trip, as wonderful as it was, I was beginning to have a sense of déjà vu. If there's one thing I've come to understand about my life, it's that whenever I start to repeat myself, it's time to move on.

So, earlier this year, when someone made me an offer I couldn't refuse, I sold the *Griff II*. *Turn the page.*

*T*he wacky comedian Rip Taylor once told this joke on my show:

Q: What do you call a short pyschic who just broke out of prison?
A: A small medium at large!

I've always been interested in astrology and psychic phenomena, especially after meeting a number of famous astrologers like Carroll Righter and Sydney Omarr and psychics like Jeane Dixon, Kenny Kingston, and the Amazing Kreskin when they were guests on my talk show. (Think about this: Kreskin used to get lost on the way to my studio.)

I don't have any firsthand experience with the psychic world, but I know someone who does. In the spring of 1982, even before she was considered as a possibility to replace Susan Stafford on *Wheel of Fortune* (Susan hadn't given her notice yet), Vanna White left her home in North Carolina and flew to Palm Springs on a modeling assignment.

Strolling through the town before her modeling job began, Vanna passed a sign that advertised psychic readings and decided to give it a try. In the course of a long session, she was told the following: "In November you will sign a long-term television contract with a man whose last name is Schwartz." The psychic had difficulty determining the man's first name, finally deciding that it was "McCoy." Vanna, who had no television experience at that point, thought the reading was interesting, but gave it little credence.

Six months later Vanna was back in Los Angeles, signing a long-term television contract with a man named Schwartz—*Murray* Schwartz, then the president of my company.

I can't explain how that happened, but it did.

Every day before breakfast, I go to the Calendar Section of the *Los Angeles Times* and read my horoscope to see if I'm going to live through the day. If it says, "You're going to drop dead today," I'd eat a bigger breakfast.

I've personally seen astrology work. And Ronnie Ward was a witness to it; he was in the room with me when it happened.

Here's the story: I'd heard about a woman named Dana (pronounced "Danna") Haynes who lives in Palm Springs and who was said to be a highly skilled astrologer. I arranged to have her do a chart reading and, as I mentioned, Ronnie was also present as an observer. She came to my office in Los Angeles. We chatted briefly about some of the successful forecasts she'd made in the past, then she started looking at my chart.

"Do you plan any travel?" asked Dana.

"In my plane." Having long ago outgrown the Beechcraft, I now owned a Challenger jet that could make transatlantic trips, although it needed to take on fuel along the way. The refueling stop would be Newfoundland, in the town of Gander.

"And what day will you be traveling?" I looked at Ronnie, who knew the date in his head, and told it to her.

"Don't go."

I studied her face. There was nothing the slightest bit ambiguous about her expression. She was clearly serious.

"I have to go," I said, wondering if that was really true. "Maybe I could look at it over the Internet, with a live Web cam. . . ."

"Well, can you fly directly from Los Angeles to Ireland?" She kept looking imploringly from me to the chart and back again, as if hoping I would change my mind or the stars would change their meaning.

"No, we have to stop for fuel, why?"

She said, "Well, you're eventually going to be safe, but you will have a terribly dangerous landing in Gander."

"But we're *going* to be safe?"

"Yes, but you'll be very uncomfortable." She was still scrutinizing my chart. "What did you say you were going to be doing in Ireland?"

"Looking at a house to buy, as a possible hotel."

"Check the water in the well outside. And the pipes that leak inside the main house. Is it a very old house?"

"Yes," I said, thinking that there's something wrong with the plumbing in almost any house, so she was very likely to be right. "It's an Irish manor house. It's over two hundred years old."

"Check the water," she repeated. "There's a problem."

That was the end of the reading. I thanked her and she left.

After she was gone, I said to Ronnie, "Why would she be so specific? If those two predictions don't happen, who will ever believe her again?"

A month later, I flew to Ireland, along with my dear friends Mort and Judy Lindsey. It was in the middle of the night when we were approaching our refueling stop, so my pilot, John, came on the intercom to wake us up. "Merv, we're going to have a little bumpy landing here. There's some rough weather in Gander."

We began our descent and the turbulence was really bad. As we came in for the landing, just before the wheels touched the ground, John shoved the gears back up and we shot into the air again, right back into the turbulence.

I looked at Ronnie, whose face was white (as I'm sure mine was), and we both said, "Dana." He carefully made his way up to the cockpit to investigate. The Lindseys and I gripped our armrests and held on.

When Ronnie came back, his eyes were wide and he spoke in a flat tone, as if he couldn't believe the words he now heard himself saying. "They cleared us to the wrong runway. Had we landed there, we probably wouldn't have made it. The crosswinds were so strong, the plane would have been blown completely off the landing strip."

I could hear John through the open cockpit door screaming at the control tower. "Is anyone *awake* down there?! Are you paying any *attention?!!* You could have killed us!"

Eventually we were given the coordinates for the right runway and we landed safely, although everyone was extremely shaken by the experience.

The next day I traveled to the town of Loughrae, twenty minutes outside of Galway to inspect that two-hundred-year-old manor house, which I had seen once before, many years ago.

I remembered it vividly. In the sixties I'd gone to Ireland, the land of my ancestors (my maternal great grandparents were Thorntons from Clonmel, County Tipperary, and my father's family, the Griffins, were from Liscannor, County Clare), to do a television special. One of my guests was John Huston, the larger-than-life director of films such as *Treasure of the Sierra Madre* and *The African Queen.*

While I was in Ireland, Huston invited me to visit him at St. Clerans, his magnificent estate near Galway. John had purchased the eighteenth century Georgian manor house for £10,000 in 1954, shortly after he'd finished shooting *The African Queen.*

Over the next two years he spent fifty times that amount restoring the house and filling it with eclectic items from all over the globe. The master bedroom included a hand-carved canopied bed from Florence, a chest of drawers he'd found in a French cathedral, a thirteenth-century Greek statue, and two Louis XIV chairs. John had a traditional Japanese bath with shoji doors and mats installed in his bathroom. The Red Sitting Room got its name after he had the walls re-covered with bright red silks and placed Chinese porcelain drum stools on either side of its entryway.

On his travels, John had collected many objets d'art, including Arezzo, Etruscan, and Magna Grecia ceramics, as well as paintings by Monet, Juan Gris, and Morris Graves. All of these expensive pieces eventually made their way to St. Clerans.

The minute I saw St. Clerans, I loved everything about it and the way he lived in it. He regaled me with stories of the many lavish dinner parties he'd given in the formal dining room where, on any given night, you'd find men like Marlon Brando, Paul Newman, or Montgomery Clift dressed in black tie and women such as Elizabeth Taylor and Olivia de Havilland clad in long, elegant gowns. They would dine by the light of fifty candles, a fire roaring on the hearth, the conversation as sparkling as the crystal. John said it was "as beautiful and fantastic as a masquerade."

After owning it for eighteen years, John had finally been forced to sell St. Clerans due to the great expense of maintaining it. He later wrote, "The decision was forced on me. I sometimes feel that I sold a little of my soul when I let St. Clerans go." St. Clerans had a succession of owners after John, including the two American families who had been using it as a vacation home and had now put it back on the market.

Now there I was, back in Ireland after a thirty-year absence, once again walking past the giant stone lions that guarded the main entryway of St. Clerans. It was every bit as magical a place as I'd remembered it to be, although it had clearly suffered some in the years since Mr. Huston had been lord of the manor.

Back outside, I encountered an old caretaker who lived on the grounds and chatted with him about the property.

"That's a beautiful waterfall," I said, referring to a stretch of the clear river that runs through the property. "We must have wonderful water in the house."

He gave me a funny look, but said nothing.

Picking up on it, I pressed him. "Is something the matter with the water?"

Knowing that I was interested in the house and that his candor could jeopardize the sale (and maybe his job), he admitted, very reluctantly, "Well, sir, you see the well is down. The pipes are all corroded. We don't *have* water right now."

"Oh my God," I said, stunned. Dana had been right again. I still bought St. Clerans, but until we repaired the water system, I only drank Evian in the house . . .

Fixing the water wasn't the only thing that needed to be done to convert St. Clerans into a world-class destination. I approached the restoration of the house with the same enthusiasm that John Huston brought to the task forty years earlier. Unlike John, however, my intention was to return St. Clerans to its original Irish splendor, rather than use it as a showcase for exotic art from almost everywhere *but* Ireland.

I completely redid the interior. Even though I had a staff of designers and no formal design experience of my own, I knew exactly what I wanted. For example, the Irish practice of hanging pictures high on the walls made no sense to me. I got a stiff neck from looking up at the art, so I made them lower everything to eye level. Sometimes the best design sense is common sense.

Picture this scene: I was stretched out on the floor of the great living room of St. Clerans surrounded by books with photographs of different rooms, swatches of fabric for the drapes, samples of paint for the walls, wallpaper panels, and pieces of carpet. The designers were all hovering over me, a bit tremulously, as I told them what I wanted done. Periodically, one of them would raise a protest, "But, Mr. Griffin, you can't *mix* stripes with checks. It doesn't match."

"Trust me," I said. "It will."

Meanwhile, in the midst of all this chaos, Ronnie Ward called me from the other room.

"Merv, come in here. You've got to see what's on television."

I picked myself up off the floor and went into the next room, where Ronnie was watching what appeared to be a cooking show on the BBC.

"What's so important?" I asked.

"Just watch this guy, Merv. He's great. We should sign him."

I looked at the screen. Ainsley Harriott was a 6'4" chef from London whose clever monologues even made chopping vegetables interesting and funny to watch. According to Ronnie, his program, *Ready Steady Cook*, was a huge hit in England. I could see why.

"You're right, Ron," I said, chuckling at Harriott's witty patter over chicken pâté. "Let's see if we can get him."

Ronnie got immediately on the phone to Ernie Chambers, the former producer of my show who now ran my production unit, and made arrangements for him to fly to London from L.A. I went back to my swatches and samples.

Two months later, I'd completely redone twelve bedrooms and the dining room of St. Clerans and my production team had signed a syndication deal for *The Ainsley Harriott Show* with Buena Vista Television in America. As my old friend Lucille Ball used to say, "If you want something done, give it to a busy person."

Today, St. Clerans is one of the most critically acclaimed and highly photographed houses in the world. But the biggest vote of confidence for my restoration came from one of its former residents, John Huston's daughter Anjelica.

Anjelica Huston has mixed emotions about growing up in Galway. In interviews she's talked about the idyllic setting and her memories of riding horses and playing games in the fields. While all that was true, there was also a darker side to her childhood, which she's only rarely discussed. Anjelica and her mother, John's fourth wife, didn't live in the main house. They shared a stable house a half mile away, while inside the manor John entertained a series of mistresses.

When I called Anjelica to tell her that I'd bought her childhood home, she was delighted. She said, "I don't know anybody in the world who I would rather have own that house other than you, Merv."

Anjelica has never been back to St. Clerans, although she's seen pictures of the restoration. In her honor, I've converted her childhood playroom/studio into a guest bedroom and named it the Anjelica Suite.

Ironically, I haven't been back to St. Clerans in three years myself, although it's not because of John Huston's lingering presence.

The reason is someone named Charlie Chan.

All my life I've never been without a dog. Even when I first moved to New York City and only had a one-room, fourth-floor walk-up apartment, I kept one. There was no elevator and my dog always had to go to the bathroom. Instead of trudging up and down four flights of stairs, I went out on my balcony and put him on the roof next door. This was in the fifties when the Soviet Union had just launched a dog into space. So, like everyone else in those days, I blamed the Russians for the mysterious rooftop droppings.

Four years ago, as a Christmas present to myself, I decided to get a third dog. At the time, my two older dogs, Patrick, a purebred Irish setter, and Lobo, a half-Malamute, half-wolf mix, were living primarily on the ranch in Carmel.

It was a Saturday and I'd been visiting Tony, Tricia, and my grandchildren at their home in Malibu. On the way back to the Beverly Hilton, I stopped into the Pet Headquarters, a wonderful pet shop in Malibu. I used to drop by there quite often because they're so sweet with their animals. On weekends they take them out of their cages and let kids come in and play with them. Cats, dogs, everything.

When I walked into the store I ran into my friend Linda Foster (who is both the wife and writing partner of David Foster, the Grammy Award–winning producer, composer, and arranger). There was a crowd gathered in the center of the pet store, and they were all looking down at something on the floor, but I couldn't see what it was. So I asked Linda what was going on.

"Oh Merv," she said, looking a bit downcast. "If I didn't already have eight dogs at home . . ." Her voice trailed off wistfully. She suggested that I push through the crowd and see for myself.

There on the floor, in the center of a circle of adoring adults and children, was a three-month-old Chinese Shar-Pei puppy. I don't know if you're familiar with the breed, but it's very different from almost any other kind of dog in the world.

The name "Shar-Pei" literally means "sand-skin." Translated more loosely it's also come to mean "rough, sandy coat," which describes the unique qualities of the Shar-Pei's skin. It hangs loose in folds on certain parts of their bodies, giving rise to the nickname "wrinkle dog."

There's an amazing story about this breed. Almost two thousand years old, it had survived everything from Genghis Khan to the Boxer Rebellion. But when the Chinese communists came to power in the late forties, they decided that dogs as pets were a bourgeois decadence, so they systematically eliminated millions of dogs from the cities and the countryside. Twenty years later, when the U.S. restored diplomatic relations with China, animal lovers in the West were shocked to discover the devastating effects of this policy of canine genocide. The Shar-Pei had been all but eliminated. If it were not for a dog breeder in Hong Kong named Matgo Law who, in 1973, issued a worldwide plea to save the Shar-Pei, it's entirely possible that it would be extinct today.

I knew none of this when I saw that adorable, crinkly-faced puppy with his unusually long hair on the floor of the pet shop. In fact, I only saw him for about five seconds. That was all it took. I walked to the front of the store, got out my credit card, and said, "Whatever that dog costs, I'll take him."

It was love at first sight. He came home with me that afternoon and he hasn't left my side for four years.

I was looking for a famous Chinese name to give him. I decided on Charlie Chan because I was a big fan of the Warner Oland–Sidney Toler detective movies of the thirties and also because I couldn't think of Mao Tse-tung's name at the time. Good thing too.

I got on to the subject of Charlie because of St. Clerans. As I said, he's the reason I haven't been back there since shortly after the renovation. Here's why: like all island nations, the Irish have a strict quarantine policy for pets entering the country. They are isolated for *six months* before they're released back to their owners.

When I flew to Ireland while Charlie was still a puppy, I was unaware of the rigidity of this policy. When the plane landed, I tried to take Charlie onto the tarmac to pee and a man from the Minister for Agriculture and Food stopped us. He told me that Charlie would have to go back on the plane and, I guess, *go* back on the plane, as well.

I don't get angry very often, but this idiot really got my Irish up.

"Let me see if I understand you, *pal* (just a tip—when I call someone my "pal," they're definitely not), you'll allow those horses over there [a plane across the field was letting off some racehorses from England] to come into your country when they could very well have mad cow disease, but you won't let my dog take a leak on the runway?"

I fought their absurd policy all the way up to the president's office, but to no avail. I even spoke to our former ambassador to Ireland, Jean Kennedy Smith. She was also helpless to do anything, but told me to keep fighting. "Merv, you're absolutely right," said Jean. "They even made *me* put my dogs in quarantine when I arrived here and they both died." Personally, I think there's an even greater scrutiny of American pets than there is of animals from other countries. We have the healthiest, most "vetted" animals in the world, yet that doesn't seem to matter when it comes to their travel abroad.

Ireland is a beautiful country and I love it dearly. If you don't have a pet, I hope you'll go and stay at St. Clerans. But while you're there, ask the front desk for the number of the Irish Ministry for Agriculture and Food and let them know how you feel about their policy. I won't charge you for the call.

Since 1987, I've bought and sold fourteen hotels. Throughout this period, the value of my hotel portfolio has increased significantly. But my joy has always come from taking a property and remaking it into something more attractive, more exciting and, yes, more lucrative.

For the time being, I'm down to three: the Beverly Hilton, St. Clerans, and the Scottsdale Hilton Resort and Villas in Arizona.

I love running the hotels and there are so many priceless moments that happen, most of which I can't tell you about without violating my hotelier's oath. (There really *isn't* an oath, but if there were, it would probably be just one word: SHHHHH!)

There are a few stories that I can talk about. Here's one:

You probably remember Heidi Fleiss, the famed Hollywood Madam. What you may not recall is the hotel that she was arrested in was the Beverly Hilton; we don't include that happy fact in our brochures. When I got the call that she'd been arrested and led away by the vice squad, I couldn't help but wonder, "Did she charge *extra* for the handcuffs?"

Then there's the satisfaction that comes from being able to provide a home away from home for your friends. Wayne Gretzky, the legendary "Great One" of hockey, has become a good friend over the years, especially because I helped him to meet his wife, the beautiful Janet Jones. Janet was a dancer in the eighties when Wayne agreed to serve as a judge on my show, *Dance Fever.* I introduced them and they've been together ever since. Not long ago, Wayne's people called Shaun Robinson, the manager of the Scottsdale Hilton, and tried to reserve a few rooms for Wayne, Janet, and their children. We were overbooked, but he managed to find them their rooms. But in the time it took Shaun to get back to Wayne's office, they'd already booked them elsewhere. Wayne's assistant was grateful to Shaun for his efforts, but said that it would now be awkward to call the other hotel back and cancel. Apparently Wayne overheard the call and quickly interceded, saying, "We only stay at Merv's hotel." That's loyalty.

A few months ago, I sold the Givenchy Hotel and Spa in Palm Springs, thus making it impossible for me to continue honoring one of the oddest requests I've ever had since getting into the hotel business.

You may remember that several years ago, Robert Downey, Jr., the highly talented and equally troubled young actor, was arrested at a Palm Springs hotel for possession of narcotics.

Want to take a guess whose hotel it was?

Anyway, Downey's publicist called and asked me if I was angry. I said, "No, I just hope he's getting the help he needs." (As of this writing, I gather he's been clean and sober for several years, which is terrific news.)

The funniest part about the whole thing was that we had people calling from all over the world wanting to stay in room 311, the bungalow where Downey was arrested. I'm not sure if they were hoping he'd left something behind (he didn't) or if it was simply morbid fascination, but it didn't let up for quite a while. Tourists even stopped outside just to get their pictures taken next to the hotel sign. I even thought about changing the numbers on another twenty rooms to "311."

I'm really sorry if this ruins your vacation plans, but now that I've sold the Givenchy, I can't get you into room 311 anymore. However, if you're interested in the Heidi Fleiss suite at the Beverly Hilton, I'm sure we can work something out. Of course, that's what *she* said too . . .

I don't watch *Survivor.* I have no interest in it. If something requires cheating, lying, and cruelty to other people to stay on top, it's nothing I want any part of. Where's the joy in that? Merely surviving has never been my purpose in life.

There's another word that makes more sense to me—it's the word "thrive." The dictionary defines "thrive" in three ways: "1) to grow vigorously: flourish; 2) to gain in wealth or possessions: prosper; 3) to progress toward or realize a goal." That's how I've always lived my life. Not just to survive, but to thrive. I don't define my success by personal wealth. My measure of success is when I'm as happy in the rest of my life as I am in my professional life.

Nor does my happiness depend on living up to people's various ideas of who the "real" Merv Griffin is. If it did, they would have had to commit me years ago. Since the day I first went on the air, people have asked, "What is Merv *really* like?" Just like they asked it about Jack Paar and Johnny Carson. Yes, there are other parts of my life and I understand why people are curious, especially because I never injected my personal opinions into my show. Neither did I reveal my religion or my politics. I believe there must be some division between what is public and what is private. If you don't leave something for yourself, who are you?

I've been in the public eye for more than fifty years as Merv Griffin, not as somebody else's creation. I've never pretended to be someone I wasn't. If there were anything really important that people didn't know about me by now, then I would have to be the world's greatest actor. Forget Brando, forget Hoffman, forget De Niro—I would have to be the best.

When I look back, my whole life has been about challenging myself. I was quoted once as saying that "retirement is what you do after you're dead." For me, that's really true.

I've always seemed to reinvent myself every couple of years. I surprised a lot of people when I sold *Wheel* and *Jeopardy*, even though it was for a big amount of money and it was the right decision financially. I surprised people when I sold Resorts, because I was so involved in all the aspects of marketing it. If somebody knocked on my door tomorrow and offered me a trophy price for the Beverly Hilton, I'd think about it seriously. As much as I love that hotel, I'm not attached to it. I'm attached to *people*, not things.

Larry Cohen has brought me projects where I could make a lot of money, and I've just looked at him and said, "I'm not going to have fun with that" or "That's going to be too tough on my people," so we've passed on them. I think that's part of the reason why people stick with me for such a long time, because it goes beyond just making a profit.

My days now are just like they were when I was doing *The Merv Griffin Show*. When I hosted my show, I loved the wonderful variety of guests, music, and subject matter, as well as the ability to improvise a question or a song whenever I wanted. Today, it's the same with all my businesses—variety and spontaneity. My life is still being ad-libbed.

When I'm at the Beverly Hilton, I stay in an apartment on one of the upper floors overlooking the corner of Wilshire and Santa Monica Boulevards, the busiest intersection in the world.

My "commute" to work begins with Marguerita, my housekeeper who's been with me for more than a dozen years, bringing me my coffee and newspapers. Then I read the daily schedule that my infallible (and unflappable) assistant, Michael Hathaway, had faxed up to me the night before.

Promptly at 10:00 A.M., Ronnie Ward, who's now vice president of the Griffin Group, arrives at my door and we review what's on tap for the day. Then, Ronnie, Charlie, and I take the elevator down to my office, one floor below the lobby. By the way, the Beverly Hilton is now the most renowned and successful hotel in Southern California, not to mention the largest employer and taxpayer in Beverly Hills.

The morning hours are spent on the phone to my New York office, talking to Gloria Redlich, who has now been an integral part of my professional and personal life for forty-two years, or to my CEO, Larry Cohen, unless he's with me in Los Angeles. (It's often hard to keep up with Larry's whereabouts, since he travels so often. Because of his peripatetic movements, Princess Elizabeth dubbed him "Coast to Coast Cohen," a name he's deservedly proud of.)

After lunch, I'll often meet with the key members of my film and television production team: Ernie Chambers and Jim Bradley. Jim has worked with me in virtually every capacity since he started out writing cue cards on my show in the late sixties. He is more than a valued colleague; he's a trusted friend whom I've relied on gratefully for more than thirty years.

As of this moment, four of our top projects are in various stages of pre- or post-production: *Shade*, a feature film starring Gabriel Byrne, Melanie Griffith, and Sylvester Stallone that will be released in 2003; *Barnes*, a feature film based on a short story by James Michener that he personally gave me permission to produce shortly before his death; a remake of *Hello, Dolly!* for television; and a fabulous big screen story based on the life of George Hamilton's mother, Anne, a glamorous southern belle who was linked socially with Hollywood legends like Clark Gable and Humphrey Bogart.

Later in the day, I'll sit down with my nephew, Michael Eyre, and talk about what's on the calendar for Merv Griffin Productions, my event management company. Under Michael's talented leadership, MGP has organized special events ranging from the Golden Globes parties to a film premiere on the deck of an aircraft carrier to the launch party for the Rolling Stones North American tour.

Before going back upstairs for the night, I'll often get a call telling me that one of my racehorses, Thunderlad or Mon Ange (among more than twenty others), had a great workout that day.

There's always so much going on and I enjoy it all. But I'm always reminded of that brilliant John Lennon line, "Life is what happens to you while you're busy making other plans." My life today is full of lots of plans, yet dependent on none.

My real pride (and joy) comes from seeing Tony's success as a filmmaker; his short film *Squint*, which he wrote, produced, directed, and starred in (shades of Orson Welles), just won first prize at the prestigious Malibu Film Festival. You remember that Oscar I never won? I may yet get to hold one, but I think it will be Tony's. And I'll be the guy sitting in the audience bawling his eyes out.

My other moments of pure pleasure come from watching my beloved grandchildren, Farah and Donovan, discover the world, either in our travels together, or right in their own backyard.

Let me preface this final observation by saying that I feel great and that I plan on being around for quite a while. But I've never been afraid of death. If you live your life in fear of dying, you might as well be dead already.

So lately, in idle moments, I've been toying with what I'd like my headstone to read. (You don't think I'm going to let anybody *else* write my last line, do you?)

There's always the hypochondriac's epitaph: "I *told* you I was sick." Or perhaps the talk show host's final exit line would be more appropriate: "I will *not* be right back after this message."

Hey, you know what? I've just figured out what I want it to say:

"Stay tuned."

A Picture Is Worth a Billion Words

1

2

3

4

5

6

7

8

9

10

11

12

13

Photo Captions

Dedication page: (clockwise from left) Farah Griffin, Tricia Griffin, Merv (holding picture of Tony Griffin and Elmer Griffin), and Donovan Griffin—Beverly Hills Country Club

Chapter One: Merv, age four—San Mateo

Chapter Two: Merv and Tallulah Bankhead—*The Merv Griffin Show*, New York City

Chapter Three: Play Your Hunch contestants and Merv, New York City

Chapter Four: Arthur Treacher and Merv—*The Merv Griffin Show*, New York City

Chapter Five: Merv and President Ronald Reagan—Reagan ranch, Santa Ynez

Chapter Six: Merv and Ron Ward—aboard Merv's plane

Chapter Seven: Donald Trump and Merv—Resorts, Atlantic City

Chapter Eight: Eva Gabor and Merv—The Cliffs of Moher, Ireland

Chapter Nine: Nancy Reagan and Merv—Washington, D.C.

Photo Montage (all pictures left to right):
1. Mort Lindsey and Merv—La Quinta
2. Matthew Perry, Merv, and Dr. Phil—Beverly Hills Country Club
3. Michael Jackson, Elizabeth Taylor, and Merv—Laguna Beach
4. Merv, Armand Hammer, H.R.H. Prince Charles, Eva Gabor, H.R.H. Princess Diana, Frances Hammer—The Breakers, Palm Beach
5. Bob Murphy's birthday; front row: Bob Murphy, Katie Murphy, Pat Sajak, and Alex Trebek; back row: Tricia & Tony Griffin, Lynn Murphy (Bob's wife), Monica Murphy, Liz Murphy, Merv, Rob Murphy, Lois Murphy, Ed Murphy, Jean Trebek, Jean Plant, and George Vosburgh—The Beverly Hilton
6. Merv and Rosemary Clooney—The Beverly Hilton
7. H.S.H. Prince Rainier, H.S.H. Princess Grace, Murray Schwartz, H.S.H. Princess Antoinette de Monaco, and Merv—Monte Carlo Tennis Club

8. Tom Hanks and Merv—Golden Globes award ceremony, The Beverly Hilton

9. Ernie & Veronica Chambers, Merv, Audrey & Bob Loggia, and Charlie Chan—Brantome, France

10. Eva Gabor, Merv, and Sidney Poitier—Paradise Island, The Bahamas

11. Back row: Kim Sinatra, Merv, Gloria Redlich; front row: Larry Cohen, Charlie Chan, Ron Ward—The Scottsdale Hilton Resort and Villas

12. Senator Trent Lott, Senator John McCain, Merv, and Bo Derek—Washington, D.C.

13. Magda Gabor, Jolie Gabor, Eva Gabor, and Merv—Palm Springs